MCSE:
Windows 2000 Network
Infrastructure Administration

Exam Notes

MCSE:
Windows® 2000 Network Infrastructure Administration

Exam Notes™

John Wm. Jenkins, Jr.
with Paul Robichaux and James Chellis

San Francisco • Paris • Düsseldorf • Soest • London

SYBEX

Associate Publisher: Neil Edde
Contracts and Licensing Manager: Kristine O'Callaghan
Acquisitions and Developmental Editors: Bonnie Bills, Brenda Frink
Editor: Kathy Simpson
Production Editors: Edith Kaneshiro, Liz Burke
Technical Editor: Donald Fuller
Book Designer: Bill Gibson
Electronic Publishing Specialists: Jill Niles, Judy Fung
Proofreaders: Nanette Duffy, Camera Obscura, Laurie O'Connell
Page Layout: Brianne Agatep, Rachel Boyce, Liz Paulus
Indexer: Ted Laux
Cover Designer: Archer Design
Cover Illustrator/Photographer: Natural Selection

Library of Congress Card Number: 00-106236

ISBN: 0-7821-2761-4

This book is dedicated to Kristen Lee Eggertsen,
the Love of my Life.

Acknowledgments

I would like to thank my family: Kristen, Aubrey, and Brooke; John Wm., Sr.; Julia; Jeff; and Jim. I am very grateful for the help and technical assistance from Jamie Chellis, Mathew Peter Bulkeley, Rick Collin, Floyd Patterson, Jared Dixon, Star Place, Ralph Edwards, and Geoff Keochakian. I would like to thank all of the great people at Sybex who helped make this book a reality; they include Neil Edde, Bonnie Bills, Brenda Frink, Kathy Simpson, Donald Fuller, Edith Kaneshiro, Liz Paulus, Jill Niles, Judy Fung, and Liz Burke.

Contents

Introduction

Microsoft's new Microsoft Certified Systems Engineer (MCSE) track for Windows 2000 is the premier certification for computer-industry professionals. Covering the core technologies around which Microsoft's future will be built, the MCSE certification is a powerful credential for career advancement.

This book has been developed, in cooperation with Microsoft Corp., to give you the critical skills and knowledge you need to prepare for one of the core requirements of the new MCSE certification program for Windows 2000 Network Infrastructure Administration. You will find the information you need to acquire a solid understanding of Windows 2000 network infrastructure administration, to prepare for Exam 70-216: Implementing & Administering a Microsoft® Windows® 2000 Network Infrastructure, and to progress toward MCSE certification.

Is This Book for You?

The MCSE Exam Notes books are designed to be succinct, portable exam-review guides that can be used in conjunction with a more complete study program (book, CBT courseware, or classroom/lab environment) or as an exam review for those who don't feel the need for more extensive test preparation. The goal is not to give the answers away, but to identify the topics on which you can expect to be tested and to provide sufficient coverage of these topics.

Perhaps you're already familiar with the features and functionality of Windows 2000. The thought of paying a great deal of money for a specialized MCSE exam-preparation course probably doesn't sound too appealing. What can these courses teach you that you don't already know, right? Be careful, though—many experienced network administrators have walked confidently into test centers, only to walk sheepishly out of them after failing an MCSE exam. As they discovered, there's the Microsoft of the real world and the Microsoft of the MCSE exams. It's our goal in these Exam Notes books to show you where the two converge and where they diverge. When you finish reading this book, you should have a clear idea of how your understanding of the technologies involved matches up with the expectations of the MCSE test makers in Redmond.

Or perhaps you're relatively new to the world of Microsoft networking, drawn to it by the promise of challenging work and higher salaries. You've just waded through an 800-page MCSE Windows 2000 Study Guide or taken a class at a local training center. That's a lot of information to keep track of, isn't it? But by organizing the Exam Notes books according to the Microsoft exam objectives, and by breaking the information into concise, manageable pieces, we've created what we think is the handiest exam-review guide available. Throw it in your briefcase and carry it to work with you. As you read through the book, you'll be able to identify quickly the areas that you know best and those that require more in-depth review.

NOTE The goal of the Exam Notes series is to help MCSE candidates familiarize themselves with the subjects on which they can expect to be tested in the MCSE exams. For complete, in-depth coverage of the technologies and topics involved, we recommend the MCSE Windows 2000 Study Guide series from Sybex.

How Is This Book Organized?

This book is organized according to the official exam-objectives list prepared by Microsoft for the 216 exam. The chapters coincide with the broad objectives groupings, such as Planning, Installation and Configuration, Monitoring and Managing, and Troubleshooting. These groupings also are reflected in the organization of the MCSE exams themselves.

Within each chapter, the individual exam objectives are addressed in turn. The objectives sections are further divided according to the type of information presented.

Critical Information

This section presents the greatest level of detail on information that is relevant to the objective. This is the place to start if you're unfamiliar with or uncertain about the technical issues related to the objective.

Necessary Procedures

Here, you'll find instructions for procedures that must be completed on a lab computer. From installing operating systems to modifying configuration defaults, these sections address the hands-on requirements for the MCSE exam.

NOTE   Not every objective has procedures associated with it. For such objectives, the "Necessary Procedures" section has been left out.

Exam Essentials

This section provides a concise list of the most crucial topics that you need to understand fully before taking the MCSE exam. This section can help you identify topics that may require more study on your part.

Key Terms and Concepts

This section is a mini-glossary of the most important terms and concepts related to the specific objective. You'll understand what all those technical words mean within the context of the related subject matter.

Sample Questions

Each objective includes a selection of questions similar to those that you'll encounter on the actual MCSE exam. Answers and explanations are provided so that you can gain some insight into the test-taking process.

How Do You Become an MCSE?

Attaining MCSE certification always has been a challenge. In the past, people could acquire detailed exam information—even most of the exam questions—from online "brain dumps" and third-party "cram" books or software products. For the new MCSE exams, how-ever, this possibility simply will not exist.

To prevent "paper-MCSE syndrome" (a devaluation of the MCSE certification because unqualified people manage to pass the exams), Microsoft has taken strong steps to protect the security and integrity of the new MCSE track. Prospective MCSEs need to complete a course of study that provides not only detailed knowledge of a wide range of topics, but also true skills derived from working with Windows 2000 and related software products.

In the new MCSE program, Microsoft heavily emphasizes hands-on skills. Microsoft has stated, "Nearly half of the core required exams' content demands that the candidate have troubleshooting skills acquired through hands-on experience and working knowledge."

Fortunately, if you are willing to dedicate time and effort to Windows 2000, you can prepare for the exams by using the proper tools. If you work through this book and the other books in this series, you should meet the exam requirements.

Exam Requirements

Successful candidates must pass a minimum set of exams that measure technical proficiency and expertise:

- Candidates for MCSE certification must pass seven exams, includ-ing four core-operating-system exams, one design exam, and two electives.

- Candidates who have already passed three Windows NT 4 exams (70-067, 70-068, and 70-073) may opt to take an "accelerated" exam, plus one core design exam and two electives.

NOTE If you do not pass the accelerated exam after one attempt, you must pass the five core requirements and two electives.

The following tables show the exams that a new certification candidate must pass. All of these exams are required:

Exam #	Title	Requirement Met
70-216	Implementing and Administering a Microsoft® Windows® 2000 Network Infrastructure	Core (Operating System)
70-210	Installing, Configuring, and Administering Microsoft® Windows® 2000 Professional	Core (Operating System)
70-215	Installing, Configuring, and Administering Microsoft® Windows® 2000 Server	Core (Operating System)
70-217	Implementing and Administering a Microsoft® Windows® 2000 Directory Services Infrastructure	Core (Operating System)

One of these exams is required:

Exam #	Title	Requirement Met
70-219	Designing a Microsoft® Windows® 2000 Directory Services Infrastructure	Core (Design)
70-220	Designing Security for a Microsoft® Windows® 2000 Network	Core (Design)
70-221	Designing a Microsoft® Windows® 2000 Network Infrastructure	Core (Design)

Two of these exams are required:

Exam #	Title	Requirement Met
70-219	Designing a Microsoft® Windows® 2000 Directory Services Infrastructure	Elective
70-220	Designing Security for a Microsoft® Windows® 2000 Network	Elective
70-221	Designing a Microsoft® Windows® 2000 Network Infrastructure	Elective
Any current MCSE elective	Exams cover topics such as Exchange Server, SQL Server, Systems Management Server, Internet Explorer Administrators' Kit, and Proxy Server; new exams are added regularly.	Elective

NOTE For a more detailed description of the Microsoft certification programs, including a list of current MCSE electives, check Microsoft's Training and Certification Web site at www.microsoft.com/trainingandservices.

Exam Registration

You can take the exams at any of more than 1,000 Authorized Prometric Testing Centers (APTCs) and VUE Testing Centers around the world. For the location of a testing center near you, call Sylvan Prometric at (800) 755-EXAM (755-3926), or call VUE at (888) 837-8616. Outside the United States and Canada, contact your local Sylvan Prometric or VUE registration center.

You should determine the number of the exam that you want to take and then register with the Sylvan Prometric or VUE registration center nearest to you. At this point, you will be asked for advance payment for the exam. The exams are $100 each. Exams must be taken within one year of payment. You can schedule exams up to six weeks in advance or as late as one working day before the date of the exam. You can cancel or reschedule your exam if you contact the center at least two working days before the exam. Same-day registration is available in some locations, subject to space availability. Where same-day registration is available, you must register a minimum of two hours before test time.

TIP   You may also register for your exams online at www .sylvanprometric.com or www.vue.com.

When you schedule the exam, you will be provided instructions about appointment and cancellation procedures, ID requirements, and information about the testing-center location. In addition, you will receive a registration- and payment-confirmation letter from Sylvan Prometric or VUE.

Microsoft requires certification candidates to accept the terms of a nondisclosure agreement before taking certification exams.

What Exam 70-216: Implementing and Administering a Microsoft Windows 2000 Network Infrastructure Measures

The 216 Network Infrastructure Administration exam could also be called the network protocol routing, security, and naming exam. The objectives include the three Windows 2000 naming services: DNS, DHCP, and WINS. Using Windows 2000 as a multiprotocol router is explored, along with remote access procedures, issues and security concerns. Network infrastructure security processes—implementing certificate authorities and IPSec—are included as well.

Tips for Taking Your Exam

Here are some general tips for taking your exam successfully:

- Arrive at the exam center early so that you can relax and review your study materials, particularly tables and lists of exam-related information.

- Read the questions carefully. Don't be tempted to jump to an early conclusion. Make sure that you know exactly what the question is asking.

- Don't leave any unanswered questions; they count against you.

- When answering multiple-choice questions you're not sure about, use a process of elimination to get rid of the obviously incorrect questions first. This technique will improve your odds if you need to make an educated guess.

- This test has many exhibits (pictures). It can be difficult, if not impossible, to view both the questions and the exhibit simulation on the 14- and 15-inch screens commonly used at the testing centers. Call around to the centers and see whether 17-inch monitors are available. If not, perhaps you can arrange to bring in your own. Failing this, some people have found it useful to draw the diagram on the scratch paper provided by the testing center and use the monitor to view just the question.

- Many participants run out of time before they are able to complete the test. If you are unsure of the answer to a question, you may want to choose one of the answers, mark the question, and go on; an unanswered question does not help you. When your time is up, you cannot go on to another question. You can, however, remain on the question you are on indefinitely when the time runs out. Therefore, when you are almost out of time, go to a question that you feel you can figure out, given enough time, and work until you feel you have the answer (or the night security guard boots you out).

- You are allowed to use the Windows calculator during your test. It may be better, however, to memorize a table of the subnet addresses and to write it down on the scratch paper supplied by the testing center before you start the test.

When you complete an exam, you receive immediate online notification of your pass or fail status. You also receive a printed Examination Score Report, indicating your pass or fail status and your exam results by section. (The test administrator gives you the printed score report.) Test scores are forwarded to Microsoft automatically within five working days after you take the test; you do not need to send your score to Microsoft. If you pass the exam, you receive confirmation from Microsoft, typically within two to four weeks.

Contact Information

To find out more about Microsoft Education and Certification materials and programs, to register with Sylvan Prometric, or to get other useful information, check the following resources. Outside the United States or Canada, contact your local Microsoft office or Sylvan Prometric testing center.

Microsoft Certified Professional Program—(800) 636-7544

Call the MCPP number for information about the Microsoft Certified Professional program and exams and to order the latest Microsoft Roadmap to Education and Certification.

Sylvan Prometric Testing Centers—(800) 755-EXAM

Contact Sylvan to register to take a Microsoft Certified Professional exam at any of more than 800 Sylvan Prometric testing centers around the world.

Microsoft Certification Development Team—Web: http://www.microsoft.com/trainingandservices/default.asp

Contact the Microsoft Certification Development Team through its Web site to volunteer to participate in one or more exam-development phases or to report a problem with an exam. Address written correspondence to Certification Development Team; Microsoft Education and Certification; One Microsoft Way; Redmond, WA 98052.

Microsoft TechNet Technical Information Network—(800) 344-2121

This network is an excellent resource for support professionals and system administrators. Outside the United States and Canada, call your local Microsoft subsidiary for information.

How to Contact the Publisher

Sybex welcomes reader feedback on all its titles. Visit the Sybex Web site at www.sybex.com for book updates and additional certification information. The site also provides online forms for submitting comments and suggestions on this book or any other Sybex book.

Chapter

1

Installing, Configuring, Managing, Monitoring, and Troubleshooting DNS in a Windows 2000 Network Infrastructure

---

MICROSOFT EXAM OBJECTIVES COVERED IN THIS CHAPTER:

▶ **Install, configure, and troubleshoot DNS.** *(pages 3 – 35)*

- Install the DNS Server service.
- Configure a root name server.
- Configure zones.
- Configure a caching-only server.
- Configure a DNS client.
- Configure zones for dynamic updates.
- Test the DNS Server service.
- Implement a delegated zone for DNS.
- Manually create DNS resource records.

▶ **Manage and monitor DNS.** *(pages 35 – 47)*

Windows 2000 includes three *network naming services* that you need to understand to pass Microsoft Exam 70-216: the Dynamic Host Configuration Protocol (DHCP), the Domain Name Service (DNS), and the Windows Internet Name Service (WINS). These services provide network name and address information to applications that request it.

The *Domain Name System* is a set of protocols and services that allows users of the network to use hierarchical, user-friendly names instead of IP addresses when looking for network resources. This system is used extensively on the Internet and in many private enterprises. If you've used a Web browser, Telnet application, FTP utility, or similar TCP/IP utilities on the Internet, you probably have used a DNS server.

DNS is a distributed database of host information. Programs called *name servers* perform the server side of client-server transactions, providing information to the querying clients, known as *resolvers*. DNS and other common standards such as DHCP have become more important with the release of Windows 2000. As TCP/IP has become the protocol suite of choice for network operations both on and off the Internet, TCP/IP services such as DNS have similarly risen as a necessary infrastructure resource.

Installing, configuring, and troubleshooting DNS servers and clients and working with the *zones* (sets of names that servers are authoritative for) are major parts of the network infrastructure information that you must understand for this exam. This chapter focuses on the critical information you must understand about DNS and the procedures you must master to pass the exam.

The first objective covers the major territory you need to know about DNS. You review how to choose the type of DNS server to use: primary or secondary, root, or caching-only. You practice configuring the zones and the resolver or client. You review how to integrate DNS with Windows 2000 and Active Directory and how to update addresses dynamically with DHCP (which is covered in more depth in Chapter 2).

The first objective includes the term *troubleshooting*, which the sub-objectives do not expand upon further. The distinction between mastering and monitoring DNS and troubleshooting DNS is a nebulous one. The skills that are covered in the second objective—mastering and monitoring DNS—can also be tools for troubleshooting DNS.

Install, configure, and troubleshoot DNS.

- **Install the DNS Server service.**
- **Configure a root name server.**
- **Configure zones.**
- **Configure a caching-only server.**
- **Configure a DNS client.**
- **Configure zones for dynamic updates.**
- **Test the DNS Server service.**
- **Implement a delegated zone for DNS.**
- **Manually create DNS resource records.**

Before you can focus on working with DNS, it is important to review how DNS works. All units of information in the DNS database are indexed by name. These names are really paths in an inverted tree that is known as the *domain name space*. It is similar to the structure of the Unix file system with a single root at the top. Like a file system, the tree can branch any number of ways at each intersection, called a *node*. The tree's depth is limited to 127 levels—which as it turns out, is plenty.

Small companies with few nodes might not implement the infrastructure discussed in this book. If you have only a few host names, you might find an Internet Service Provider to manage your domain for you. But to learn these objectives for Exam 70-216, you need to learn to install, configure, test, and troubleshoot DNS.

This section focuses on the subobjectives and the different types of DNS servers that can be configured after installation. It also discusses how to configure the *resolver* (the client that makes queries) and how to work with the partial subdomains known as *zones*.

This first objective reviews some DNS basics so that you can learn to administer DNS in your network. Pay attention to the way DNS works with Windows 2000's Active Directory and other naming services, such as DHCP.

Critical Information

DNS is a necessary service for Windows 2000 networks to use to translate information from text-based names to numbered IP addresses and back again. It performs this function throughout company intranets and on the Internet. DNS allows use of all the names we like to call ourselves, our companies, our governments, and so on.

DNS probably has been adopted as the standard to be used with Windows 2000 networks because it is essential for working with the Internet. The world is moving toward supporting the TCP/IP protocol suite.

NOTE The primary specifications for DNS are defined as all such standards are, in Requests for Comments (RFCs) 974, 1034, and 1035. The Windows 2000 DNS server also supports the requirements in RFCs 1033, 1034, 1035, 1101, 1123, 1183, 1536, and 2136. For a less-boring and more user-friendly discussion of the basics of DNS, check out *MCSE: Windows 2000 Network Infrastructure Administration Study Guide* by Paul Robichaux (Sybex, 2000).

NOTE   Although complete instructions are beyond the scope of this book, you should get experience creating each type of DNS resource record.

Understanding DNS and the Internet

You may know how DNS works on the Internet; if you've sent or received Internet e-mail or browsed Web pages, you've got first-hand experience using DNS. Internet DNS depends on a set of top-level domains that serve as the root of the DNS hierarchy. The top-level domains are just below the root. These top-level domains and their authoritative name servers are managed by the Internet Network Information Center (http://www.internic.com). The top-level domains are organized in two ways: by organization and by country.

Understanding the DNS Database

DNS is a widespread, highly distributed system that, for the most part, works remarkably well and with little fuss. Knowing how servers and resolvers communicate with one another and what kind of queries are passed around is critical to configuring your network properly. That knowledge begins with understanding what's in the DNS database.

The programs that store information about domain name spaces are called *name servers*. Name servers usually store information about some portion of the domain name space that is called a *zone*. The difference between zones and domains is a subtle one. Domain names can be larger than a zone handled on a specific DNS server. The space that the name server handles is referred to as a zone, and the name server is said to have authority over that zone. Name servers can be authoritative for multiple zones as well.

No matter how many servers store your *zone* information, you can rest assured that it contains many items, some of which are new for Windows 2000. Although the DNS snap-in makes it unlikely that you'll ever need to edit these files by hand, it's good to know exactly what data they contain.

The first thing to understand is the fact that each zone file consists of resource records. Each *resource record*, or RR, contains information about some resource on the network, such as its IP address. You need to know about several types of resource records to manage your DNS servers effectively.

Start of Authority (SOA) Records

The first record in any database file is the Start of Authority (SOA) Record, which looks like this:

```
@ IN SOA <source host> <contact e-mail> <ser. no.>
<refresh time>
<retry time> <expiration time> <TTL>
```

The SOA defines the general parameters for the DNS zone, including the authoritative server for the zone. *MCSE: Windows 2000 Network Infrastructure Administration Study Guide* by Paul Robichaux (Sybex, 2000) lists the attributes stored in the SOA record.

Name Server (NS) Records

NS records list the name servers for a domain; these records allow other name servers to look up names in your domain. A zone file may contain more than one name-server record. The format of these records is simple:

```
<domain> @ IN NS <nameserver host >
```

domain is the name of your domain, and nameserver host is the fully qualified domain name (FQDN) of a name server in that domain. A couple of interesting shortcuts can be used in DNS records, such as the following:

- In a zone file, the @ symbol represents the root domain of the zone. The IN in the records stands for *Internet*.

- Any domain name in the database file that does *not* terminate with a period has the root domain appended to the end.

The Host Record

A *host record* (also called an *address* or an *A record*) is used to associate a host's name statically with its IP addresses. The A record ties a host name (which is part, you may recall, of a FQDN) to a specific IP address. This fact makes them suitable for use when you have devices with statically assigned IP addresses; in that case, you'd create these records manually by using the DNS snap-in. As it turns out, if you enable Dynamic DNS (DDNS), your DHCP server can create these records for you. That automatic creation is what enables DDNS to work.

The Pointer Record

A records probably are the most visible components of the DNS database, because Internet users depend on them to turn FQDNs such as www.microsoft.com and www.delta-air.com into IP addresses so that browsers and other components can find them. The host record has a lesser-known but still-important twin: the *pointer (PTR) record*. The A record maps a host name to an IP address, and the PTR record does just the opposite. Having both types of records makes it possible to do *reverse lookups*, in which a resolver asks a DNS server to cough up the FQDN associated with a particular IP address. This function is useful for, among other things, preventing people with made-up or illegal domain names from using services such as e-mail and FTP servers.

The Alias Record

Almost every company on the Web has a URL in the format www.companyname.com. This format is fairly standard. But did you ever stop to consider whether all those domains actually have machines named www? In fact, many (if not most) of them don't; they use DNS alias records (more properly known as *canonical name*, or *CNAME*, entries, which allow them to use more than one name to point to a single host).

The Mail Exchange Record

The mail exchange, or MX, record tells you which servers can accept mail bound for this domain. Each MX record contains two parameters—a preference and a mail server—as shown in the following example:

```
<domain> IN MX <preference> <mailserver host>
```

Even though most mailers will deliver mail to a host with just an address and no MX records, it is a good idea to have at least one MX record for each host. The mailer's local name server then caches the MX record for future use.

Service Records

Windows 2000 depends on some (relatively) new services, such as LDAP and Kerberos. These protocols postdate the DNS system by quite a while. Normally, clients use DNS to find the IP address of a machine whose name they already know. Microsoft wanted to extend this system by devising a way for a client to locate a particular *service* by making a DNS query. A Windows 2000 client, for example, can query DNS servers for the location of a domain controller, which makes it much easier (for both the client and the administrator) to manage and distribute logon traffic in large-scale networks. For this approach to work, Microsoft had to have some way to register the presence of a service (really, a TCP/IP protocol) in DNS, but none of the RR types you've read about so far offers any way to do so. Enter the *service record (SRV)*.

SRV records tie together the location of a service (such as a domain controller) with information about how to contact the service. Think of a CNAME record: It ties a name to an IP address. The MX record extends the concept by adding another parameter: the preference. SRV records add even more information, with seven parameters.

NOTE You can define other types of service records. If your applications support them, these records can query DNS to find the services they need.

Understanding How DNS Resolves Names

A client can make three types of queries to a DNS server: recursive, iterative, and inverse. Remember that the client of a DNS server can be a *resolver* (what you'd normally call a client) or another DNS server.

Iterative queries are the easiest to understand: A client asks the DNS server for an answer, and the server returns the best kind of answer it has. Most resolvers, however, use recursive queries, which are different from iterative queries. In a *recursive* query, the client sends a query to one name server, asking it to respond either with the requested answer or with an error.

Inverse queries use PTR records. Instead of supplying a name and then asking for an IP address, the client first provides the IP address and then asks for the name. Because there's no direct correlation in the DNS name space between a domain name and its associated IP address, this search would be fruitless without the use of a special trick: the `in-addr.arpa` domain. Nodes in the `in-addr.arpa` domain are named after the numbers in the dotted-octet representation of IP addresses, but because IP addresses get more specific from left to right and domain names get less specific from left to right, the order of IP address octets must be reversed when building the `in-addr.arpa` tree.

When the domain tree is built into the DNS database, a special pointer record is added to associate the IP addresses to the corresponding host names.

Caching and Time to Live

When a name server is processing a recursive query, it may be required to send several queries to find the definitive answer. Name servers are allowed to cache all the received information during this process; each record contains a *time to live* (TTL). The name-server owner sets the TTL for each RR on its server. If your data changes frequently, you can use smaller TTL values to help ensure that data about your domain is more consistent across that network. If you make the TTL too small, however, the load on your name server goes up.

Queries for Services

Windows 2000 uses some special domains (not unlike the in-addr.arpa domain that you just read about) to make it possible for domain clients to look up services they need. It turns out that RFC 2052—"A DNS RR for specifying the location of services (DNS SRV)"—specifies how this mechanism should work. There's a Microsoft twist, however: The underscore (_) character isn't legal in domain names, so Microsoft uses it to mark its special domains and to keep them from colliding with RFC 2052-compliant domains. There are four of these trick Windows 2000 domains:

- **_msdcs:** This domain contains a list of all the Windows 2000 domain controllers in a domain. Each domain controller, global catalog, and PDC emulator is listed here.

- **_sites:** Each site has its own subdomain within the _sites domain. In AD parlance, a site is a group of connected network subnets that have high bandwidth among them.

- **_tcp:** This domain lists service records for services that run on TCP: LDAP, Kerberos, the kpasswd password changer, and the global catalogs.

- **_udp:** This domain lists services that run on UDP: Kerberos and the kpasswd service.

When any network client wants to find a service (such as a domain controller), it can query its DNS server for the appropriate SRV record. By making a recursive query, the client can force the local DNS server to poke around in the domain until it finds the desired information.

Installing DNS

DNS can be installed before, during, or after the installation of Windows 2000 Active Directory service. If the Active Directory Installation wizard cannot locate a DNS server, it asks whether you want it to install and configure a DNS server for you. Using this feature is the simplest method of installing a DNS server for your Windows 2000 Active Directory service.

When you install the DNS server, you get the DHCP snap-in installed, too. You can open it by using the Start ➤ Programs ➤ Administrative Tools ➤ DNS command. The snap-in follows the standard MMC model. The left pane shows you which servers and zones are available. You can connect to servers in addition to the one to which you're already talking. Each server contains subordinate items grouped in folders. Each zone has a folder, which is named after the zone itself.

Configuring a Root Name Server

On the Internet, root name servers know where to locate the name servers authoritative for all top-level domains. If all the Internet root name servers were unreachable for an extended period, all resolution on the Internet would fail.

If your Windows 2000 servers aren't directly connected to the Internet, or if you want to prevent them from referring queries to the Internet, you can configure them to contain their own root zone. Root zones are treated as the authoritative source of information for a top-level domain. By creating your own root zones, you can control the domains for which your clients can resolve queries.

The process is simple; you can use the Configure DNS Server wizard on a machine that you haven't previously configured, or you can do it manually, as shown in the "Necessary Procedures" section for this objective.

Creating and Configuring Zones

The directive *NS records* lists the name servers for a domain, allowing other name servers to look up names in your domain. A zone file may contain more than one name-server record. The format of these records is simple:

```
<domain> @ IN NS <nameserver host >
```

`domain` is the name of your domain, and `nameserver host` is the FQDN of a name server in that domain. A couple of interesting shortcuts that can be used in DNS records, such as the following:

- In a zone file, the @ symbol represents the root domain of the zone. The `IN` in the records stands for *Internet*.

- Any domain name in the database file that does *not* terminate with a period has the root domain appended to the end. An entry that has just the name `sales`, for example, is expanded by adding the root domain to the end, but `sales.microsoft.com` is not expanded.

Configuring Zones

You can use the New Zone wizard to create a new forward or *reverse lookup zone*. The process is substantially the same, even though the steps and wizard pages differ somewhat. In either case, you create a new zone first by right-clicking the server that you want to host the zone and then by using the New Zone command; this kicks off the New Zone wizard.

Creating a New Forward Lookup Zone

When you pass the initial wizard page, the first choice you have to make is on the Zone Type page. What kind of zone do you want this to be? You can choose Active Directory-integrated, standard primary, or standard secondary. Which option you use depends on what you're doing:

- If you want to store zone data in Active Directory, use an AD-integrated zone.

- If you need to transfer zone data manually to other DNS servers by moving the actual zone data, or if you're not using Active Directory, choose the Standard Primary radio button.

- If you want to set up your server as a secondary zone server, choose the Standard Secondary radio button. Later in the process, you'll be prompted to specify the primary zone from which you want to transfer data.

No matter which zone type you choose, the next step is to specify whether you want to create a forward or reverse lookup zone.

Forward zones need to have names. You specify the name of the zone in the Zone Name page of the wizard. For an AD-integrated or primary zone, you have to specify the name (including the suffix— `microsoft` isn't a valid name, but `microsoft.com` is). If you're creating a secondary zone, you can use the Browse button to locate the primary zone that you want to copy.

If you're building a new AD-integrated zone, you're done after you specify the name. If you're setting up a standard primary zone, however, you must specify where you want the zone data to be stored on the zone file page. The default file name is the same as the zone name with `.dns` tacked on the end, but you can modify it freely. You also can combine multiple zones' data into a single zone file, though that practice makes it a little harder to sort out what's what.

Because secondary zones have to transfer their zone data from somewhere else, you have to specify where exactly that data comes from. Use the controls in the Master DNS Servers page of the New Zone wizard to specify which DNS servers your server will contact to request zone transfers. If you specify more than one server in this page, your server tries the servers in the order you specify.

Creating a New Reverse Lookup Zone

The process of creating a reverse lookup zone is a little different, because reverse lookup zones tie addresses to names. The Reverse Lookup Zone page allows you to specify the reverse lookup zone's name in two ways. The easy way is to specify the network ID portion of the network that the zone covers, using the Network ID radio button and field. The more complex, but equivalent, way is to fill in the name of the reverse zone itself.

After you select the network to which you want your reverse zone to point, you have to select a zone file, just as you do when you create a forward lookup zone.

Setting Zone Properties

You get six tabs in the Properties dialog box when you use the Properties command for a forward or reverse lookup zone. You use the Security tab only to control who can change properties and make dynamic updates to records on that zone. The other tabs are discussed in the following sections.

NOTE Secondary zones don't have a Security tab, and their SOA tab shows you the contents of the master SOA record, which you can't change.

The General Tab   Like General tabs everywhere in Windows 2000, the controls in this one are fairly straightforward, because they're dedicated mostly to settings that don't belong elsewhere. These settings include the following:

- The Status indicator (and the associated button) lets you see and control whether this zone can be used to answer queries. When the zone is running, the server can use it to answer client queries; when it's paused, the server won't answer any queries it gets for that particular zone.

- The Type indicator and button allow you to change the zone type between standard primary, standard secondary, and AD-integrated. As you change the type, the controls you see below the horizontal dividing line change too. The most interesting controls are the ones you see for AD-integrated zones. For primary zones, you see a field that lets you select the zone file name; for secondary zones, you get controls that allow you to specify the IP addresses of the primary servers.

- The Allow Dynamic Updates field gives you a way to specify whether you want to support dynamic DNS updates from compatible DHCP servers. The DHCP server or DHCP client must know about and support dynamic DNS to use it, but the DNS server has to participate, too. You can turn dynamic updates on or off, or you can require that updates be secured.

By default, a standard primary zone won't accept dynamic updates, but an AD-integrated zone will. You can change these settings at will. (A standard primary does accept updates as long as dynamic updates are enabled. Active Directory integrated zones can be configured only on a domain controller that supports dynamic updates— but by default, the standard primary has dynamic updates turned off.)

The Start of Authority (SOA) Tab   The controls in the Start of Authority (SOA) tab control the contents of the SOA record for this zone. The first record in any database file is the Start of Authority (SOA) record. The SOA defines the general parameters for the DNS zone, including the host server and various time parameters in the zone. The following list describes these controls:

- The Serial Number field indicates which version of the SOA record the server currently holds. Every time you change another field, you should increment the serial number so that other servers will notice the change and get a copy of the updated record.

- The Primary Server and Responsible Person fields indicate the location of the primary NS for this zone and the responsible administrator, respectively.

- The Refresh Interval field controls how often any secondary zones of this zone must contact the primary and get any changes that have been posted since the last update.

- The Retry Interval field controls how long secondary servers wait after a zone transfer fails before they try again. The servers keep trying at the interval you specify (which should be shorter than the refresh interval) until they succeed in transferring zone data.

- The Expires After field tells the secondary servers when to throw away zone data. The default setting—24 hours—means that a secondary that hasn't gotten an update in 24 hours will delete its local copy of the zone data.

- The Minimum (Default) TTL field sets the default TTL for all RRs created in the zone. You can still assign different TTLs to individual records, if you want.

- The TTL for This Record field controls the TTL for the SOA record itself.

The Name Servers Tab   The NS record for a zone indicates which name servers are authoritative for a zone—normally, the zone primary and any secondaries you've configured for the zone. (Remember that secondaries are authoritative read-only copies of the zone.) You edit the NS record for a zone by using the Name Servers tab. To be more specific, the tab shows you which servers are listed; you use the Add, Edit, and Remove buttons to specify which name servers you want to include in the zone's NS record.

The WINS Tab   The WINS tab allows you to control whether this zone uses WINS forward lookups. These lookups pass queries that DNS can't resolve to WINS for action, which is a useful setup if you're stuck using WINS on your network. You must explicitly turn this option on by checking the Use WINS Forward Lookup check box in the WINS tab for a particular zone.

The Zone Transfers Tab   Zone transfers are necessary and useful, because they're the mechanism used to propagate zone data between primary and secondary servers. For primary servers (whether AD-integrated or not), you can specify whether your servers allow zone transfers and, if so, where. The Zone Transfers tab allows you to specify these settings per zone by using the following controls:

- The Allow Zone Transfers check box controls whether the server answers zone-transfer requests for this zone. When this option is unselected, no zone data is transferred.

- Next, the three radio buttons control where zone-transfer data will go when you have zone transfers enabled.

  To Any Server is the default setting; this option allows any server, anywhere on the Internet, to request a copy of your zone data.

Only to Servers Listed on the Name Servers Tab limits transfers to those servers listed in the Name Servers tab for this zone. This setting is more secure than the default because it limits zone transfers to other servers for the same zone.

Only to the Following Servers, along with the corresponding IP address controls, gives you even more control because you can specify exactly which servers are allowed to request zone transfers. This list can be larger or smaller than the list specified in the Name Servers tab.

- The Notify button allows you to set up automatic notification triggers that are sent to secondary servers for this zone. Those triggers signal the secondary servers that changes have occurred on the primary; that way, the secondaries can request updates sooner than the normally scheduled interval.

Delegating Zones for DNS

DNS provides the ability to divide the name space into one or more zones, which then can be stored, distributed, and replicated to other DNS servers. When you decide whether to divide your DNS name space to make additional zones, consider the following reasons to use additional zones:

- A need to delegate the management of part of your DNS name space to another location or department within your organization.

- A need to divide one large zone into smaller zones to distribute traffic loads among multiple servers, improve DNS name resolution performance, or create a more fault-tolerant DNS environment.

- A need to extend the name space by adding numerous subdomains at the same time, such as to accommodate the opening of a new branch or office site.

You can store DNS data in Active Directory (AD) instead of in regular disk files. Although it might seem odd to use AD to store information that AD will have to run, doing so makes sense. Consider a typical DNS zone data file on disk—plain text, easy to edit. The file is not replicated, it's probably not secured, and there's no way to delegate control over it. All these limitations go away when you build what Microsoft calls an *Active Directory-integrated (ADI) zone*. In an ADI zone, Active Directory stores all the DNS zone data in AD, so it gains all of the benefits of AD—especially improved security and seamless replication. Note that there's no such thing as an ADI secondary zone.

The *domainName* File

Each domain that has a forward lookup zone on your server has its own database file in the system's DNS directory (%systemroot%\ system32\DNS). The file is essentially empty when you create the zone: it contains only an SOA record for the domain and one NS record listing the name of the server you just created. As you add A records to the domain, they're stored in this file.

The Reverse Lookup File

This database file holds information on a single reverse lookup zone. These zones usually are named after the IP address ranges they cover. A reverse lookup zone that can handle queries for the 172.30.1.* block, for example, is named 1.30.172.in-addr.arpa. Remember that the reverse lookup database allows a resolver to provide an IP address and request a matching host name. It looks like the domain database file (it has SOA and name-server records), but instead of A records, it has one PTR record for each host designated in the reverse lookup zone.

The Cache File

The cache file contains host information needed to resolve names outside the authoritative domains—in short, it holds a list of the names and addresses of root name servers. If your DNS server can connect to the Internet, you can leave this file alone; if not, you can edit it so that it lists the authoritative roots for your private network.

The Boot File

Consider what a *primary DNS server* must do when it boots. Somehow, it has to figure out what zones it's supposed to be serving, decide whether it's authoritative for any of them, and link up with other servers in the zone (if any). You can choose the method by which Windows 2000 DNS servers get this information: from AD, from the registry, or from a BIND-style

boot file. The boot file, which must be named %systemroot%\system32\
dns\boot, controls the DNS server's startup behavior. Boot files support
only four commands:

- **Directory:** The directory command specifies where the other
  files named in the boot file are located—almost always, the
  %systemroot%\system32\dns directory. You use the command
  along with a directory path, as follows:

  ```
  directory f:\winnt\system32\dns
  ```

- **Cache:** The cache command specifies the file of root hints used to
  help your DNS service contact name servers for the root domain.
  This command, *and* the file to which it refers, *must* be present. The
  command cache cache.dns, for example, points the DNS server
  to the default cache.dns file shipped with Windows 2000.

- **Primary:** The primary command specifies a domain for which this
  name server is authoritative, as well as a database file that contains
  the resource records for that domain. You can use multiple primary commands in a single boot file, as in this example:

  ```
  Primary xyzcorp.com
  xyzcorp.com.dns
  primary acct.xyzcorp.com
  acct.xyzcorp.dns
  ```

- **Secondary:** The secondary command designates a domain as
  being one that your server handles as a *secondary*. This designa-
  tion means that your server is authoritative but pulls DNS information from one or more of the specified master servers. The
  command also defines the name of the local file for caching this
  zone. Multiple secondary command records may exist in the boot
  file. The secondary command takes three parameters, as follows:

  ```
  Secondary xcorp.com
  ns.pair.com
  xcorp.dns
  Secondary ycorp.com
  ns2.pair.com
  ycorp.dns
  ```

Configuring a Caching-Only DNS Server

Configuring a DNS server ranges from very easy to very difficult, depending on what you're trying to make it do. The simplest configuration is a caching-only server, in which you don't have to do anything except make sure that the server's root hints are set correctly.

Although all DNS name servers cache queries that they have resolved, caching-only servers are DNS name servers that only perform queries, cache the answers, and return the results. They are not authoritative for any domains, and the information that they contain is limited to what has been cached while resolving queries. Accordingly, they don't have any zone files, and they don't participate in zone transfers. When a caching-only server is first started, it has no information in its cache; the cache is gradually built up over time. As a name server sends out queries, it continues to find information including addresses of DNS servers that are authoritative for different zones. This information is cached in a caching-only server, which speeds future resolutions that involve the same information.

This cached data does not live forever, however. The administrator of the zone determines a TTL or *time to live* for the information.

Configuring a DNS Client

The DNS client is also called a *resolver*. The client is responsible for translating a request for host information into a query to a name server and for translating the response into a recognizable answer. If you need the clients to do more than perform default duties, they must be configured.

DNS configuration seems to be easy: After all, the only thing you have to do is click one radio button and fill in one or two IP addresses. The process involves some subtleties, though, created by the presence of a DNS tab in the Advanced TCP/IP Settings dialog box. You should start with the fundamentals of DNS client configuration: using the controls in the standard Internet Protocol (TCP/IP) Properties dialog box.

Basic DNS Configuration

The Internet Protocol Properties dialog box reveals the main features of the DNS configuration. The Obtain DNS Server Address Automatically and the Use the Following DNS Server Addresses radio buttons control whether your client picks up DNS information from the DHCP server or from the following two IP address fields:

- When you select the Obtain DNS Server Addresses Automatically button (which you can do only when DHCP is enabled), whatever DNS addresses you've put into your DHCP server configuration—or none, if you don't provide any—will be used by the client, with no way for you to override them. This button can be selected only when you've selected the Obtain an IP Address Automatically radio button.

- When you choose the Use the Following DNS Server Addresses button, you must enter an address in the Preferred DNS Server field. You can enter the address of another server in the Alternate DNS Server field; if you want to specify more than two servers, it'll cost you a trip to the Advanced button.

In a welcome departure from previous versions of Windows, you can change DNS modes and server addresses without having to reboot.

Advanced DNS Configuration

To do more advanced configuration of the DNS configuration, you must click to the Advanced button in the Internet Protocol (TCP/IP) Properties dialog box to access the DNS tab of the Advanced TCP/IP Settings dialog box. The tab seems to be fairly busy, but all the controls are reasonably easy to understand.

You must understand the following settings for the DNS server list itself:

- The DNS Server Addresses, In Order of Use list shows all the DNS servers currently defined for this client. Any DNS query is sent to the first server; if that server doesn't produce an answer, the query goes to the next one in the list. The DNS server physically closest to the client computer should be first in the list. This process continues until a server returns a valid answer or until all the servers have been tried.

You can add, edit, and remove servers by using the buttons below the list, and you can change the order of a server in the list by selecting it and then clicking the up and down arrows to the right of the list.

NOTE The DNS server list is used only for the network interface you're configuring. This list allows you to use different DNS servers for NICs that are connected to different networks.

The remaining settings pertain only to this connection (or network adapter, to be more precise):

- The Append Primary and Connection Specific DNS Suffixes radio button controls whether the DNS resolver automatically appends the *primary DNS suffix* and any connection-specific suffixes when it makes DNS requests.

- The Append Parent Suffixes of the Primary DNS Suffix check box (which is active only when Append Primary and Connection Specific DNS Suffixes is selected) forces the resolver to tack on parent suffixes of the primary suffix.

- The Append These DNS Suffixes (In Order) radio button and its associated controls allow you to provide a canned list of suffixes for the resolver. These suffixes are used in place of the primary and connection-specific suffixes, and they override any suffixes passed by the DHCP servers.

- The DNS Suffix for This Connection field specifies the default connection suffix you want to append to DNS queries. This setting overrides any suffix that may be specified by the DHCP server.

- The Register This Connection's Address in DNS check box, which is checked by default, tells the DHCP client to register its name and IP address with the nearest dynamic DNS (DDNS) server.

- The Use This Connection's DNS Suffix in DNS Registration check box controls whether the primary or connection-specific DNS suffix is used when your client registers itself with the DDNS service.

Configuring Zones with Dynamic DNS (DDNS)

In Windows NT, when you use DHCP to assign IP addresses to clients, you have no way to keep the corresponding DNS records up to date. If you have a DNS entry pointing to an IP address, that's great until the DHCP lease is released and the entry gets a new address. At that point, you get the choice of either fixing the DNS record by hand or relying on NetBIOS and WINS for name resolution. You may have a similar problem if you use a dial-up ISP; every time you dial up, you get a different IP address.

The *Dynamic DNS (DDNS) standard*, described in RFC 2136, was designed to solve this problem. DDNS allows DNS *clients* (not resolvers) to update information in the DNS database files. A Windows 2000 DHCP server, for example, can automatically tell a DDNS server to which IP addresses it's assigned and to what machines. (Windows 2000 DHCP clients can do this, too, but for security reasons it's better to let the DHCP server do the job.) The result: IP addresses and DNS records stay in sync so that you can use DNS and DHCP together seamlessly.

Because DDNS is a proposed Internet standard, you can even use Windows 2000's DDNS-aware parts with Unix-based DNS servers. Dynamic updates enable DNS client computers to register and dynamically update their resource records with a DNS server whenever changes occur. This arrangement reduces the need for manual administration of zone records. The DNS service allows dynamic update to be enabled or disabled on a per-zone basis at each server.

Windows 2000 Registration

A Windows 2000 client that has a statically assigned IP address attempts to register its IP address with a dynamic DNS server when the IP address changes or when the machine reboots. DHCP clients update DNS records whenever an IP address assignment changes (when a lease is renewed or issued). In both cases, the DHCP service on the client is responsible for sending the update for all IP addresses assigned to the machine, even those that aren't using DHCP.

Turning on secure updates has no initial effect on clients, because they always try unsecured updates first. If an unsecured update fails, the client tries again with a secure update. If that attempt fails, the update fails.

The Windows 2000 DHCP server can register DNS data for machines to which it issues leases; in this role, it's called a *DNS proxy,* because it's acting on behalf of another set of machines. Although this DNS proxy system gives all your computers access to dynamic DNS registrations, it opens some worrisome security issues, because you must add the DHCP servers you want to act as proxies to the DnsProxyUpdate group in Active Directory. This tells the OS that you want those DHCP servers to be able to register clients, but it also means that any DHCP server running on an AD controller has full access to the DNS registration information— meaning that a malicious DHCP client could threaten your DNS information.

Testing the DNS Server Service

You can use the DNS snap-in to do some basic server testing The Monitoring tab of the DNS snap-in gives you some simplistic testing tools. The A Simple Query Against This DNS Server test asks for a single record from the local DNS server; it's useful for verifying that the service is running and listening to queries, but not much else. The A Recursive Query to Other DNS Servers test is more sophisticated, using a recursive query to see whether forwarding is working. The Test Now button and the Perform Automatic Testing at the Following Interval control allow you to run these tests now or later, as you require.

TIP If the simple query fails, make sure that the local server contains the zone 1.0.0.127.in-addr.arpa. If the recursive query fails, make sure that your root hints are correct and that your root servers are running.

Implementing a Delegated Zone for DNS

When delegating zones within your name space, be aware that for each new zone you create, you need delegation records in other zones that point to the authoritative DNS servers for the new zone. This pointing is necessary both to transfer authority and to provide correct referral to other DNS servers and clients of the new servers that are being made authoritative for the new zone.

Creating DNS Records Manually

From time to time, you may find it necessary to add resource records manually to your Windows 2000 DNS servers. Although dynamic DNS frees you from the need to fiddle with A and PTR records, other resource types (including MX records, required for the proper flow of SMTP e-mail) still have to be created manually. You can create A, PTR, MX, SRV, and 15 other record types manually. You must remember two important things: you must right-click the zone and then use either the New Record command or the Other New Records command, and you must know how to fill in the fields of whatever record type you're using. To create an MX record, for example, you need three pieces of information (the domain, the mail server, and the priority), but to create an SRV record, you need several more parameters.

Troubleshooting Problems

You will benefit by examining and framing some basic monitoring and management issues when troubleshooting DNS problems on your network. When working with DNS issues, ask yourself the following basic questions:

- What application is failing? What works? What doesn't work?

- Is the problem basic IP connectivity, or is it name resolution? If the problem is name resolution, does the failing application use NetBIOS names, DNS names, or host names?

- How are the things that do and don't work related?

- Have the things that don't work ever worked on this computer or network?

- If so, what has changed since they last worked?

By the process of elimination, you should be able to narrow down the problem and then use of the management tools discussed in the next objective of this chapter.

Necessary Procedures

You will find procedures that cover the various subobjectives for this Microsoft test objective in this section. You can practice installing DNS servers and installing a root name server and a caching-only server. You get some basic practice doing some simple DNS testing and learning to configure a delegated DNS zone. Finally, you get a procedure for manually creating an MX resource record.

NOTE   Microsoft has based its certification exams on testing from the hands-on perspective and from stressing real-life scenarios. This is even more true and refined with Windows 2000 MCSE Exams. Therefore, it is very important to put this book down and perform all the procedures in this book until the techniques are second nature.

Installing a DNS Server

Installing the DNS server service is easy, because you install it with the same tools you use to add other components. Follow these steps to install the DNS server:

NOTE   This procedure works only on computers running Windows 2000 Server or Advanced Server. Microsoft strongly recommends that you configure your DNS servers to use static IP addresses. There are problems installing DNS servers without static IP addresses.

---

1. Open the Windows Components wizard by opening Add/Remove Programs in the Control Panel (Start ➤ Settings ➤ Control Panel ➤ Add/Remove Programs).

2. Click the Add/Remove Windows Components icon. The Installation wizard opens, listing all the components it knows how to install or remove.

3. Choose the Networking Services item from the Component list; then click the Details button.

4. When the Subcomponents of Network Services list appears, select Domain Name System (DNS); then click OK.

5. If prompted, enter the path to the Windows 2000 distribution files.

Configuring a DNS Server as a Root Name Server

This procedure walks you through the process of configuring the DNS server as a root server with one forward lookup zone:

1. Open the DNS management snap-in (Start ≻ Programs ≻ Administrative Tools ≻ DNS).

2. Click the DNS server to expand it; then right-click the server and choose the Configure the Server command. When the Configure DNS Server wizard starts and begins guiding you through the process of setting up DNS, click Next.

3. Click the option titled This Is the First DNS Server on This Network. This option makes the server a root server. A root server can gain access to second-level domains on the Internet. Click Next.

4. Click the option titled Yes, Create a Forward Lookup Zone; then click Next. A *forward lookup zone* is a name-to-address database that helps computers translate DNS names into IP addresses and provides information about available resources.

5. Click the Standard Primary option; then click Next. This action stores a master copy of the new zone in a text file and facilitates the exchange of DNS data with other DNS servers that use text-based storage methods.

6. Type the name of your new zone; then click Next.

7. Click the Create a New File With This Filename radio button; then click the Next button. You can keep or change the name of the zone file.

8. Click the No, Do Not Create a Reverse Lookup Zone radio button; then click Next.

9. Click Finish to complete the Configure DNS Server wizard.

Installing a Caching DNS Server

Follow these steps to install a DNS server and configure it as a caching-only server:

NOTE This procedure works only on computers running Windows 2000 Server or Advanced Server.

---

1. Install a DNS server.

2. Open the DNS management snap-in (Start ➤ Programs ➤ Administrative Tools ➤ DNS).

3. Notice that the Forward and Reverse Lookup Zone folders are empty. You want them that way.

4. Right-click your DNS server and choose the Properties command. When the Properties dialog box appears, switch to the Root Hints tab. If your server is connected to the Internet, you should see a list of root hints for the root servers maintained by InterNIC. If not, click the Add button to add root hints as defined in the root.dns file.

5. Close the Properties dialog box by clicking OK.

Configuring a Windows 2000 Client to Use DNS

To configure basic DNS name resolution on a client machine, follow these steps:

1. Choose Start ➤ Settings ➤ Network and Dial-Up Connections.

2. Right-click the Local Area Connection icon, and choose the Properties command. If you have more than one LAN adapter, choose the one that you want to configure. The Local Area Connection Properties dialog box appears.

3. Select Internet Protocol (TCP/IP) in the Components Checked Are Used by This Connection list.

4. Click the Properties button. The Internet Protocol (TCP/IP) Properties dialog box appears.

5. Choose the Use the Following DNS Server Addresses radio button.

6. Enter an IP address in the Preferred DNS server field.

7. (Optional) Enter a different IP address in the Alternate DNS Server field.

8. Click OK to close the Internet Protocol (TCP/IP) Properties dialog box.

9. Click OK to close the Local Area Connection Properties dialog box.

Configuring Zones and Using WINS to Allow Dynamic Updates

In this procedure, you modify the properties of a forward lookup zone, configuring the zone to use WINS to resolve names not found by querying the DNS name space. In addition, you configure the zone to allow dynamic updates. Follow these steps:

1. Open the DNS management snap-in (Start ➤ Programs ➤ Administrative Tools ➤ DNS).

2. Click the DNS server to expand it; then expand the Forward Lookup Zones folder.

3. Right-click the zone that you want to modify (the zone you created in "Configuring a DNS Server as a Root Name Server"); then choose the Properties command.

4. Switch to the WINS tab; then click the Use WINS Forward Lookup check box.

5. Enter the IP address of any valid WINS server on your network, click Add, and then click OK. Notice that there's now a new WINS Lookup RR in your zone.

6. Repeat step 3 to reopen the Zone Properties dialog box, and this time stay on the General tab.

7. Change the value of the Allow Dynamic Updates control to Yes.

8. Close the Properties dialog box.

Performing Simple DNS Testing

In this procedure, you enable logging, use the DNS MMC to test the DNS server, and view the contents of the DNS log. Follow these steps:

1. In the Control Panel, double-click Administrative Tools; then double-click DNS.

2. Right-click the DNS server that you want to test; then choose the Properties command.

3. Switch to the Logging tab, check all the Debug logging options, and then click the Apply button.

4. Switch to the Monitoring tab, and check the check boxes titled A Simple Query Against This DNS Server and A Recursive Query to Other DNS Servers.

5. Click the Test Now button several times; then click OK.

6. Using Windows Explorer, navigate to the %windir%\System32\ Dns folder, and use WordPad to view the contents of the dns.log file, which is in Rich Text Format (RTF).

Creating a Delegated DNS Zone

In this procedure, you create a delegated *subdomain* of a domain. Follow these steps:

1. Open the DNS management snap-in (Start ➤ Programs ➤ Administrative Tools ➤ DNS).

2. Click the DNS server to expand it; then expand the Forward Lookup Zones folder.

3. Expand the DNS server; then locate a zone you want to use as the parent (for which you want to create the delegated subdomain).

4. Right-click the zone; then choose the New Delegation command. The New Delegation wizard appears.

5. Click Next to get rid of the initial wizard page.

6. Enter whatever name you want to use in the Delegated Domain field of the Delegated Domain Name page. This is the name of the domain for which you want to delegate authority to another DNS server. It should be a subdomain of the primary.

7. When the Name Servers page appears, click the Add button to add the IP address(es) of the server(s) that will be hosting the newly delegated zone.

8. Click the Finish button. The New Delegation wizard disappears, and the new zone you created appears below the zone you chose in step 4. The newly delegated zone's folder icon is displayed in gray to indicate that control of the zone is delegated.

Exam Essentials

Know how DNS functions to translate user-friendly domain names into IP addresses and back again.   Be familiar with the inverted tree that makes up the domain name space, and know the difference among top-level domains, subdomains, and zones. Understand that domain name data is contained in resource records (RRs) and how to read their basic syntax.

Know about the various types of name servers and their functions. Be familiar with both primary and secondary masters and their relationship. Understand the roles of root name servers, both on and hidden from the Internet. Be aware of the role that caching servers play and how they make the process more efficient.

Know about resolvers (clients) and how they handle queries, interpret responses, and return information to the requesting programs. These clients can be just sets of library routines in programs called stub resolvers, such as FTP or Telnet. Most of the burden of name resolution is on the server, but be aware that there are implementations of DNS with smarter resolvers.

Know the difference between recursive and iterative queries. In recursion, a resolver sends a recursive query about a certain domain name to a name server. The server must respond to that recursive query with the requested data or a denial. Iterative resolution doesn't require the server to respond with its best information.

Know about reverse DNS lookups. The IP address appears backward as a domain name, because it is read leaf to root. Be familiar with the in-addr.arpa domain space and pointer (PTR) records that the Internet uses to make these reverse lookups possible.

Know the types of records or information that is stored in the DNS database. Be familiar with MX records, alias or CNAME records, pointer records, host records, NS records, and SOA records, as well as their various functions.

Know that Windows 2000 can query for various network services. Protocols such as LDAP and Kerberos can be located on the network via DNS.

Know the four boot-file commands in DNS and their purposes. Be familiar with the directory, cache, primary, and secondary commands, as well as how they are used.

Know the four special Windows 2000 trick domains that use an underscore to look up specific services. These domain names are not read as domains due to their initial underscore: _msdocs, _tcp, _sites, _udp.

Know the ordering of resource records in the db files. The order is as follows: SOA record, NS record, other records. It also is good to know about other records, such as **A**-Name-to-address mapping, **PTR**-Address-to name mapping, **CNAME**-Canonical name (for aliases), **TXT**-Textual information, and **RP**-Responsible Person.

Key Terms and Concepts

Active Directory-integrated zone   In a Windows 2000 ADI zone, Active Directory stores all the DNS zone data in AD, so it gains all of the benefits of AD—especially improved security, fault tolerance, and seamless replication.

DNS server   A server that uses *DNS* to resolve domain or host names to *IP addresses*.

domain name server   An Internet host dedicated to the function of translating fully qualified domain names into *IP addresses*.

Domain Name Service (DNS)   The *TCP/IP* network service that translates textual Internet network addresses into numerical Internet network addresses.

Dynamic DNS (DDNS)   A naming process that allows DNS clients to dynamically update information in the DNS database files.

fully qualified domain name (FQDN)   An absolute domain name that ends with a period and a null space for the root.

name server   A server that can give an authoritative answer to queries about its domain.

network naming   Three services—DNS, DHCP, and WINS—that provide network name and address information to applications that request it.

pointer record (PTR)   A record that associates an IP address to a host name.

primary DNS server   The owner of the zones defined in its database. The primary DNS server has authority to make changes in the zones it owns.

resolver   A DNS client computer that makes requests to a name server. These requests ask the server to resolve a client DNS name into the corresponding IP address, or vice versa.

resource records   Records that contain information about some resource on the network. There are several types of resource records.

secondary DNS server   A server that pulls a copy of zone data from the specified master server. Secondary DNS servers receive a read-only copy of zones. The secondary DNS server can resolve queries from this read-only copy, known as a *zone transfer*, but cannot make changes or updates.

service record (SRV)   A record that links the location of a service, such as a domain controller, with information about how to contact the service. It provides seven items of information: service name, transport protocol, domain name for which the service is offered, priority, weight, port number on which the service is offered, and DNS name of the server that offers the service.

time to live (TTL)   The amount of time that any name server is allowed to cache data.

zone   Subtree of the DNS database that is considered to be a single unit. Name servers are said to have authority for this part of the domain name space for the zone.

zone transfer   A process that copies information from a primary DNS server to a secondary DNS server.

Sample Questions

1. What is necessary for a reverse DNS lookup?

    A. The presence of at least one DHCP server

    B. A forward lookup zone and an A record for the IP address

    C. A reverse lookup zone and a PTR record for the IP address

    D. The existence of a proper SRV record

    Answer: C. The Reverse DNS lookup uses the reverse octets in the `in-addr.arpa` tree and the pointer (PTR) records within that reverse lookup zone to resolve IP addresses back to user-friendly names.

2. A primary DNS server performs which of the following functions?

A. It is authoritative for the zones it hosts.

B. It holds data that can be copied to a secondary DNS server.

C. Neither A nor B

D. A and B

Answer: D. The primary server is authoritative for its zone; it also holds the master copy of the zone data, which is replicated to secondary and cache servers.

Manage and monitor DNS.

Now that your DNS name server has been set up, configured, and has some resource records, you want to confirm that your DNS name server is resolving and replying to client DNS requests. The simplest test is to use the *ping* command to make sure that the server is alive.

A more exhaustive test would be to use management tools such as the directive tool nslookup to verify that you can actually resolve addresses for items on your DNS server.

This objective has no subobjectives, and as you read at the beginning of this chapter, there is a question as to whether these tools are best described as tools for managing and monitoring DNS or for troubleshooting problems. Whatever the case, you need to learn to use them and to understand their syntax to manage DNS on your network.

Critical Information

You can use the DNS snap-in to do some basic server testing and monitoring. More important, you use the snap-in to monitor and set logging options. The Logging tab allows you to specify which events you want to log. The more of these options you turn on, the more log information you get. This information is useful when you're trying to track what's happening with your servers, but it can result in a very large log file if you're not careful.

Management Tools for DNS

Windows 2000 provides several useful tools that can help you diagnose and solve problems with DNS:

- You can use nslookup to perform DNS queries and to examine the contents of zone files on local and remote servers.

- You can use ipconfig to view DNS client settings, display and flush the resolver cache, and force a dynamic-update client to register its DNS records.

- You can use Event Viewer to view DNS client and server error messages.

- The network redirector allows you to stop the DNS client and flush its cache by stopping and restarting it with the Net Stop and Net Start commands.

- You can configure the DNS server to monitor certain events and log them in the DNS log for your edification.

- You can perform test queries by using the Controls options on the Monitoring tab in the DNS console.

Understanding *nslookup*

nslookup is a standard command-line tool provided in most DNS server implementations, including Windows 2000. nslookup offers the capability to perform query testing of DNS servers and to obtain detailed responses at the command prompt. This information can be useful for diagnosing and solving name-resolution problems, for verifying that resource records are added or updated correctly in a zone, and for debugging other server-related problems. You can do several useful things with nslookup:

- Use it in noninteractive mode to look up a single piece of data.

- Enter interactive mode and use the debug feature.

- From within interactive mode, perform these steps:

  1. Set options for your query

  2. Look up a name

  3. Look up records in a zone

  4. Perform zone transfers

  5. Exit `nslookup`

NOTE   When you are entering queries, it generally is a good idea to enter FQDNs so that you can control what name is submitted to the server. If you want to know which suffixes are added to unqualified names before they are submitted to the server, however, you can enter *nslookup* in debug mode and then enter an unqualified name.

You can start using `nslookup` in plain old command-line mode:

```
nslookup <name> <server>
```

This code looks up a DNS name or address named *name*, using a server at an IP address specified by *server*. `nslookup`, however, is much more useful in interactive mode, because you can enter several commands in sequence. Running `nslookup` by itself (without specifying a query or server) puts it in interactive mode, where it stays until you type **exit** and press Enter. Before that point, you can look up a great deal of useful information.

While you are in interactive mode, you can use the `Set` command to configure how the resolver carries out queries. Table 1.1 shows a few of the option settings available for `Set`.

TABLE 1.1: Command-Line Options Available for the *Set* Command

Option	Purpose
Set all	Shows all the options available with the Set option.
Set d2	Puts nslookup in debug mode so you can examine the query and response packets between the resolver and the server.
Set domain=<*domain name*>	Tells the resolver what domain name to append for unqualified queries.
Set timeout=<*time-out*>	Tells the resolver which time-out to use. This option is useful for slow links in which queries frequently time out and the wait time must be lengthened.
Set type=<*record type*>	Tells the resolver which type of resource records to search for (A, PTR, or SRV, for example). If you want the resolver to query for all types of resource records, type **Set type=all**.

While you are in interactive mode, you can look up a name just by typing it, as follows:

```
<name> [server]
```

name is the owner name of the record you are looking for, and *server* is the server that you want to query.

You can use the wildcard character (*) in your query. If you want to look for all resource records that have *K* as the first letter, type **k*** as your query.

If you want to query for a particular type of record (such as an MX record), use the Set type command.

```
Set type=mx
```

This example tells nslookup that you're interested in seeing only MX records that meet your search criteria.

nslookup has other management options. You can get a list of the contents of an entire domain by using the Ls command. To find all the hosts in the xyzcorp.com domain, for example, you type the following:

```
Set type=a
Ls -t xyzcorp.com
```

You also can simulate zone transfers by using the Ls command with the -d switch. This switch helps you determine whether the server that you are querying allows zone transfers to your computer.

Type the following:

```
ls -d <domain name>
```

Identifying What's Wrong

A successful nslookup response looks like this:

```
Server: <Name of DNS server>
Address: <IP address of DNS server>
<Response data>
```

nslookup might also return an error. The following message means that the resolver did not locate a PTR resource record (containing the host name) for the server IP address. nslookup can still query the DNS server, and the DNS server can still answer queries.

```
DNS request timed out.
Timeout was <x> seconds.
*** Can't find server name for address <IP Address>:
Timed out
*** Default servers are not available
Default Server: Unknown
Address: <IP address of DNS server>
```

The following message means that a request timed out. This might happen, for example, if the DNS service was not running on the DNS server that is authoritative for the name.

 *** Request to <Server> timed-out

The following message means that the server is not receiving requests on UDP port 53:

 *** <Server> can't find <Name or IP address queried for>: No response from server

The following message means that this DNS server was not able to find the name or IP address in the authoritative domain. The authoritative domain might be on that DNS server or on another DNS server that this DNS server is able to reach.

 *** <Server> can't find <Name or IP address queried for>: Non-existent domain

The following message generally means that the DNS server is running but is not working properly. It might have a corrupted packet, or the zone in which you are querying for a record might be paused. This message also may be returned if the client queries for a host in a domain for which the DNS server is not authoritative and the DNS server cannot contact its root servers, is not connected to the Internet, or has no root hints.

 *** <Server> can't find <Name or IP address queried for>: Server failed.

Understanding *ipconfig*

You can use the command-line tool ipconfig to view your DNS client settings, to view and reset cached information used locally for resolving DNS name queries, and to register the resource records for a dynamic update client. If you use ipconfig with no parameters, it displays DNS information for each adapter, including the domain name and DNS servers used for that adapter. Table 1.2 shows some command-line options available for ipconfig.

TABLE 1.2:   Command-Line Options Available for the *ipconfig* Command

Command	What it does
ipconfig /all	Displays additional information about DNS, including the FQDN and the DNS suffix search list.
ipconfig /flushdns	Flushes and resets the DNS resolver cache.
ipconfig /displaydns	Displays the contents of the DNS resolver cache.
ipconfig /registerdns	Refreshes all DHCP leases and registers any related DNS names. This option is available only on Windows 2000–based computers that run the DHCP Client service. For more information about this option, see the section "Creating and Configuring Zones" earlier in this chapter.
ipconfig /release *[adapter]*	Releases all DHCP leases.
ipconfig /renew *[adapter]*	Refreshes all DHCP leases and dynamically updates DNS names. This option is available only on systems that are running the DHCP Client service.

DNS Log

You can configure the DNS server to create a log file that records the following types of events:

- Queries
- Notification messages from other servers
- Dynamic updates
- Content of the question section for DNS query message
- Content of the answer section for DNS query messages

- Number of queries this server sends

- Number of queries this server receives

- Number of DNS requests received over a UDP port

- Number of DNS requests received over a TCP port

- Number of full packets sent by the server

- Number of packets written through by the server and back to the zone

The DNS log appears in:

```
%SystemRoot%\System32\dns\Dns.log.
```

Because the log is in RTF format, you must use WordPad to view it.

You can change the directory and file name in which the DNS log appears by adding the following entry to the registry with the REG_SZ data type:

```
HKEY_LOCAL_
MACHINE\SYSTEM\CurrentControlSet\Services\DNS\
Parameters\LogFilePath
```

Set the value of `LogFilePath` equal to the file path and file name where you want to locate the DNS log.

By default, the maximum file size of `Dns.log` is 4MB. If you want to change the size, add the following entry to the registry with the REG_DWORD data type:

```
HKEY_LOCAL_
MACHINE\SYSTEM\CurrentControlSet\Services\DNS\
Parameters\LogFileMaxSize
```

Set the value of `LogFileMaxSize` equal to the desired file size in bytes. The minimum size is 64KB.

When the log file reaches the maximum size, Windows 2000 writes over the beginning of the file. If you make the value higher, data persists for a longer time, but the log file consumes more disk space. If you make the value smaller, the log file uses less disk space, but the data persists for a shorter time.

WARNING   Do not leave DNS logging turned on during normal operations, because it uses up both processing and hard disk resources. It is best to enable it only when you are diagnosing and solving DNS problems.

Necessary Procedures

In this section, you start performing some simple DNS monitoring and working with the nslookup directive tool. You may want to get more experience with this important tool. You also may want to check out the directive command dig. This command provides similar functionality, and some people prefer its interface.

NOTE   As you gain facility with DNS and understand the different concerns in managing this important infrastructure resource, you will develop confidence with these first two exam objectives. Make sure that you perform all the hands-on procedures. Remember, that is the perspective from which questions will be asked!

Simple DNS Monitoring

In this procedure, you get some hands-on practice with the nslookup directive tool, a simple but effective way to manage DNS problems. Follow these steps:

1. Open a Windows 2000 command prompt (Start ➤ Run; then type **cmd.exe** in the Run dialog box).

2. When the command prompt window opens, type **nslookup** and press the Enter key. (For the rest of the exercise, press the Enter key to terminate each command.)

3. nslookup starts, printing a message that tells you the name and IP address of the default DNS server. Write down this information; you'll need it later.

4. Try looking up a well-known address by typing http://www.microsoft.com. Notice that the query returns several IP addresses. (Microsoft load-balances Web traffic by using multiple servers in the same DNS record.)

5. Try looking up a nonexistent host by typing http://www.xvuwssssio.com. Your server complains that it can't find the address. This is normal behavior.

6. Change the server to a nonexistent host. Try making up a private IP address that you know isn't a DNS server on your network, such as 10.10.10.10.

7. Try doing another lookup of a known DNS name. Type microsoft.com. Notice that nslookup contacts the server you specified and that the lookup times out after a few seconds. This lookup operates in a similar but not identical way to a resolver query.

8. Reset your server to the address that you wrote down in step 3.

9. If doing so won't disrupt your network, unplug your computer from the network and repeat steps 4 through 8. Notice the differences.

Exam Essentials

Know how to use *nslookup* to perform DNS queries and to examine the contents of zone files on local and remote servers. Remember that nslookup also can be used to simulate zone transfers with the Ls command and the -d switch. nslookup behaves similarly to a resolver but does differ slightly. The tool has a great deal of functionality that is not described in this text. You can find information on compiling nslookup in Appendix B of the source of the 4.9.4 version of BIND at http://www.isc.org/isc/bind.html.

Know how to use the *ipconfig*'s option setting-*Set* commands-to configure how the resolver carries out queries.   Be familiar with the command-line options for the Set command displayed in Table 1.1.

Know how to use *ipconfig* to view DNS client settings, display and flush the resolver cache, and force a dynamic update client to register its DNS records.   Be familiar with all the command-line options shown in Table 1.2.

Know how to use Event Viewer to view DNS client and server error messages.   Be familiar with the different error messages, as they are likely to appear in some test versions.

Know how to stop the DNS client and flush its cache.   Practice stopping and restarting the network redirector with the Net Stop and Net Start commands.

Know the benefits and limitations of using the DNS log.   You can use the DNS log to have the DNS server monitor certain events and record them in the DNS log for your edification. Be sure to keep this log under reasonable size constraints.

Know how to use the DNS console's Monitoring tab.   Practice test queries by using the Controls options in the Monitoring tab of the DNS console.

Key Terms and Concepts

DNS log   A log file created by the DNS server that records the following types of events:

- Queries

- Notification messages from other servers

- Dynamic updates

- Content of the question section for DNS query message

- Content of the answer section for DNS query messages

- Number of queries this server sends

- Number of queries this server receives
- Number of DNS requests received over a UDP port
- Number of DNS requests received over a TCP port
- Number of full packets sent by the server
- Number of packets written through by the server and back to the zone

IP address A four-byte number that uniquely identifies a computer on an IP *internetwork*. InterNIC assigns the first bytes of Internet IP addresses and administers them in hierarchies. Organizations not attached to the Internet are free to assign IP addresses as they please.

ipconfig A command-line tool provided by Windows 2000, used to configure and to display the configuration of TCP/IP interfaces on your local machine.

nslookup A directive tool that allows you to query a DNS server to see what information it holds for a host record. A greater understanding of nslookup will result from practicing the different options that can be used with the Set command in interactive mode.

Sample Questions

1. What tab of the DNS snap-in allows you to choose which events you want to log?

   A. DNS Log

   B. Configure Events

   C. Logging

   D. Events Channel

   Answer: A. Choosing only the events that you want to log helps keep log files to a reasonable size.

2. If you want to query for a particular type of record with an
ipconfig option setting, you should use:

A. Set record

B. Set type

C. Set /t

D. Set /d

Answer: B. Set type is the correct option setting to use to look for
a particular type of record, such as an MX record.

Chapter

2

Installing, Configuring, Managing, Monitoring, and Troubleshooting DHCP in a Windows 2000 Network Infrastructure

MICROSOFT EXAM OBJECTIVES COVERED IN THIS CHAPTER:

▶ **Install, configure, and troubleshoot DHCP.** *(pages 51 – 78)*

- Install the DHCP Server service.
- Create and manage DHCP scopes, superscopes, and multicast scopes.
- Configure DHCP for DNS integration.
- Authorize a DHCP server in Active Directory.

▶ **Manage and monitor DHCP.** *(pages 78 – 81)*

his chapter examines the second of Windows 2000's three *network naming services* that you need to understand to pass Microsoft Exam 70-216: the Dynamic Host Configuration Protocol (DHCP). The Dynamic Host Configuration Protocol is designed to automate configuration of TCP/IP clients. You can put one or more DHCP servers on your network, program them with a range of network addresses and other configuration parameters, and let clients obtain IP addressing information automatically, without manual intervention. With appropriate DHCP configurations, your TCP/IP clients—running any OS that has DHCP support—can be configured without manual intervention from you.

To prepare you for the exam, this chapter shows you how to install the DHCP service and how to manage the IP addresses you have to work with as DHCP scopes, superscopes, and multicast scopes. You add on to what you learned in Chapter 1 about integrating DHCP with DNS, and you see how to authorize a DHCP server in Active Directory.

Managing and monitoring DHCP is not very complex, as you'll see in the second objective in this chapter. As long as you configure your DHCP properly, troubleshooting, managing, and monitoring DHCP are relatively easy tasks.

Install, configure, and troubleshoot DHCP.

- **Install the DHCP Server service.**
- **Create and manage DHCP scopes, superscopes, and multicast scopes.**
- **Configure DHCP for DNS integration.**
- **Authorize a DHCP server in Active Directory.**

This objective covers installing, configuring, and troubleshooting DHCP. You may have worked with DHCP on the Internet or back in the Windows NT 4 days, but it has become so important in Windows 2000 networks that you should take a closer look at the details that make up the DHCP process.

Critical Information

DHCP's job is to centralize the process of IP address and option assignment. You can configure a DHCP server with a range of addresses and then sit back and allow it to assign IP parameters such as addresses, default gateways, and DNS server addresses. In brief, the DHCP process works this way: When TCP/IP starts up on a DHCP-enabled host, a special message is sent, requesting an IP address and a subnet mask from a DHCP server.

Any DHCP server that hears the request checks its internal database and then replies with a message containing the information the client requested. When the client accepts the IP offer, the offer is extended to the client for a specified period called a *lease*. If the DHCP server has given out all the IP addresses in its range, it won't make an offer; if no other servers make an offer, the client's TCP/IP initialization fails.

The DHCP service in Windows 2000 is moderately different from the one included in Windows NT. For starters, you manage DHCP servers by using the DHCP snap-in for the Microsoft Management Console (MMC). A larger, though less visible, change is that DHCP and the Domain Name Service (DNS) are now integrated, as you saw in Chapter 1, so that DNS records can be updated whenever a DHCP-assigned address changes as the result of a lease issue or release.

Ideally, you'll integrate Dynamic DNS and DHCP on your Windows 2000 networks. When a DHCP client receives an IP address, the DHCP server dictates how dynamic updates occur. By default, here's what happens:

1. The DHCP client computer updates the DNS record that identifies which IP address is associated with that computer's name.

2. The DHCP server updates the corresponding DNS resource record that identifies which name belongs with the newly issued IP address.

Understanding DHCP Functionality

Because an IP address is required to communicate with other devices on a TCP/IP network, the DHCP negotiation happens very early in the Windows 2000 boot cycle.

NOTE Each network adapter in a system has its own IP address. If you have multiple NICs that are configured to use DHCP, you'll see that the process happens once for each DHCP-aware NIC.

The first step in the DHCP process is the *lease-request* stage. This stage is triggered the first time that a client's DHCP-configured TCP/IP stack starts or when you switch from using an assigned IP address to using DHCP. Just to complicate things further, the lease-request stage also can occur when a specific IP address is requested but unavailable or immediately after a formerly used IP address was released.

Stage One: IP Lease Request

At the time of any lease request, the client doesn't know what its IP address is; neither does it know the IP address of the server. To work around this problem, the client uses 0.0.0.0 as its address and 255.255.255.255 as the server's address; then it sends out a broadcast *DHCP discover message* on UDP ports 67 and 68. The discover message contains the hardware MAC address and NetBIOS name of the client.

When the first discover message is sent, the client waits 1 second for an offer. If no DHCP server responds within that time, the client repeats its request three more times at 9-, 13-, and 16-second intervals. If the client still doesn't hear an answer, it continues to broadcast discover messages every five minutes until it gets an answer. If no DHCP server ever becomes available, no TCP/IP communications will be possible.

The Windows 2000 client automatically picks what it thinks is an unused address (from the 169.254.x.y address block) at this point instead of waiting indefinitely for an answer. Even though a static address has been assigned, the DHCP client continuously polls for a DHCP server every five minutes and switches back to using a DHCP-assigned address when the server becomes available. Remember that the discover-message broadcasts won't be heard outside the client's local subnet unless your routers support BootP forwarding.

Stage Two: IP Lease Offer

In the second phase of the DHCP process, any DHCP server that received the discover-message broadcast and that has valid address information to offer responds with an offer message. The Windows 2000 DHCP server registers itself in Active Directory, and it doesn't begin offering leases until it successfully registers in the directory. The offer message is a proposal from the server to the client; it contains an IP address, a subnet mask, a lease period (in hours), and the IP address of the DHCP server offering the proposal. The IP address being offered is temporarily reserved so that the server doesn't offer the same address to multiple clients. All offers are sent directly to the requesting client's hardware MAC address.

Stage Three: IP Lease Selection

When the client receives at least one offer, the third phase of the DHCP process begins. In this phase, the client machine selects an offer from those it received. Windows 2000 always accepts the first offer that arrives. To signal acceptance, the client broadcasts an acceptance message containing the IP address of the server it selected. This message has to be broadcast so that the servers whose offers weren't selected can unreserve (pull back) the addresses that they offered.

Stage Four: IP Lease Acknowledgment

When the chosen DHCP server receives the acceptance message from the client, it marks the selected IP address as leased; then it sends an acknowledgment message, called a *DHCPACK*, to the client. The server might instead send a negative acknowledgment, or *DHCP-NACK*, to the client. DHCPNACKs are most often generated when the client is attempting to renew a lease for its old IP address after that address has been reassigned elsewhere. Negative acceptance messages also can mean that the requesting client has an inaccurate IP address, resulting from a physical change in locations to an alternative subnet.

The DHCPACK message includes any DHCP options specified by the server, along with the IP address and subnet mask. When the client receives this message, it puts the parameters into the TCP/IP stack, which then proceeds just as though the user gave it new configuration parameters manually.

NOTE   Manually configured entries on the client override any DHCP-supplied entries.

TIP   To remember these stages, just think "I please ROSA" ("IP lease," followed by the four phases: R-request, O-offer, S-selection, and A-acknowledgement).

DHCP Lease Renewal

No matter how long the lease period is, the client sends a new lease-request message to the DHCP server when the lease period is half over. If the server hears the request message and has no reason to reject it, it sends a DHCPACK to the client. This message resets the lease period.

If the DHCP server isn't available, it sends an "eviction notice," indicating that the lease can't be renewed. The client can use the address for the rest of the lease period. When 87.5 percent of the lease period has elapsed, the client sends another renewal request. At that point, any DHCP server that hears the renewal could respond to this *DHCPREQUEST* message with a DHCPACK and renew the lease.

Any time the client gets a DHCPNACK message, it must stop using its IP address immediately and start the leasing process over from the beginning by requesting a new lease.

When a client initializes TCP/IP, it always attempts to renew its old address. As in any other renewal, if the client has time left on the lease, it continues to use the lease until its end. If the client is unable to get a new lease by that time, all TCP/IP functions stop until a new, valid address can be obtained.

DHCP Lease Release

Although leases can be renewed repeatedly, at some point they're likely to run out. Furthermore, the lease process is an "at will" process, meaning that the client or server can cancel the lease before it ends. In addition, if the client doesn't succeed in renewing the lease before it expires, out it goes. This release process is an important function that's useful for reclaiming extinct IP addresses formerly used by systems that have moved or switched to a non-DHCP address.

Installing DHCP

Before you can configure a DHCP server, you must install it. When you install the DHCP server, you get the DHCP snap-in installed, too; you can open it by using the Start ➤Programs ➤ Administrative Tools ➤

DHCP command. The snap-in follows the standard MMC model. The left pane shows you which servers are available, allowing you to connect to servers other than the one to which you're already talking. Each server contains subordinate items grouped in folders.

Each scope has a folder, which is named after the scope's IP address range. A *scope* is nothing more than a contiguous range of IP addresses. A separate folder, Server Options, holds options that are specific to a particular DHCP server. Within each scope are four subordinate views that show you interesting things about the scope, such as the following:

- The Address Pool view shows you what the address pool looks like.

- The Address Leases view shows one entry for each current lease. Each lease shows the computer to which the lease was issued, the corresponding IP address, and the current lease-expiration time.

- The Reservations view shows you which IP addresses are reserved and which devices hold them.

- The Scope Options view lists the set of options you've defined for this scope. The three options are the default gateway (003 Router), the default DNS server (006 DNS Servers), and the default DNS domain name (015 DNS Domain Name).

Understanding Scopes and Superscopes

To learn how to configure your servers to hand out leases, you need to understand scopes. There's usually one scope per physical subnet, and a scope can cover a class A, class B, class C, or class D (with multicast) network address. DHCP uses scopes as the basis for managing and assigning IP addressing information.

A *superscope* is an administrative convenience that allows you to group two or more scopes even though they're actually separate. In reality, a superscope is just a list of its child scopes. Microsoft's DHCP snap-in allows you to manage IP address assignment in the superscope, though you still must configure other scope options individually for each child scope.

Each scope has a set of parameters you can set. These parameters, or scope options, control what data are delivered to DHCP clients to complete the DHCP negotiation process with that particular server. For example, the DNS server name, default gateway, and default network time server are all separate options that can be assigned.

More properly, these settings are called option types; you can use any of the types provided with Windows 2000, or you can roll your own. What about IP addresses? The scope defines what addresses potentially could be assigned, but you can influence the assignment process in two additional ways by specifying the following:

- Any IP addresses within the range that you *never* want to be assigned automatically. These addresses are called excluded addresses or just *exclusions*, and they're off limits to DHCP. You typically use exclusions to tag any addresses that you never want the DHCP server to assign.

- Any IP addresses within the range for which you want a permanent DHCP lease. These addresses are known as *reservations*, because they essentially reserve a particular IP address for a particular device.

TIP How do you know whether to use a reservation or an exclusion? The key is what you want to do with the addresses. If you have a range of addresses reserved for devices such as routers, gateways, and printers, you normally exclude their addresses so that they don't participate in DHCP. Alternatively, if you're using devices such as laptops, and you want them to get DHCP settings without getting a new address each time they restart, you can use reservations.

The range of IP addresses that the DHCP server actually can assign is called its *address pool*.

Creating and Managing DHCP Scopes

Like many other things in Windows 2000, the process of creating a new scope is driven by a wizard. In this case, the New Scope wizard is your helper. The overall process is simple, as long as you know beforehand what the wizard is going to ask. If you think about what defines a scope, you'll be well prepared. You need to know the following:

- The IP address range for the scope you want to create
- Which IP addresses, if any, you want to exclude from the address pool
- Which IP addresses, if any, you want to reserve
- Values for the DHCP options you want to set, if any

This last item isn't strictly necessary for creating a scope, because the wizard doesn't ask for any options. You probably will have *some* options to specify for the clients, however.

To create a scope, select a superscope or DHCP server in the DHCP snap-in; then choose the Action ➤ New Scope command. That command starts the New Scope wizard. The operation of this wizard is discussed in detail in the following sections, with each wizard page described in its own section.

Warming Up

The first two wizard pages are fairly uneventful. The first page tells you that you've launched the New Scope wizard, and the second allows you to enter a name and description for your scope. These tidbits are displayed by the DHCP snap-in, so it's a good idea to pick a sensible name for your scopes so that other administrators will be able to figure out what the scope is *for*.

Defining the IP Address Range

The next wizard page, the IP Address Range page, is where you enter the start and end IP addresses for your range. The wizard does minimal checking on the addresses you enter, but it automatically calculates the appropriate subnet mask for the address range you enter. You can modify the subnet mask if you know what you're doing.

Adding Exclusions

The Add Exclusions page allows you to create exclusion ranges as part of the scope-creation process. To exclude one address, put it in the Start IP Address field; to exclude a range, fill in a start and end address. Remember that you can always add exclusions later, but it's best to include them when you create the scope so that no excluded addresses are ever passed out to clients.

Setting a Lease Duration

The Lease Duration page allows you to set the lease duration. By default, new leases start with a duration of eight days and zero hours. This setting isn't a bad default, but you may find that a shorter or longer duration makes sense for your network. If your network is highly dynamic, with many arrivals, departures, and moving computers, set the lease duration to be short; if the network is less active, set the duration for a longer period. Remember that renewal attempts begin when half the lease period is over, so don't set them *too* short.

Configuring Basic DHCP Options

The Configure DHCP Options page allows you to choose whether you want to configure basic DHCP options (including the default gateway and DNS settings). If you choose to configure these options, you'll have to go through some additional pages, all of which are fairly simple. If you choose not to configure options, you can go back and do so later; if you take that route, make sure that you don't activate the scope until you've configured the options you to assign.

CONFIGURING A ROUTER

The first option-configuration page is the Router (Default Gateway) page, which allows you to enter the IP addresses of routers that you want to use as gateways for outbound traffic. Type in the IP addresses of the routers you want to use; then click the Up and Down buttons to put the list in the order you want clients to use when attempting to send outgoing packets.

PROVIDING DNS SETTINGS

The Domain Name and DNS Servers page allows you to specify the set of DNS servers and the parent domain you want to pass down to DHCP clients. Normally, you need to specify at least one DNS server by filling in its DNS name or IP address. You also can specify the domain that you want Windows 2000 to use as its base domain for all connections that don't have their own connection-specific suffixes defined.

PROVIDING WINS SETTINGS

If you're still using WINS on your network, you can configure DHCP so that it passes WINS -server addresses to your Windows clients (though if you want the Windows clients to honor it, you also need to define the WINS/NBT Node Type option for the scope). Like the Domain Name and DNS Servers page, the WINS Servers page allows you to enter the addresses of several servers, moving them into the order in which you want clients to try them. You can enter the DNS or NetBIOS name of each server, or you can enter an IP address. An IP address is recommended in case name resolution fails.

ACTIVATING THE SCOPE

The final page gives you the option of activating the scope immediately after creating it. By default, the wizard assumes that you want the scope to be activated unless you select the No, I Will Active [sic] This Scope Later radio button, in which case the scope remains dormant until you activate it manually.

WARNING   Be sure to verify that no other DHCP servers are assigned to the address range you choose!

Setting Scope Properties

Each scope has a set of properties associated with it. Except for the set of options assigned by the scope, these properties are listed in the General tab of the Scope Properties dialog box. Some of these properties, such as Scope Name and Description, are self-explanatory. The following require a little more explanation:

- The Start IP Address and End IP Address fields allow you to set the size of the scope. The subnet mask is calculated for you automatically, based on the IP addresses you enter.

- The controls in the Lease Duration for DHCP Clients group control how long leases in this scope will be valid. Your two choices are set by the Limited To and Unlimited radio buttons. If you choose to set lease-duration limits, you use the Days, Hours, and Minutes controls to govern how long the leases will remain in use.

TIP   Don't confuse setting the properties of the scope with setting the options associated with the scope—those two operations are entirely different.

Managing Reservations and Exclusions

After defining the address pool, the next step is creating whatever reservations and exclusions you want to use to reduce the size of the pool.

ADDING AND REMOVING EXCLUSIONS

When you want to exclude an entire range of IP addresses, you need to add that range as an exclusion. Normally, you want to add the exclusion before you enable a scope, because that prevents you from issuing any of the excluded IP addresses accidentally. In fact, you can't create an exclusion that includes a leased address; you have to get rid of the lease first.

When you add exclusions, they appear in the Address Pool node below the scope where you added them. To remove an exclusion, just right-click it and then choose the Delete command. After confirming your command, the snap-in removes the excluded range and makes it available for immediate issuance.

ADDING AND REMOVING RESERVATIONS

Adding reservations is simple, as long as you have the MAC address of the device for which you want to create a reservation. Because reservations belong to a single scope, you create and remove them within the Reservations node below each scope. You add reservations by right-clicking the scope and then choosing the New Reservation command. That command displays the New Reservation dialog box.

At minimum, when you create a new reservation, you must enter the IP address and MAC address for the reservation. If you want, you also can enter a name and description for the reservation. You can choose whether the reservation will be made by DHCP only, BOOTP only (useful for remote-access devices that use BOOTP), or both.

To remove a reservation, right-click it and then choose the Delete command. This command removes the reservation but does nothing to the client device (which, after all, doesn't have a lease to revoke).

NOTE There's no way to change a reservation after it's been created; to change any of the associated settings, you have to delete it and then re-create it.

Setting Scope Options

After you've installed a server (and possibly authorized it in Active Directory) and fixed up the address pool, the next step is to set the options that you want to be sent to clients. You *must* configure the options that you want sent out before you activate a scope; if you don't, clients may register in the scope without getting any options, rendering them useless. There are five different (and slightly overlapping) ways to control which DHCP options are doled out to clients.

PREDEFINED OPTIONS

You predefine options so that they'll be available in the Server, Scope, or Client Options dialog box. Think of predefining options as making those options available.

SERVER OPTIONS

Server options are assigned to all scopes and clients of a particular server. That means if you want *all* clients of a DHCP server to have a certain setting, no matter what scope the clients are in; these settings are assigned to them.

Notice, however, that more specific options (such as those that are set at class, scope, or client level) override server-level options. That gives you an escape valve. It's a better idea, though, to be careful about which options you assign if your server manages multiple scopes.

SCOPE OPTIONS

If you want a particular option value to be assigned only to those clients in a certain subnet, select that scope as the base for the option. It's common practice to specify different routers for different physical subnets, for example. If you have two scopes corresponding to different subnets, each scope probably would have a separate value for the router option.

CLASS OPTIONS

The idea behind class options is that you should be able to assign different options to clients in different classes. Windows 2000 machines, for example, recognize several DHCP options that Windows 98 and Mac OS machines ignore. By defining a new Windows 2000 class, you could assign those options only to machines that report themselves as being in that class. The problem is that you need to have clients that are smart enough to do so, and most of them aren't.

CLIENT OPTIONS

If you want to force certain options onto a specific client, you can do so—provided that the client is using a DHCP reservation. You actually attach client options to a particular reservation; these options override any scope, server, or class option. In fact, the only way to override a client option is to configure the client manually. The DHCP server manages client options.

Assigning Options

You can use the DHCP snap-in to assign options at the scope, server, reserved address, or class level. The mechanism you use to assign these options is identical; the only difference is where you set the options. When you create an option assignment, remember that it applies to all the clients of the server or in the scope *from that point forward*. Option assignments aren't retroactive, and they don't migrate from one scope to another.

To actually *create* a new option and have it assigned, select the scope or server where you want the option to be assigned; then select the corresponding Options node and choose the Action ➢ Configure Options command. (To set options for a reserved client, right-click its entry in the Reservations node and then choose the Configure

Options command.) This command displays the Configure Options dialog box, which lists all the options you might want to configure.

To select an individual option, check the check box next to it; then use the controls in the Data Entry control group to enter the value that you want to associate with the option. Continue to add options until you've specified all the ones you want to attach to the server or scope; then click the OK button.

Activating and Deactivating Scopes

When you've completed the preceding steps, and you're ready to unleash your new scope so that it can be used to make client assignments, the final required step is activating the scope. Activating a scope just tells the server that it's OK to start handing out addresses from that scope's address pool. As soon as you activate a scope, addresses from its pool can be assigned to clients. Activation, of course, is a necessary precondition to getting any use out of your scope.

If you later want to stop using a scope, you can, but beware: the change is permanent. You turn off a scope by deactivating it, but when you do, DHCP tells all clients registered with the scope that they need to release their leases and renew them someplace else. Don't deactivate a scope unless you want clients to stop using it immediately.

Creating a Superscope

A superscope allows the DHCP server to provide multiple logical subnet addresses to DHCP clients on a single physical network. You create superscopes by choosing the New Superscope command. It shouldn't surprise you to learn that this command triggers the New Superscope Wizard. This wizard is so simple, however, that it really didn't need to be a wizard.

NOTE You can have only one superscope per server.

Adding and Removing Scopes

Adding a scope to an existing superscope is easy. Find the scope that you want to add; then right-click it and choose the Action ➤ Add to

Superscope command. This command causes the snap-in to display a dialog box listing all the scopes known to this server; pick the one you want to append to the current superscope and then click the OK button.

If you later want to remove a scope from a superscope, open the superscope and right-click the target scope. The context menu provides a Remove from Superscope command that will do the deed.

Activating and Deactivating Superscopes

Just as you can with regular scopes, you can activate and deactivate superscopes. The same restrictions and guidelines apply—that is, you must activate a superscope before it can be used, and you must not deactivate it until you want all your clients to lose their existing leases and be forced to request new ones.

Creating Multicast Scopes

IP multicasting is becoming increasingly common as the amount of network bandwidth available on the average network increases. It's much more efficient to *multicast* a video or audio stream to multiple destinations than it is to broadcast it to the same number of clients, and the increased demand for multicast-friendly network hardware has resulted in some head-scratching about how to automate the multicast configuration.

DHCP normally is used to assign IP configuration information for *unicast* (one-to-one) network communications. It turns out that a separate type of address space is assigned just for multicasting: 224.0.0.0 -239.255.255.255. Multicast clients, however, also need to have an "ordinary" IP address; clients can participate in a multicast just by knowing (and using) the multicast address for the content they want to receive.

How do clients know what address to use? Ordinary DHCP won't help, because it's designed to assign IP addresses and option information to one client at a time. Realizing this, the Internet Engineering Task Force (IETF) defined a new protocol: the *Multicast Address Dynamic Client Allocation Protocol*, or *MADCAP*. MADCAP provides an analog to DHCP, but for multicast use. A MADCAP server issues leases for multicast addresses only. MADCAP clients can request a multicast lease when they want to participate in a multicast.

There are some important differences between DHCP and MADCAP. First, you have to realize that the two protocols are totally separate. A single server can be a DHCP server, a MADCAP server, or *both*; there's no implied or actual relation between the two. Likewise, clients can use DHCP and/or MADCAP at the same time; the only requirement is that every MADCAP client has to get a unicast IP address from somewhere. The multicast address is used only to *receive* packets.

Next, remember that DHCP can assign options as part of the lease process, but MADCAP cannot. The only thing that MADCAP does is assign multicast addresses dynamically.

TIP The Windows 2000 Server online help system has a comprehensive checklist that covers how to set up IP multicasting, just in case you're interested. Exam questions have been known to come from sources such as this.

Building Multicast Scopes

When you want to create a new multicast scope, right-click the server on which you want to create the scope and then choose the New Multicast Scope command. Most of the steps you follow to create a multicast scope are identical to those required for creating an ordinary unicast scope.

Setting Multicast Scope Properties

After you create a multicast scope, you can adjust its properties by selecting it and choosing the standard Properties command. This command displays the Multicast Scope Properties dialog box, which has two tabs. The General tab allows you to change the scope's name, its start or end address, its TTL value, its lease duration, and its description—in essence, all the settings that you provided when you created it in the first place. The Lifetime tab allows you to limit how long your multicast scope will hang around. By default, a newly created multicast scope lives forever, but if you're creating a scope to provide MADCAP assignments for a single event (or a set of events that cover a limited duration), you can specify an expiration time for the scope. When that time is reached, the scope disappears from the server, but not before making all its clients give up their multicast address leases. This multicast lease return is a nice way to make sure the lease cleans up after itself when you're done with it.

Enabling DDNS-DHCP Integration

DHCP integration with Dynamic DNS is a great Windows 2000 feature. It's simple in concept but powerful in action, because by setting up that integration, you can pass out addresses to DHCP clients while maintaining the integrity (and utility!) of your DNS services.

There are actually two separate ways that the DNS server could be updated. One way is for the DHCP client to tell the DNS server, "Hey, my address is now XYZ." This method is easy to understand, but it's insecure, because there's no way to trust the client to tell the truth. The default Windows 2000 method is better: the DHCP server tells the DNS server when it registers a new client. This method relies on the likelihood that the DHCP server is more trustworthy than some random client.

Neither of these updates, however, will take place unless you configure the DHCP server to use Dynamic DNS. You can make this change in two different ways. If you make the change at scope level, the change applies only to that scope, but if you make the change at server level, it applies to all scopes and superscopes served by the server. Whichever of these options you choose depends on how widely you want to support Dynamic DNS. Most sites have enabled DNS updates at server level.

NOTE Don't forget that you also have to instruct the DNS server to *accept* Dynamic DNS updates. For more information on how to do so, see Chapter 1.

To actually update the settings at either the server or scope levels, you need to open the scope or server properties, which you do by right-clicking the appropriate object and choosing the Properties command. When you do, you'll see the General tab, which allows you to adjust some general settings for the object you've just opened. Next to the General tab is the DNS tab, which contains the stuff you're interested in for this purpose.

The DNS tab controls are:

- The Automatically Update DHCP Client Information In DNS check box controls whether this DHCP server attempts to register lease information with a DNS server. It must be checked to enable Dynamic DNS.

- The Update DNS Only If DHCP Client Requests radio button (which is selected by default) tells the DHCP server to register the update only if the DHCP client asks for DNS registration. When this option is active, DHCP clients that aren't configured to DDNS won't have their DNS records updated. Windows 98 and Windows 2000 DHCP clients, however, are smart enough to ask for the updates.

- The Always Update DNS radio button forces the DHCP server to register *any* client to which it issues a lease. This setting may add DNS registrations for DHCP-enabled devices that really don't need them (such as printer servers), but it allows other clients (such as Mac OS, Windows NT, and Linux machines) to have their DNS information updated automatically.

- The Discard Forward (Name-to-Address) Lookups When Lease Expires check box has a long name but a simple function. When a DHCP lease expires, what should happen to the DNS registration? Obviously, it would be nice if the DNS record associated with a lease vanished when the lease expired, and when this check box is checked (as it is by default), that's exactly what happens. If you uncheck this box, your DNS will contain entries for expired leases that are no longer valid. When a particular IP address is reissued on a new lease, the DNS is updated, but between leases, you'll have incorrect data in your DNS—something to avoid.

- The Enable Updates for DNS Clients That Do Not Support Dynamic Update check box allows you to handle older clients, that don't support Dynamic DNS, making the updates via a separate mechanism.

Authorizing DHCP for Active Directory

After you've installed a server, your next step is to authorize the DHCP server in Active Directory. Authorization, which actually creates an Active Directory object representing the new server, helps keep unauthorized servers off your network. These renegade servers can cause two kinds of problems: they may hand out bogus leases, or they may fraudulently deny renewal requests from legitimate clients.

When you install a DHCP server by using Windows 2000, and if Active Directory is present on your network, the server won't be allowed to provide DHCP services to clients until it's been authorized. If you install DHCP on a member server in an Active Directory domain or on a stand-alone server, you'll have to authorize the server manually. When you authorize a server, you're really adding its IP address to the Active Directory object that contains a list of the IP addresses of all authorized DHCP servers.

At start time, each DHCP server queries the directory, looking for its IP address in the "authorized" list. If a server can't find the list, or if it can't find its IP address on the list, the DHCP service fails to start. Instead, the server logs an event-log message, indicating that it couldn't service client requests because it wasn't authorized. This mechanism works only with Windows 2000 DHCP servers; there's no way to monitor or restrict the presence of DHCP servers running under other operating systems, including Windows NT.

Necessary Procedures

Installing DHCP is easy, because it uses the new Windows 2000 installation mechanism. Unlike some of the other services described in this book, the actual installation installs just the service and its associated snap-in, starting the service when it's done. At that point, the installation mechanism is not delivering any DHCP service, but at least you don't have to reboot or answer intrusive wizard questions.

As part of this objective's procedures, you get to create a scope for a private class C network and also create a new superscope. You get hands-on experience adding an exclusion range on a scope and get some practice creating a multicast scope. You enable DNS/DHCP integration and also practice the steps to authorize a DHCP server.

Installing the DHCP Service

Follow these steps to install the DHCP server:

NOTE This procedure works only on computers running Windows 2000 Server or Advanced Server.

---

1. Open the Windows Components wizard by opening Add/Remove Programs in Control Panel (Start ➤ Settings ➤ Control Panel ➤ Add/Remove Programs).

2. Click the Add/Remove Windows Components icon. The Installation wizard opens, listing all the components that it knows how to install or remove.

3. Select the Networking Services item in the component list; then click the Details button.

4. When the Subcomponents of Network Services list appears, make sure that Dynamic Host Configuration Protocol (DHCP) is selected; then click the OK button.

5. If prompted, enter the path to the Windows 2000 distribution files.

Creating a New Scope

Follow these steps to create a new scope for a private class C network:

1. Open the DHCP snap-in (Start ➤Programs ➤ Administrative Tools ➤ DHCP).

2. Right-click the server on which you want to create the new scope, and choose the New Scope command. The New Scope wizard appears.

3. Click the OK button to dismiss the first wizard page.

4. Enter a name and a description for your new scope; then click the Next button.

5. In the IP Address Range page, enter the start IP address for the scope and the end IP address. Leave the subnet-mask controls alone (although when creating a scope on a production network, you might need to change them). Click the Next button.

6. In the Add Exclusions page, click Next without adding any excluded addresses, (unless you want to exclude some, as you will do in the next procedure).

7. In the Lease Duration page, set the lease duration to however many days you want your lease to run; then click the Next button.

8. In the Configure DHCP Options page, click the Next button to indicate that you want to configure default options for this scope.

9. Enter a router IP address in the IP address field; then click the Add button. When the address is added, click the Next button.

10. In the Domain Name and DNS Servers page, enter the IP address of a DNS server on your network in the IP address field; then click the Add button. When you're done, click the Next button.

11. In the WINS Servers page, click the Next button to leave the WINS options unset and display the Activate Scope page.

If your network is currently using the range of IP addresses you selected, select the No, I Will Active This Scope Later radio button. Click the Next button. When the Wizard Summary page appears, click the Finish button to create the scope.

Adding an Exclusion Range

Follow these steps to add an exclusion range of IP addresses you want set aside:

1. Open the DHCP snap-in, and find the scope to which you want to add an exclusion.

2. Expand the scope so that you can see its Address Pool item.

3. Right-click Address Pool; then choose the New Exclusion Range command. (Alternatively, you can choose the Actions ➤ New Exclusion Range command.)

4. When the Add Exclusion dialog box appears, use it to enter the IP addresses that you want to exclude. To exclude a single address, type it in the Start IP address field; to exclude a range, put the end address of the range in the End IP address field.

5. Click the Add button to add the exclusion.

Creating a New Superscope

Follow these steps to create a superscope:

1. Open the DHCP snap-in (Start ➤Programs ➤ Administrative Tools ➤ DHCP).

2. Follow the instructions in "Creating a New Scope" earlier in this chapter to create two scopes with different sets of contiguous IP addresses.

3. Right-click your DHCP server; then choose the New Superscope command. The New Superscope wizard appears. Dismiss the first wizard page by clicking the Next button.

4. In the Superscope Name page, name your superscope; then click the Next button.

5. The Select Scopes page appears, displaying a list of all scopes on the current server. Select the two scopes that you created in step 2; then click the Next button.

6. The Wizard Summary page appears; click the Finish button to create your superscope.

7. Verify that your new superscope appears in the DHCP snap-in.

NOTE You may notice that you can delete a superscope by right-clicking it and then choosing the Delete command. Because a superscope is just an organizational convenience, you can safely delete one scope at any time; doing so doesn't affect the "real" scopes that make up the superscope.

Creating a New Multicast Scope

Follow these steps to create a new multicast scope:

1. Open the DHCP snap-in (Start ➤Programs ➤ Administrative Tools ➤ DHCP).

2. Right-click your DHCP server; then choose the New Multicast Scope command. The New Multicast Scope wizard appears. Dismiss the first wizard page by clicking the Next button.

3. In the Multicast Scope Name page, name your multicast scope (and add a description, if you'd want); then click the Next button. The IP Address Range page appears.

4. Enter a start IP address and an end IP address. Adjust the TTL to 1 to make sure that no multicast packets escape your local network segment. Click the Next button when you're done. The Add Exclusions page appears.

5. Click the Next button. The Lease Duration page appears.

6. Normally, you leave multicast scope assignments in place somewhat longer than their unicast brethren—hence, the default lease length of 30 days. Click the Next button.

7. The wizard asks whether you want to activate the scope now. Click the No radio button; then click the Next button. The Wizard Summary page appears.

8. Click the Finish button to create your scope.

Verify that your new multicast scope appears in the DHCP snap-in. Delete it at your convenience.

Enabling DHCP-DNS Integration

Follow these steps to enable a scope to participate in Dynamic DNS updates:

1. Open the DHCP snap-in (Start ≻Programs ≻ Administrative Tools ≻ DHCP).

2. Right-click your DHCP server; then choose the Properties command. The Server Properties dialog box appears.

3. Click the DNS tab.

4. Check the Automatically Update DHCP Client Information in DNS check box.

5. Check the Discard Forward (Name-to-Address) Lookups When Lease Expires check box.

Click the OK button to apply your changes and dismiss the Properties dialog box.

Authorizing a DHCP Server

Follow these steps to authorize a DHCP server in Active Directory:

1. Open the DHCP snap-in (Start ≻Programs ≻ Administrative Tools ≻ DHCP).

2. Right-click the server you want to authorize; then choose the Authorize command.

3. Wait a short time (30 to 45 seconds) to allow the authorization to take place.

Right-click the server again. Verify that the Unauthorize command appears in the context menu; this command indicates that the server is authorized. You can unauthorize a previously authorized server by right-clicking it and then choosing the Unauthorize command.

Exam Essentials

Know how DHCP services work in a Windows 2000 network. Be familiar with how IP leases are requested and granted by DHCP. Also be familiar with lease renewal and release, and with the conditions that result in the absence of an IP lease for a client.

Know and plan how you will assign your IP addresses before you install DHCP. You must understand which addresses you plan to hold permanently as reservations and which you will exclude from the address pool.

Know the differences between scope properties and options, and how and why they are assigned. Be sure that you understand DHCP options, as well as scope options and how they differ from scope properties.

Know the time frames involved with DHCP leases. Understand that the client always requests a lease extension or new lease when half the time has expired and again when 87.5 percent of the time is up.

Know how to install and configure DHCP. Gain experience working with the folders for the address pool, the address lease, reservations, and scope options.

Know about scopes, superscopes, and multicast scopes. Be knowledgeable about the necessary parameters and steps involved in creating scopes, grouping them into superscopes, and creating multicast scopes.

Know how to integrate DNS with DHCP. Be clear about the steps for integrating Dynamic DNS with DHCP to keep your network's records correct and current as DHCP manages your IP address pool.

Know how to authorize DHCP servers in Active Directory. Take advantage of Active Directory and incorporate your DHCP process into Windows 2000 fully by knowing these steps.

Key Terms and Concepts

address pool   The range of IP addresses that the DHCP server can actually assign.

DHCPACK   An acknowledgment message sent by the DHCP server to the client after the server marks the selected IP address as leased.

DHCP authorization   The process of enabling a DHCP server to lease addresses by registering the server in Active Directory.

DHCP discover message   A message broadcast by a DHCP client that's looking for a nearby DHCP server. The discover message contains the hardware MAC address and NetBIOS name of the client, which the server can use to direct the request.

DHCP integration   A feature that allows you to pass out addresses to DHCP clients while still maintaining the integrity of your DNS services.

DHCP lease request   A request sent by a DHCP client for assignment of an IP address (and related parameters) from a DHCP server.

DHCPNACK   A negative acknowledgment sent by the DHCP server to the client. This situation generally occurs when the client is attempting to renew a lease for its old IP address after that it has been reassigned.

DHCP relay agent   A functional entity that enables DHCP on a multi-segment network, you can use a DHCP relay agent or proxy to forward requests.

DHCP server   A server configured to provide DHCP clients with all of their IP configuration information automatically.

exclusion   An IP address within the range that you *never* want the DHCP server to assign automatically.

host record   A record that associates a host's name to its IP address (also known as an address or A record).

lease   The offer of service provided by a DHCP server to a client upon successful negotiation.

Multicast Address Dynamic Client Allocation Protocol (MAD-CAP)   A protocol that issues leases for multicast addresses only.

multicast routing   A transportation process that allows one machine to send packets to an entire network.

multicast scope   A range in which multicast addresses can be assigned.

reservation   An IP addresses within the range for which you want a permanent DHCP lease for a specific device.

scope   A contiguous range of IP addresses.

superscope   A management convenience that allows you to group two or more scopes even though they're actually separate.

unicast routing   A transportation process that allows one machine to send packets directly to one destination address.

unicast scope   A DHCP scope used to assign unicast (point-to-point) addresses. Compare with *MADCAP*.

Sample Questions

1. Which of the following statements about superscopes are true? (Choose all that apply.)

    A. Only one superscope is allowed for every DHCP server.

    B. A superscope is an administrative convenience that allows you to group scopes.

    C. A superscope allows one server to handle multiple logical subnets on one physical network.

    D. You must name your superscope.

    Answer: A, B, C, and D. All of the above statements are true.

2. To take advantage of Dynamic DNS and to integrate it with DHCP, you must do which of the following?

    A. Configure it with multicast scopes.

B. Enable DNS updates on the DHCP server.

C. Enable dynamic updates on the DNS server.

D. Enable it on only one scope or the entire server.

Answer: B, C, and D. You must enable Dynamic DNS support on the DNS server and on the DHCP server, as well as choose whether to enable it on the entire server or for a single scope.

Manage and monitor DHCP.

To understand the ongoing duties of DHCP administration and to understand this second chapter objective, you need to familiarize yourself with the following information on monitoring and removing leases, as well as the procedures for inspecting leases and reconciling scopes.

Critical Information

As you saw with DNS, the difference between DHCP management and troubleshooting is a nebulous objective difference that possibly is clear only to Microsoft. You need to understand some processes, however, to accomplish these goals should your DHCP automated processes go awry. It can be useful to be able to see your DHCP leases, for example.

Monitoring DHCP Leases

You monitor which DHCP leases have been assigned by using the Address Lease view associated with a particular scope. When you open the scope and choose this view, you see an easy-to-read list of all the leases that are currently in force for that scope. This view shows the client IP address, the client's DNS name, the lease's duration, and the client's unique DHCP ID (if there is one).

Removing Client Leases

If you want to remove a client lease, you can do so by right-clicking it and then choosing the Delete command. This command actually removes the lease, but not before canceling it. Normally, it's better to let leases expire than to cancel them manually, but circumstances sometimes dictate otherwise.

Necessary Procedures

On larger networks with broader scopes and more information to study, you can create a text file for recordkeeping, troubleshooting, or analysis. You also should be aware of the process of *reconciling* a scope, which means checking for inconsistencies with your assigned leases.

Inspecting Leases

Follow these steps to create a tab-delimited text file containing information about all leases in a scope:

1. Open the DHCP snap-in (Start ➤Programs ➤ Administrative Tools ➤ DHCP).

2. Expand the target server's node in the MMC until you see the Address Leases node.

3. Right-click the Address Leases node; then choose the Export List command.

4. When the Save As dialog box appears, select a location for the list file. Type a meaningful name in the Filename field; then click the Save button.

Open the file that you just created with WordPad, Word, Excel, or any other tool that honors tab settings. Notice that the contents of the file mirror what you saw in the DHCP snap-in.

Reconciling a Scope

Follow these steps to reconcile a single scope on your server:

1. Open the DHCP snap-in (Start ➢ Programs ➢ Administrative Tools ➢ DHCP).

2. Expand the target server's node in the MMC until you see the target scope.

3. Right-click the target scope; then choose the Reconcile command. The Reconcile dialog box appears, but it's empty.

4. To start the reconciliation, click the Verify button.

If the database is consistent, a dialog box tells you so. If there are any inconsistencies, the dialog box lists them and allows you to repair them.

You can use a similar procedure to reconcile all scopes on a server. You just right-click the DHCP server and choose the Reconcile All Scopes command instead of reconciling the individual scope. To recover a broken DHCP server the preferred way, first remove the database files and then reconcile all scopes on the server to rebuild the database.

Exam Essentials

Know the method for monitoring and removing leases. Although it is better to remove an address and let a client find a new DHCP lease, it may be necessary in some situations to remove one. Be familiar with this process, as well as the method of viewing leases and the parameters that are visible when you do.

Know how to make a text file listing all leases. This file may be a useful baseline record to keep for your network at certain intervals.

Know how to reconcile a scope. This knowledge is important if you have problems or need to rebuild your DHCP database.

Key Terms and Concepts

scope reconciliation   A procedure that checks the assigned leases in DHCP scopes for inconsistencies in preparation for their repair. If no consistencies exist, or if you repair any that you find, the scope is reconciled.

Sample Question

1. What method would you use to recover a broken DHCP server?

A. First reconcile all the scopes and then remove the database files.

B. First remove the database files and then reconcile the scopes.

C. Configure new scopes, and don't worry about reconciling the scopes.

D. None of the above.

Answer: B. First remove the database; then you can reconcile the scopes. This procedure can be much easier than reconfiguring all the scopes.

Chapter

3

Configuring, Managing, Monitoring, and Troubleshooting Remote Access in a Windows 2000 Network Infrastructure

---

MICROSOFT EXAM OBJECTIVES COVERED IN THIS CHAPTER:

▶ **Configure and troubleshoot remote access.**
(pages 85 – 119)

- Configure inbound connections.
- Create a remote access policy.
- Configure a remote access profile.
- Configure a virtual private network (VPN).
- Configure multilink connections.
- Configure Routing and Remote Access for DHCP Integration.

▶ **Manage and monitor remote access.**
(pages 119 – 126)

▶ **Configure remote access security.**
(pages 126 – 138)

- Configure authentication protocols.
- Configure encryption protocols.
- Create a remote access policy.

Some Windows 2000 features are thinly disguised retreads from Windows NT and its various service and option packs; others are wholly new. The remote access service component of the Routing and Remote Access Service (RRAS) falls somewhere in between. RRAS itself dates back to the NT 4 Option Pack, but the Windows 2000 implementation of remote access adds a ton of new features that are not present in the older version.

Before you can get into the details of what these features do and how you configure them to provide remote access for your network, you need to understand some of the terms and concepts specific to RRAS remote access and to details about virtual private networks (VPNs).

After reviewing those basic details, you move on to reviewing the details of the configuration subobjectives of remote access configuration, inbound connection configuration, remote access policy configuration, remote access profile configuration, VPN configuration, multilink connection configuration, and the methods of configuring RRAS for DHCP integration.

You then take a closer look at managing and monitoring remote access and at configuring remote access security. Within the security objective section of this chapter, you look at configuring authentication protocols, configuring encryption protocols, and creating a remote access policy.

Finally, you study the procedures and concepts that you need to learn to meet the exam objectives.

Configure and troubleshoot remote access.

- Configure inbound connections.
- Create a remote access policy.
- Configure a remote access profile.
- Configure a virtual private network (VPN).
- Configure multilink connections.
- Configure Routing and Remote Access for DHCP Integration.

Remote access services provide another way to carry the network protocols you're already using. In the case of RRAS, they also provide some security services necessary to provide remote access effectively. You'll probably want to have the ability to restrict user dial-up access by group membership, time of day, or other factors, and you'll need a way to specify the various callback, authentication, and encryption options that the protocols support.

Critical Information

In the bad old days, remote access was part of few networks. It was too hard to implement, too hard to manage, and too hard to secure. Securing your networks against unauthorized physical access is reasonably easy, but doing so for remote access was perceived (rightly or wrongly) as being much harder. Several security policies, protocols, and technologies have been developed to ease this problem.

Understanding User Authentication

One of the first steps in establishing a remote access connection involves allowing the user to present some credentials to the server. This process is like showing your invitation to the doorkeeper at a fancy party; some parties have more elaborate authentication mechanisms than others. The same is true of remote access. You can use any or all of the following five authentication protocols that Windows 2000 supports:

Password Authentication Protocol (PAP)   PAP is the simplest—and least secure—authentication protocol. It transmits all authentication information in clear text with no encryption, which makes it vulnerable to snooping. In addition, it has no way for a client and server to authenticate each other. Because other protocols offer better security, PAP is falling out of favor, and Microsoft recommends turning it off unless you have clients that cannot use a more secure protocol.

Shiva Password Authentication Protocol (SPAP)   SPAP is a slightly more secure version of PAP that's intended primarily for talking to remote-access hardware devices made by Shiva (which is now owned by Intel). It's included for backward compatibility, but isn't in wide use.

Challenge Handshake Authentication Protocol (CHAP)   CHAP (sometimes called MD5-CHAP, because it uses the RSA MD5 hash algorithm) has a major security advantage over PAP: it doesn't transmit password information in the clear. Instead, the server sends a challenge encrypted with the DES algorithm to the client, which must decrypt it and return the correct response. This setup allows the server to verify the user's credentials without sending those credentials across an insecure link.

Although NT's RAS client can use MD5-CHAP when dialing into a third-party device, an unmodified NT RAS server will not support MD5-CHAP clients, because MD5-CHAP requires the server to store passwords in clear text. For security purposes, the SAM database stores NT passwords as a hash—never in clear text.

Microsoft CHAP (MS-CHAP)   Microsoft has extended the CHAP protocol to allow the use of Windows authentication information (among other things, that's what the Log on With Dial-Up Networking check box in the Windows 2000 logon dialog box does). There are two separate versions of MS-CHAP. Version 2 is much more secure than version 1, and all Microsoft operating systems support version 2.

Extensible Authentication Protocol (EAP)   EAP is fairly nifty. Instead of hard-wiring any single authentication protocol, a client-server pair that understands EAP can negotiate an authentication method. The computer that asks for authentication is called the *authenticator*. The authenticator is free to ask for several different pieces of information, making a separate query for each one. This system allows the use of almost any authentication method, including secure access tokens such as SecurID, one-time password systems such as S/Key, or ordinary username/password systems.

Each authentication scheme supported in EAP is called an *EAP type*. Each EAP type in turn is implemented as a plug-in module. Windows 2000 can support any number of EAP types at the same time; the RRAS server can use any EAP type to authenticate if (a) you've allowed that module to be used and (b) the client has the module in question. Windows 2000 comes with the following two EAP types:

EAP MD5-CHAP implements the version of CHAP that uses the MD5 hash algorithm. The EAP version of CHAP is identical to the regular version, but the challenges and responses are packaged and sent as EAP messages. This means that if you turn EAP MD5-CHAP on and disable regular CHAP on the server, plain CHAP clients won't be able to authenticate.

EAP Transport Level Security (TLS) allows you to use public-key certificates as an authenticator. TLS is very similar to the familiar Secure Sockets Layer (SSL) protocol used for Web browsers. When EAP TLS is turned on, the client and server send TLS-encrypted messages back and forth. EAP TLS is the strongest authentication method you can use; as a bonus, it supports smartcards. EAP TLS, however, requires your RRAS server to be part of a Windows 2000 domain.

A third EAP authentication method is included with Windows 2000, but it's not really an EAP type. EAP-RADIUS is a fake EAP type that passes any incoming message to a RADIUS server for authentication. (*RADIUS* stands for *Remote Authentication for Dial-In User Service*.)

Using Virtual Private Networks

Most people think the Internet was the first true wide-area network, but several others can legitimately argue that they deserve the title. Private networks used for credit-card authorization and time-sharing access to mainframes provided wide-area networking before the Internet took hold as a consumer technology.

Private networks offer superior security: Because you own the wires, you control what they're used for, who can use them, and what kind of data passes over them. These networks are not very flexible, however. If each of those networks is in a separate city, that implies a requirement for leased lines to implement the internetwork connection, and leased lines are expensive. To make things worse, most private networks face a dilemma: implementing enough capacity to handle peak loads almost guarantees that much of that capacity will sit idly much of the time, even though it still has to be paid for.

One way to work around this problem is to maintain private dial-up services so that a field rep can dial the home office. Dial-ups are expensive, and they have the same excess-capacity problem that truly private networks do. As an added detriment, users who need to dial in from long distances have to pay long-distance charges unless they use toll-free numbers (in which case the remote access cost goes up dramatically).

Virtual private networks (VPNs) offer a solution: you get the security of a true private network with the flexibility, ubiquity, and low cost of the Internet. To understand how VPNs work, as well as the PPTP and L2TP encapsulation process, check out *MCSE: Windows 2000 Network Infrastructure Administration Study Guide* by Paul Robichaux (Sybex 2000).

Understanding What Multilink Is All About

Many parts of the world don't have high-speed broadband access yet. In fact, many places don't have ISDN or even phone lines that support 56K modems. Wouldn't it be nice if there were some way to aggregate multiple analog or ISDN lines to make them act like one faster connection? In fact, there is. The multilink extensions to Point-to-Point Protocol (PPP) provide a way to gang up several independent PPP connections so that they act as a single connection. The multilink PPP software on the Windows 2000 machine and on the ISP's router takes care of stringing all the packets together to make this process seamless.

Windows 2000's RRAS service supports multilink PPP for inbound and outbound calls; the dial-up networking client supports it too. The primary drawback to multilink calls is they take up more than one phone line apiece.

Configuring IP-Based Connections

TCP/IP is far and away the most commonly used remote access protocol; coincidentally, it's also the most configurable of the protocols that Windows 2000 supports. Both of these facts are reflected in the IP tab of the server Properties dialog box.

The controls in the tab do the following:

- The Enable IP Routing check box controls whether RRAS routes IP packets between the remote client and other interfaces on your RRAS server. When this box is checked (as it is by default), remote clients' packets can go to the RRAS server or to any other host to which the RRAS server has a route. To limit clients to accessing resources only on the RRAS server itself, uncheck this box.

- The Allow IP-Based Remote Access And Demand-Dial Connections check box controls whether clients can use IP over PPP. This option may seem to be an odd one, because the overwhelming majority of PPP connections use IP, but if you want to limit your server to NetBEUI, IPX, or AppleTalk remote clients, you can do so by making sure this box is unchecked.

- The IP Address Assignment control group allows you to specify how you want remote clients to get their IP addresses. The default setting varies, depending on what you told the RRAS wizard during setup. If you want to use a DHCP server on your network as the source of IP addresses for remote clients, select the DHCP radio button (making sure, of course, that the DHCP relay agent is installed and running). If you'd rather use static address allocation, select the Static Address Pool button and then use the controls below the address list to specify which IP address ranges you want to issue to clients.

TIP　If you choose to use static addressing, be sure that you don't use any address ranges that are part of a DHCP server's address pool. Better still, you can add the ranges you want to reserve for remote access as excluded ranges in the DHCP snap-in.

Configuring IPX-Based Connections

You may recall that IP and IPX are very similar in many respects. Even though the particulars differ, they both involve addresses that must be assigned to every device on the network. Accordingly, the IP and IPX tabs of the server Properties dialog box aren't as different as you might expect. The IPX tab includes two controls that give you power over whether this server speaks IPX.

The IPX tabs include the following:

- The Allow IPX-Based Remote Access and Demand-Dial Connections check box controls whether this server accepts IPX connections.

- The Enable Network Access for Remote Clients and Demand-Dial Connections check box controls whether IPX clients can reach only this server or other IPX-capable servers on your network.

TIP　Notice that each protocol tab has a check box but that each one is labeled differently. Make sure that you get the names straight for the exam.

In addition, the IPX Network Number Assignment control group gives you a way to have this server assign IPX network numbers to dial-up clients automatically. Your best bet is to leave the Automatically radio button selected, which tells the server to pass out numbers as it sees fit. If necessary, you can assign numbers in a specified range manually. The two other check boxes give you some additional control:

- The Use the Same Network Number for All IPX Clients check box (checked by default) indicates whether you want all IPX clients to get the same network number. Normally, you want this option to be on so that all your IPX resources are visible to clients immediately.

- The Allow Remote Clients to Request IPX Node Number check box normally is unchecked by default, because it's a potential security hole. When this option is on, clients can request a particular IPX node number; in theory, it could allow a malicious remote client to impersonate another IPX device. Leave this box unchecked.

Configuring AppleTalk and NetBEUI Connections

The AppleTalk and NetBEUI tabs control whether your server accepts remote connections using those protocols. Because AppleTalk and NetBEUI are both fairly simple, the tabs really don't have any configuration options—just check boxes that you use to specify whether your server allows incoming connections. The AppleTalk check box is labeled Enable AppleTalk Remote Access; its NetBEUI counterpart reads Allow NetBEUI-Based Remote Access Clients to Access. The NetBEUI version also has an associated pair of radio buttons that regulate whether NetBEUI clients can see only the RRAS server or the entire network.

Configuring Your Remote Access Server

Now that you've set up the server to accept incoming calls, it's time to determine who can actually *use* it. You do this in two ways: by setting up *remote access profiles* on individual accounts and by creating and managing *remote access policies* that apply to groups of users. This distinction is subtle but important, because you manage and apply profiles and policies in different places.

Most of the configuration necessary for a remote access server happens at the server level. In particular, you use the server's Properties dialog box to control whether the server allows remote connections at all, what protocols and options it supports, and so forth. You also have to configure settings for your users.

To open the RRAS server's Properties dialog box, pick the server you're interested in and use the Action ➤ Properties command (or the Properties command on the Context menu).

Setting General Configuration Options

The General tab of the server Properties dialog box has only one check box of interest for remote access configurations: when checked, the Remote Access Server check box allows the RRAS service to act as a remote access server. You need to know this so that you can switch remote access capability on and off without deactivating and reactivating the RRAS service, which causes the service to erase its settings.

The other tabs in this dialog box control specific settings for different protocols. The other tabs available in this dialog box include the following:

- The Security tab allows you to specify what authentication providers and settings you want the server to use.

- The next four tabs—IP, IPX, NetBEUI, and AppleTalk—control the specific settings applied to each protocol you have installed. In particular, these tabs govern whether the associated protocol can be used for remote access clients, as well as whether remote clients can reach the entire network or only the remote access server itself.

- The PPP tab controls which PPP protocols—including multilink—the clients on this server are allowed to use.

- The Event Logging tab controls what level of log detail is kept for incoming connections.

Understanding Remote Access Policies

Besides turning dial-in access on or off for a single user, you can use *remote access policies* to control whether users can get access. Like group policies, remote access policies give you an easy way to apply a consistent set of policies to groups of users. The policy mechanism is a little different, however: you create rules that include or exclude the users you want in the policy.

Unlike group policies, remote access policies are available only in native Windows 2000 domains (that is, in domains where no Windows NT domain controllers are present). Therefore, you may not have the option to use remote access policies until your Windows 2000 deployment is farther along. These policies are considered to be subobjectives in the exam, both from the configuring-remote-access point of view and again from the configuring-remote-access security point of view. Remember that these policies are distinct from the user profiles.

Configuring User Profiles

Windows 2000 stores a great deal of information for each user account. Collectively, this information is known as the account's *profile*, and it's normally stored in Active Directory. Some settings in the user's profile are available through the two user-management snap-ins—Active Directory Users and Computers, or Local Users and Groups—depending on whether your RRAS server is part of an Active Directory domain. In either case, the interesting part of the profile is the Dial-In tab of the user's properties dialog box. This tab has several interesting controls that regulate how the user account can be used for dial-in access.

These controls include the following:

Remote Access Permission (Dial-in or VPN) Control Group   The first, and probably most familiar, controls in this tab are in the Remote Access Permission control group; they control whether this account has dial-in permission. In addition to explicitly allowing or denying access (via the Allow Access and Deny Access radio buttons), you can leave the access decision up to a remote access policy, provided that you're using Windows 2000 in native mode.

Verify Caller-ID Check Box   If you like, you can force RRAS to verify the user's Caller ID information and use the result of that verification to decide whether the user gets access. When you check the Verify Caller-ID check box and enter a phone number in the field, you're explicitly telling RRAS to reject a call from anyone who provides that username and password but whose Caller ID information doesn't match what you enter. Be careful to get the number right.

Callback Options Control Group The Callback Options control group gives you three choices for regulating callback. The first (the default setting) is the No Callback radio button. When this option is selected, the server never honors callback requests from this account. If you choose the Set By Caller radio button instead, the calling system can specify a number at which it wants to be called, and the RRAS server calls the client back at that number. The final choice, Always Callback To, allows you to enter a number that the server calls back no matter where the client's actually calling from. This option is less flexible, but more secure, than the second option.

Assign a Static IP Check Box If you want one particular user to always get the same static IP address, you can arrange it by checking the Assign a Static IP Address check box and then entering the desired IP address. This option allows you to set up nondynamic DNS records for individual users, guaranteeing that their machines always have a usable DNS entry. On the other hand, this method is much more error-prone than the dynamic DNS-DHCP combination.

Apply Static Routes Control Group In an ordinary LAN, you don't have to do anything special to clients to enable them to route packets; you just configure them with a default gateway, and the gateway handles the rest. For dial-up connections, though, you may want to define a list of static routes that will enable the remote client to reach hosts on your network, or elsewhere, without requiring packets to be sent to a gateway in between. If you want to define a set of static routes on the client, you have to do it manually. If you want to assign static routes on the server, check the Apply Static Routes check box and then use the Static Routes button to add and remove routes as necessary.

TIP Remember that these settings apply to individual users, so you can assign different routes, Caller ID, or callback settings to each user.

Using Remote Access Policies and Profiles

Windows 2000 includes support for two configuration systems: remote access policies and remote access profiles. Policies determine who can and cannot connect; you define rules with conditions that the system evaluates to see whether a particular user is allowed to connect. Profiles contain settings that determine what happens during call setup and completion. (Don't confuse remote access profiles with the dial-in settings associated with a user profile.)

You can have any number of policies in a native Windows 2000 domain; each policy may have exactly one profile associated with it.

NOTE Settings in an individual user's profile override settings in a remote access policy.

You manage remote access policies through the Remote Access Policies folder in the RRAS snap-in. By default, only one policy is listed: Allow Access If Dial-in Permission Is Enabled. That name should give you a clue about how policies work: they contain conditions that you pick from a list. When a caller connects, the policy's conditions are evaluated one by one to determine whether the caller gets in. *All* the conditions in the policy must match for the user to gain access. If multiple policies exist, they're evaluated according to an order you specify. You learn to create policies in the third exam objective section of this chapter, which concerns configuring remote access security.

Configuring a Virtual Private Network (VPN)

Virtual private networks (VPNs) are increasingly popular because they essentially give you something for nothing. If you have users outside your network boundary, VPNs give you an easy-to-implement, easy-to-manage solution to the problem of how to give these remote users access.

Conventional dial-up access still works fine, but it can be expensive to implement, painful to manage, and vulnerable to attack. VPNs offer a way around these problems by offering low initial and ongoing cost, easy management, and excellent security. Windows 2000's Routing and Remote Access Service (RRAS) component includes two complete VPN implementations, one using Microsoft's *Point-to-Point Tunneling Protocol (PPTP)* and one using a combination of the Internet-standard IPSec and *Layer 2 Tunneling Protocol (L2TP)* protocols.

In the following sections, you learn to set up and configure RRAS as a VPN server using PPTP and L2TP + IPSec (which this chapter lumps together and calls L2TP from now on).

Comparing PPTP and L2TP

Because you can choose between two different VPN protocols, how do you know which one is the proper choice in a given situation? If you know the differences and similarities between the two protocols, you'll be better prepared to make the right choice and prepared for comparisons on the exam. The following list summarizes the most important points of interest:

- PPTP and L2TP both depend on the PPP protocol to move data. (This doesn't mean that either requires a dial-up PPP connection, though.)

- PPTP requires an IP connection. L2TP can use PPP over IP, frame relay, X.25, or ATM.

- L2TP supports header compression; PPTP doesn't.

- L2TP connections can be encrypted and authenticated, but PPTP connections are only encrypted.

- L2TP must be used with IPSec (although IPSec can be used alone). PPTP always uses Microsoft Point-to-Point Encryption (MPPE).

Installing a VPN

The basic process of setting up a VPN is simple, but you have some things to think through before plunging ahead. Getting the VPN installation right may require small hardware or networking changes, as well as proper configuration of the VPN service itself.

Stop for a minute to think about what a VPN server does. It sits between your internal network and the Internet, accepting connections from clients in the outside world.

In general, you want your VPN server to be outside any firewalls or network security measures that you have in place. The most common configuration is to use two NICs; one connects to the Internet, and the other connects either to the private network or to an intermediate network that itself connects to the private network. You can use any type of Internet connection you want for the VPN server: cable modems, DSL, T-1, ISDN, or whatever.

The point behind giving the VPN its own network adapter is that your VPN clients need a public IP address to connect to, and you probably don't want them calling directly into your internal network. That also means that things will be easiest for your VPN users if the IP address for your VPN server's external interface is assigned statically, so that it won't change on users when they least expect it.

Avoiding Some Subtle L2TP Pitfalls

IPSec uses a fairly complex process to negotiate security agreements (SAs) between two endpoints of a secure connection. Part of this process involves the use of what Microsoft calls *machine certificates*. These certificates are nothing more than digital certificates issued to machines instead of people. The certificates allow both ends of the connection to authenticate the computers involved, not just the people.

Installing RRAS as a VPN Server

To get any use from your VPN, you need two pieces: a VPN client and a VPN server. In the case of Windows 2000, having a VPN server means that you're very likely to be using RRAS.

Starting from Scratch

If you don't have RRAS installed, you need to install it, activate it, and configure it as a VPN server. The easiest way to do this is with the RRAS Setup wizard. The wizard gives you a page with several radio buttons that you use to select the kind of server you want to set up. When you install RRAS as a remote access server, the wizard automatically sets up VPN ports for you. The following sections describe the steps from the standpoint of how things look when you explicitly choose to build a VPN server.

Enabling Your VPN Server

If you're already using RRAS for IP routing or remote access, you can enable it as a VPN server without reinstalling. The General tab of the Server Properties dialog box contains controls that you use to specify whether your RRAS server is a router, a remote access server, or both. The first step in converting your existing RRAS server to handle VPN traffic is making sure that the Remote Access Server check box in this tab is checked. Making this change requires you to stop and restart the RRAS service, but that's OK, because the snap-in does it for you.

Configuring VPN Ports

VPN configuration is extremely simple, at least for PPTP. Either a server can accept VPN calls, or it can't. If it can, it has a certain number of VPN ports, all of which are configured identically. There's very little that you *have* to change or tweak to get a VPN server set up, but you can adjust a few things as you like.

The biggest opportunity to configure your VPN server is to adjust the number and kind of VPN ports that are available for clients to use. The initial release of Windows 2000 supports up to 1000 simultaneous connections, although this number may be more than your hardware can handle. In addition, you can enable or disable either PPTP or L2TP, depending on what you want your remote users to access. You accomplish this task through the Ports Properties dialog box.

For conventional remote access servers, this dialog box shows you a long list of hardware ports, but for servers that support VPN connections, there are some extra goodies: two WAN Miniport devices, one for PPTP and one for L2TP. These devices aren't really devices, of course; they're actually virtual ports maintained by RRAS for accepting VPN connections. You configure these ports with the Configure button, which displays the Configure Device dialog box. Following are the three controls that are pertinent to a VPN configuration:

- The Remote Access Connections (Inbound Only) check box, which must be activated to accept VPN connections with this port type. To disable a VPN type, uncheck this box in the corresponding device's Configure Device dialog box.

- The Demand-Dial Routing Connections (Inbound and Outbound) check box, which controls whether this VPN type can be used for demand-dial connections. By default, this box is checked; you need to uncheck it if you don't want to use VPN connections to link your network with other networks.

- The Maximum Ports control, which allows you to set the number of inbound connections that this port type supports. By default, you get 5 PPTP and 5 L2TP ports when you install RRAS; you can use 0 to 1,000 ports of each type by adjusting the number.

You also can use the Phone Number for This Device field to enter the IP address of the public interface to which VPN clients connect. You may want to do this if your remote access policies accept or reject connections based on the number called by the client. Because you can assign multiple IP addresses to a single adapter, you can control VPN traffic by throttling which clients can connect to which addresses through a policy.

Setting Up a VPN Remote Access Policy

You learned earlier in this chapter how to use the remote access policy mechanism on a Windows 2000 native-mode domain. Now it's time to apply what you've learned to the VPN world. Recall that there are two ways to control which specific users can access a remote access server: you can grant dial-up permission to individual users in each user's Properties dialog box, or you can create a remote access policy that embodies whatever restrictions you want to impose. You can do the same thing for VPN connections, but there are a few additional twists to consider.

Granting Per-User Access

To grant or deny VPN access to individual users, all you have to do is make the appropriate change in the Dial-in tab of each user's Properties dialog box. Although this method is the easiest to understand, it gets tedious quickly if you need to change VPN permissions for more than a few users. Furthermore, you have no way to distinguish between dial-in and VPN permission.

Creating a Remote Access Policy for VPNs

You may find it helpful to create remote access policies that enforce the permissions you want end users to have. You can achieve this result in several ways; which one you use depends on your overall use of remote access policies. The simplest way is to create a policy that allows all your users to use a VPN. You learn in the security objective later in this chapter how to create remote access policies and specify settings for them. One thing you may have noticed is that you can use a NAS-Port-Type attribute in the policy's conditions. That attribute is the cornerstone of building a policy that allows or denies remote access via VPN, because you use it to accept or reject connections arriving over a particular type of VPN connection. For best results, use Tunnel-Type in conjunction with the NAS-Port-Type attribute.

NOTE Remember that you can use remote access policies only if you're in a native-mode Windows 2000 domain.

Troubleshooting VPNs

The two primary VPN problems are inability to establish a connection and inability to reach some needed resource when connected. The processes of troubleshooting a VPN connection and an ordinary remote access connection have a great deal in common.

Verifying the Simple Stuff

"Is it plugged in?" That's one of the first questions that support techs at mass-market vendors such as Gateway and Packard Bell ask customers who call to report a dead computer. In the same vein, there are some extremely simple—but sometimes overlooked—things to check when your VPN clients can't connect.

Check the following things:

- Is the RRAS server installed and configured on the server?

- Is the server configured to allow remote access? (Check the General tab of the server Properties dialog box.)

- Is the server configured to allow VPN traffic? Check the Ports Properties dialog box to make sure that the appropriate VPN protocol is enabled and that the number of ports for that protocol is greater than zero.

- Are any VPN ports available? If you have only 10 L2TP ports allocated, caller 11 is out of luck.

- Do the client and server match?

- Is the VPN protocol used by the client enabled on the server? Windows 2000 clients will try L2TP first and switch to PPTP as a second choice; clients on other OSes (including Windows NT) normally can expect either L2TP or PPTP.

- Are the network protocols for all clients enabled on the server? This situation is particularly good to check if some IPX-using clients are lurking in the woodpile.

- What about authentication? Has it taken place successfully?

- Here's a favorite: Are the username and password correct? If not, don't expect to get a VPN connection.

- Does the user account in question have remote access permissions, either directly on the account or through a policy?

- Speaking of policy, do the authentication settings in the server's policies (if any) match the supported set of authentication protocols?

Checking the Slightly More Sophisticated Problems

If you check all the simple stuff and find nothing wrong, it's time to move on to some slightly more sophisticated problems. These situations tend to affect more than one user, as opposed to the simple (and, generally user-specific) issues outlined in the preceding section. The problems include the following:

Policy Problems If you're using a native-mode Windows 2000 domain, and you're using policies, those policies may have some subtle problems that show up under some circumstances. It is important to check the following.

- Are there any policies whose Allow or Deny settings conflict? Remember that all conditions of all policies must match to gain user access; if any condition of any policy fails, or if any policies deny access, it's "game over" for that connection.

- Does the user match all the necessary conditions that are in place, such as Time and Date?

Network Stuff   If you're using static IP addressing, are any addresses left in the pool? If the VPN server can't assign an address, it won't accept the connection.

If you're using IPX, make sure that the client and server settings that control whether the client can ask for its own node number match; if the server disallows the client from asking for its node number, the client won't be able to connect unless it already has an assigned number.

Domain Stuff   Windows 2000 RRAS servers can coexist with Windows NT RRAS servers, and both of them can interoperate with RADIUS servers from Microsoft and other vendors. Sometimes, though, this interoperation doesn't work exactly as you'd expect. You should check the following details if problems do arise:

- Is the RRAS server's domain membership correct? Your RRAS servers don't have to be domain members unless you want to use native-mode features such as remote access policies.

- If you're in a domain, are the server's group memberships correct? The server account must be a member of the RAS and IAS Servers security group.

Configuring a VPN Client

When you establish a virtual private network connection, you're actually building an encrypted tunnel between you and some other machine. The tunneled data is carried over an insecure network, such as the Internet. VPN connections are easy to set up and use, especially because you create and manage them with the same Network Connection wizard discussed earlier in this chapter. The first noticeable difference is that you choose the Connect to a Private Network Through the Internet button at the beginning of the wizard process; after that, things get even more different.

After you click the Next button in the first page, the next difference is the Public Network page, which allows you to tell DUN whether you want it to dial the underlying connection for you automatically. By default, the Automatically Dial This Initial Connection radio button is selected, so you can use the associated pull-down menu to choose which connection you want to dial. This feature is a terrific one, because it largely automates the process of establishing VPN connections. If you want VPN connectivity only when you're already dialed up, you can select the Do Not Dial the Initial Connection button instead.

Clicking the Next button again brings you to the Destination Address page. This page is very simple; the only thing you do is fill in the IP address (or DNS name) of the host you want to talk to over your tunnel. In other words, this entry is the address of the VPN server to which you're talking. Enter the address or name and click Next. Then you see the same two sharing pages discussed earlier in this chapter, followed by the summary page where you name the new connection. When you click Finish, you can bring up the connection right then, or you can adjust its properties by opening the connection's Properties dialog box.

Setting VPN Connection Properties

Perhaps surprisingly, most of the properties you set for a plain dial-up connection work the same way for VPN connections. In particular, the Options, Security, and Sharing tabs of the Properties dialog boxes are identical across the two connection types. The other tabs have some minor differences, which include the following:

General   The VPN version of the General tab has a field where you enter the VPN server address or hostname instead of a phone number. In addition, the First Connect group allows you to specify which dial-up connection, if any, you want brought up before the VPN connection is established.

Networking   The VPN Networking tab uses the top drop-down menu to allow you to indicate what kind of VPN call you're making. Automatic is the default setting, but you can explicitly ask for a *PPTP* or L2TP connection if you prefer.

Integrating RRAS with DHCP

If you want your RRAS clients to use a DHCP server on your network, you may need to do a little fancy dancing to get things working properly. By design, the DHCP protocol is intended to allow clients and servers on the same IP network to communicate. RFC 1542 sets out how the BOOTP protocol (on which DHCP is based) should work when the client and server are on different IP networks. If no DHCP server is available on the network where the client's located, you can use a *DHCP relay agent* to forward DHCP messages from the client to the DHCP server's network. The relay agent acts like a radio repeater, listening for DHCP client requests and retransmitting them on the server's network.

The bottom line is that each network that has a DHCP client on it must have either a DHCP server or a DHCP relay agent. Otherwise, the client has no way to reach a DHCP server and get a lease.

What does this situation mean for your remote access deployment? The answer depends on your network configuration, as follows:

- On a small or simple network, you may choose to use static IP addressing and assign each dial-in client a fixed IP address. In this case, you don't have to fool with DHCP at all.

- If your RRAS server also is a DHCP server, you're OK, because dial-in clients get an IP address from that server's address pool.

- If your RRAS server is on a different IP network from your DHCP servers, or if you want to assign client addresses out of an address range that's not part of any DHCP scope, you need a relay agent.

The RRAS package includes a DHCP relay agent that you install as an additional routing protocol; after you install and configure it, the relay agent can tie your remote access clients to whatever DHCP infrastructure you want to use.

Installing the DHCP Relay Agent

First, a couple of caveats: you can't install the relay agent on a computer that's already acting as a DHCP server, and you can't install it on a system running Network Address Translation (NAT) with the

addressing component installed. As long as you meet these requirements, the actual installation process is easy. After you have the agent
installed, you're ready to configure it to forward requests when and
where you want them to be relayed.

Configuring the DHCP Relay Agent

As is typical of other RRAS components, you actually configure the
DHCP relay agent in two places: the Relay Agent Properties dialog
box and again in each individual interface. The configuration settings
required for each of these two places are different.

Setting DHCP Relay Agent Properties

When you select the DHCP Relay Agent item below the IP Routing
node and open its Properties dialog box, the only thing you can do is
specify the DHCP servers to which you want *this particular* DHCP
relay agent to forward requests. The only restriction is that the RRAS
server that's running the DHCP relay agent must be able to route IP
packets to the destination network. The servers you specify apply to
all network interfaces to which you attach the relay agent; there's no
way to configure independent forwarding addresses for individual
network interfaces.

Assigning the Relay Agent to Specific Interfaces

After you've configured the list of servers to which you want DHCP
requests forwarded, you still have to attach the relay agent to particular network interfaces. You use the same mechanism discussed in the
preceding section to create an interface, too: right-click the DHCP
Relay Agent item and then choose the New Interface command.
When the New Interface for DHCP Relay Agent dialog box appears,
select the network interface to which you want the relay agent bound.
When you do, the interface-specific Properties dialog box appears.

Setting Interface Properties

Each relay agent-enabled interface has its own set of properties, which
are exposed through the interface-specific Relay Agent Properties dialog box. The topmost control, the Relay DHCP Packets check box,
allows you to control whether DHCP relaying is active on this interface; you can turn it on or off without restarting the RRAS service.

The other two controls affect how long relayed DHCP requests bounce around your network. The hop count controls the number of intervening routers between the client and the DHCP server that the DHCP traffic can traverse, and the boot threshold controls how long the relay agent waits before forwarding any DHCP messages it hears. If you want to give a local DHCP server first crack at incoming requests, adjust the boot threshold up so that the local server has a chance to respond before the message is forwarded.

Necessary Procedures

In this section, you gain a great deal of understanding of many processes. You practice configuring incoming connections and a user profile for dial-in access. You get practice installing RRAS as a VPN server and creating a VPN remote access policy. You better understand PPTP encapsulation.

You get to configure a Windows client as a VPN client. You learn to control multilink for incoming calls. You install DHCP Relay Agent on an RRAS server and practice configuring DHCP relay agent on a network interface. The first thing you can become proficient at is installing an RRAS server.

Some of the steps for installing and configuring an RRAS server for remote access are similar to those for installing RRAS as a router (discussed in Chapter 6); others are different. The overall process is still driven by the Routing and Remote Access Server Setup wizard; the primary difference in this case is that you use the wizard to set up a dial-up server, not an IP router. The following procedure leads you through the process of using the wizard to configure an RRAS server.

Installing the Routing and Remote Access Service

Follow these steps to install a RRAS remote access server:

1. Open the RRAS MMC console (Start ➤ Programs ➤ Administrative Tools ➤ Routing and Remote Access).

2. In the left pane of the MMC, select the server you want to configure. Right-click the server; then choose the Configure and Enable Routing and Remote Access command. The RRAS Setup wizard appears. Click the Next button.

3. In the Common Configurations page of the wizard, select the Remote Access Server radio button; then click the Next button. The Remote Client Protocols page appears, listing the protocols available for remote access clients.

4. If you need to add another protocol to the list, click the No, I Need to Add Protocols button. If all the protocols you want to use are listed, leave the Yes, All of the Required Protocols Are on the List button selected. Then click the Next button.

5. If you indicated that you need to add additional protocols, the wizard stops. If the protocols that you need are already present, the wizard continues. The Macintosh Guest Authentication page appears.

6. The Mac OS allows anonymous remote access. If you want your RRAS server to imitate this behavior, click the Allow Unauthenticated Access for All Remote Clients button. Then click the Next button. The IP Address Assignment page appears.

7. If you want to use DHCP (either a DHCP server on your network or the built-in address allocator), leave the Automatically radio button selected. If you want to choose an address range, select the From a Specified Range of Addresses button. Then click the Next button.

   If you choose to use static addressing, at this point the wizard gives you the opportunity to define one or more address ranges to be assigned to remote clients. The Managing Multiple Remote Access Servers page appears.

8. You use this page to configure your RRAS server to work with other RADIUS-capable servers on your network. In this case, you don't want to use RADIUS, so leave the No, I Don't Want to Set Up This Server to Use RADIUS Now button selected. Then click the Next button. The Wizard Summary page appears.

9. Click the Finish button to start the RRAS service and prepare your server to be configured. If the RRAS service is running on the same server as a DHCP server, you see a message indicating that you need to configure the DHCP relay agent.

Configuring Incoming Connections

For this exercise, you configure your RRAS server so that it accepts only inbound calls that use the IP protocol. You may have to skip some steps if you don't have all four network protocols loaded. To configure the connections, follow these steps:

1. Open the RRAS MMC console (Start ≻ Programs ≻ Administrative Tools ≻ Routing and Remote Access).

2. In the left pane of the MMC, right-click the server that you want to configure; then choose the Properties command. The server Properties dialog box appears.

3. Switch to the IP tab by clicking it. Verify that both the Enable IP Routing and the Allow IP-Based Remote Access and Demand-Dial Connections check boxes are marked.

4. Switch to the IPX tab, if you have one. Uncheck the Allow IPX-Based Remote Access and Demand-Dial Connections check box.

5. If your Properties dialog box has a NetBEUI tab, switch to it; then uncheck the Allow NetBEUI-Based Remote Access Clients to Access check box.

6. If your Properties dialog box has an AppleTalk tab, switch to it; then uncheck the Enable AppleTalk Remote Access check box.

7. Click the OK button. After a brief pause, the Properties dialog box disappears, and your changes become effective.

Configuring a User Profile for Dial-In Access

For security reasons, it's usually a good idea to limit access to the administrative accounts on your network. In particular, many consultants usually tell clients to restrict remote access for the Administrator account; that way, the potential exposure from a dial-up compromise is somewhat reduced. Here's how to configure the Administrator account's user profile to restrict dial-up access:

1. Log on to your computer, using an account that has administrative privileges.

2. Open the Active Directory Users and Computers snap-in (Start ➤ Programs ➤ Administrative Tools ➤ Active Directory Users and Computers) if you're using an RRAS server that's part of an AD domain. If not, open the Local Users and Groups snap-in (Start ➤ Programs ➤ Administrative Tools ➤ Local Users and Groups) instead.

3. Expand the Users folder. In the right pane, right-click the Administrator account; then choose the Properties command. The Administrator Properties dialog box appears.

4. Switch to the Dial-In tab by clicking it. On machines that participate in Active Directory, the Permission group should have the Control Access Through Remote Access Policy radio button set.

5. Click the Deny Access radio button to prevent the use of this account over a dial-in connection.

6. Click the OK button.

Installing the Routing and Remote Access Service As a VPN Server

Follow these steps to install a RRAS remote access server:

1. Open the RRAS MMC console (Start ➤ Programs ➤ Administrative Tools ➤ Routing and Remote Access).

2. In the left pane of the MMC, select the server that you want to configure. Right-click the server; then choose the Configure and Enable Routing and Remote Access command. The RRAS Setup wizard appears. Click the Next button.

3. In the Common Configurations page of the wizard, make sure that the Virtual Private Network (VPN) Server radio button is selected; then click the Next button. The Remote Client Protocols page appears, listing the protocols available for remote access clients.

4. If you need to add another protocol to the list, click the No, I Need to Add Protocols button. If all the protocols you want to use are in the list, leave the Yes, All of the Required Protocols Are on the List button selected. Then click the Next button.

5. If you indicate that you need to add additional protocols, the wizard stops. If the protocols that you need are already present, the wizard continues, and the Internet Connections page appears.

6. This page lists all the demand-dial and permanent network interfaces known to RRAS; you have to choose an interface to serve as the incoming "phone number" for VPN connections. Pick an interface; then click the Next button. The IP Address Assignment page appears.

7. If you want to use DHCP (either a DHCP server on your network or the built-in address allocator), leave the Automatically radio button selected. If you want to choose an address range, select the From a Specified Range of Addresses button. Then click the Next button.

If you choose to use static addressing, at this point the wizard gives you the opportunity to define one or more address ranges to be assigned to remote clients. The Managing Multiple Remote Access Servers page appears.

8. You use the Managing Multiple Remote Access Servers page to configure your RRAS server to work with other RADIUS-capable servers on your network. In this case, you still don't want to use RADIUS, so leave the No, I Don't Want to Set Up This Server to Use RADIUS Now button selected; then click the Next button. The wizard summary page appears.

9. Click the Finish button to start the RRAS service and prepare your server to be configured. If the RRAS service is running on the same server as a DHCP server, you see a message indicating that you need to configure the DHCP relay agent.

When you complete this exercise, you have a complete, ready-to-go VPN server that starts accepting connections immediately. You may want to configure the available ports to meet your VPN needs, however.

Creating a VPN Remote Access Policy

Follow these steps to create a remote access policy that governs VPN use:

1. Open the RRAS MMC console (Start ➤ Programs ➤ Administrative Tools ➤ Routing and Remote Access).

2. Navigate to the server on which you want to create the policy; then expand the server node until you see the Remote Access Policies node.

3. Right-click the Remote Access Policies folder; then choose the New Remote Access Policy command. This command starts the Add Remote Access Policy wizard.

4. Name the policy VPN Access or something else that clearly indicates what it's for; then click the Next button. The Conditions page of the wizard appears.

5. Click the Add button to add this condition: NAS-Port-Type Attribute Set to "Virtual (VPN)." If you want to restrict VPN users to either PPTP or L2TP, add this other condition: tunnel-type attribute set to the appropriate protocol.

6. In the Permissions page of the wizard, make sure that the Grant Remote Access Permission radio button is selected (unless you're trying to *prevent* VPN users from connecting). Click the Next button when done. The User Profile page appears.

7. If you want to create a specific profile (perhaps to restrict which authentication types VPN can may use), use the Edit Profile button to specify them. At minimum, you should clear the No Encryption option in the Encryption tab of the remote access profile. When you're done tweaking the profile, click the Finish button to create and activate the policy.

If you don't want to grant VPN access to everyone, you can make some changes in the process to fine-tune it. When you add the policy described in the exercise, it ends up after the default Allow Access If Dial-In Permission Is Enabled policy. The default policy takes effect before the VPN-specific policy, so you probably will want to move the VPN policy to the top of the list.

Suppose that you want to allow everyone dial-up access, but you also want VPN capability to be reserved for a smaller group. The easiest way to accomplish this task is to create an Active Directory group and put your VPN users in it. Then you can create a policy using the two conditions outlined in the exercise *plus* a condition that uses the Windows-Groups attribute to specify the new group. As with the ordinary VPN policy in the exercise, if you create a policy using the Windows-Groups attribute, make sure to put it ahead of the default policy.

TIP   You can delete the default remote access policy if you don't need it for dial-in users.

Understanding PPTP Encapsulation

VPNs depend on encapsulation, because their security depends on being able to keep the payload information encrypted. The following steps demonstrate what happens to a typical packet as it goes from being a regular IP datagram to a PPTP packet:

1. Some application creates a block of data bound for a remote host—in this case, a Web browser.

2. The client-side TCP/IP stack takes the application's data and turns it into a TCP/IP packet, first by adding a TCP header and then by adding an IP header. At this point, you can call the whole mess an *IP datagram*, because it contains all the necessary addressing information to be delivered by IP.

3. Because the client is connected via PPP, it adds a PPP header to the IP datagram. This PPP + IP combination is called a *PPP frame*. If you were using PPP instead of a VPN protocol, the packet would go across the PPP link without further modification. In this example, however, you *are* using a VPN, so the next step is for the VPN to encrypt the PPP frame, turning it into gibberish.

4. A Generic Routing Encapsulation (GRE) header is combined with the encrypted payload. GRE really is generic; in this case, the protocol ID fields in the GRE header tell anyone who cares that this is an encapsulated PPTP packet.

5. Now that you have a tag to tell you what's in the payload, the PPTP stack can add an IP header (specifying the destination address of the VPN server, not the original host from step 2) and a PPP header.

6. The now-innocent-looking packet can be sent out over your existing PPP connection. The IP header specifies that it should be routed to the VPN server, which can pick it apart and reverse steps 1-5 when the packet arrives.

Configuring a Windows Client As a VPN Client

To configure a Windows client as a VPN client, follow these steps:

1. Choose Start ➢ Settings ➢ Network and Dial-Up Connections.

2. Double-click the Make New Connection icon. The Network Connection wizard appears. Click the Next button.

3. Choose the Connect to a Private Network Through the Internet button; then click Next.

4. Choose the dial-up connection you want; then click the Next button.

5. Enter the IP address or DNS name of your VPN server (example: 192.168.0.25). Click Next when you're done. The Connection Availability page appears.

6. If you want to make this connection available to all users, choose the For All Users radio button. If this connection should be available only to you, choose Only for Myself. Click the Next button when you're done.

7. When the Internet Connection Sharing page appears, click Next without turning on ICS. The wizard's completion page appears.

8. Type a name for this connection in the provided field; then click Finish. A confirmation dialog box labeled Initial Connection

appears, notifying you that the dial-up connection you picked in step 4 has to be brought up first.

9. Click Yes to bring up the connection dialog box. When the connection goes through, log on to the VPN server, using the correct credential information.

Controlling Multilink for Incoming Calls

It doesn't make sense to enable multilink connections if you have only one phone line; in addition, you may want to turn them off to keep a small number of users from hogging all your lines. To control whether multilink is on or off, follow these steps:

1. Open the RRAS MMC console (Start ➤ Programs ➤ Administrative Tools ➤ Routing and Remote Access).

2. In the left pane of the MMC, right-click the server that you want to configure; then choose the Properties command. The server Properties dialog box appears.

3. Switch to the PPP tab by clicking it.

4. To turn multilink capability off, make sure that the Multilink Connections check box is turned off. To turn it back on, simply check the appropriate check box.

5. If you decide to turn multilink capability on, you also should enable the use of BAP/BACP to make it easier for your server to adjust to the load placed on it. To do so, make sure that the Dynamic Bandwidth Control Using BAP Or BACP check box is checked.

6. Click the OK button.

Installing the DHCP Relay Agent on an RRAS Server

Follow these steps to install the DHCP relay agent on an RRAS server:

1. Open the Routing and Remote Access snap-in (Start ➤ Programs ➤ Administrative Tools ➤Routing and Remote Access).

2. Locate the server on which you want to install the DHCP relay agent.

3. Expand the server's configuration until you see the General node (*serverName* ➤ IP Routing ➤ General).

4. Right-click the General node; then choose the New Routing Protocol command. The New Routing Protocol dialog box appears.

5. Select DHCP Relay Agent in the list of routing protocols; then click the OK button. The IP Routing node now has a child node named DHCP Relay Agent.

6. Select this child node, and use the Properties command to open its Properties dialog box.

7. In the DHCP Relay Agent Global Properties dialog box, add the IP addresses of the DHCP servers to which you want DHCP requests to be forwarded; then click the OK button.

Configuring the DHCP Relay Agent on a Network Interface

In this exercise, you add a new DHCP Relay Agent interface for your LAN connection and then specify configuration parameters for it. In practice, you need to add the DHCP Relay Agent to whichever interface remote clients use. Follow these steps:

1. Install the DHCP Relay Agent on your server.

2. Right-click the DHCP Relay Agent item; then choose the New Interface command. The New Interface for DHCP Relay Agent dialog box appears, listing each of the interfaces to which you could attach the relay agent.

3. Select Local Area Connection; then click the OK button. The interface-specific Properties dialog box appears.

4. If you have a DHCP server on your local network, increase the boot threshold to 5 seconds; if you don't, decrease it to 0.

5. Click the OK button. Notice that the list of DHCP Relay Agent interfaces has been updated to reflect the new interface.

Exam Essentials

Know the six authentication protocols that remote access can use and that Windows 2000 supports. Understand PAP, SPAP, CHAP, MS-CHAP, EAP, and EAP-RADIUS.

Know how VPNs leverage the Internet by making secure connections with encrypted packets. Understand the two VPN protocols— PPTP and L2TP with IPSec—and how the encapsulation process functions.

Know how multilink extensions to PPP enable several connections to act as one. Understand the necessity for multiple phone lines with multilink.

Know the two main configuration methods for remote access: remote access individual profile configuration and remote access policy configuration. Understand the distinctions unique to each method, and be conversant with the remote access server's Properties dialog box and the procedure for configuring the various protocols.

Know the User Profile controls that you can configure in the Dial-in tab of the user's Properties dialog box. Understand the Remote Access Permission control group, the Verify Caller-ID check box, the Callback Options control group, the Assign a Static IP check box, and the Apply Static Route control group.

Know the benefits of using VPNs, and be familiar with the comparative advantages of each protocol they use: PPTP and L2TP with IPSec. Understand the differences and the similarities with these protocols.

Know how L2TP uses machine certificates to authenticate the computers involved in a transaction. Understand that this process usually takes place automatically and how to configure it to do so.

Know how to troubleshoot VPNs, working with problems of varying complexity. This type of problem-solving, troubleshooting material is great for the increasing numbers of scenario questions Microsoft is putting in the exam. These questions often ask for an ideal outcome and a required outcome, and you must specify which are satisfied by various solutions.

Know how to integrate RRAS with DHCP, including how to configure a DHCP relay agent. Be clear about your IP address pool and its use, as you learned in Chapter 2.

Key Terms and Concepts

Challenge Handshake Authentication Protocol (CHAP) Remote access authentication protocol that uses encrypted challenge and response messages instead of sending passwords and usernames in plain text.

DHCP relay agent A relay agent that acts like a radio repeater, listening for DHCP client requests and retransmitting them on the server's network.

Encapsulating Security Payload (ESP) An encrypting packet function that is used to encrypt the entire payload of an IPSec packet, rendering it undecipherable by anyone other than the intended recipient. It provides only confidentiality.

encapsulation A process in which the client takes a packet with some kind of "forbidden" content, wraps it inside an IP datagram, and sends it to the server.

Layer 2 Tunneling Protocol (L2TP) A generic tunneling protocol that allows encapsulation of one network protocol's data within another protocol. L2TP is used in conjunction with IPSec to enable VPN access to Windows 2000 networks.

machine certificates Digital certificates issued to machines instead of people.

Microsoft CHAP (MS-CHAP)   A Microsoft-created protocol, compatible with CHAP, that can work with various members of the Windows family of operating systems.

Password Authentication Protocol   The simplest and least secure authentication protocol; it transmits all authentication information in clear text in the clear, which makes it vulnerable to snooping.

Point-to-Point Protocol   A protocol that enables any two computers to establish a TCP/IP connection over a dial-up modem connection, direct serial cable connection, infrared connection, or any other type of serial connection.

Point-to-Point Tunneling Protocol   A Microsoft-specific VPN protocol that encapsulates IP, IPX, or NetBEUI information inside IP packets, hiding data from onlookers.

remote access profiles   Allow an administrator to determine who can actually use dial-up capabilities. Remote access profiles work on individual accounts, whereas remote access policies work on groups of users.

Remote Access Service (RAS)   A service that allows network connections to be established over a modem connection, an Integrated Services Digital Network (ISDN) connection, or a null-modem cable. The computer initiating the connection is called the *RAS client*; the answering computer is called the *RAS server*.

Remote Authentication for Dial-In User Service (RADIUS)   A common authentication scheme used by (for example) ISPs using non-Microsoft systems.

Routing and Remote Access Service   A Windows 2000 component that provides multiprotocol routing and dial-up access.

tunnel   A private virtual circuit between a client and a server using the Internet as a transportation medium.

virtual private network (VPN)   A private network that uses links across private or public networks (such as the Internet). When data is sent over the remote link, it is encapsulated and encrypted, and it requires authentication services.

Sample Questions

1. If you want to allow your RRAS server to interoperate with your existing DHCP servers, which of the following do you need to use?

A. The DHCP relay agent

B. A Microsoft DHCP server

C. Dynamic DNS

D. The WINS proxy agent

Answer: A. The DHCP relay agent allows DHCP broadcasts to bridge routers, which usually is what you'll need to make RRAS work with an external DHCP server.

2. The VPN protocols in Windows 2000 can be used for which of the following?

A. Remote access by network clients

B. Linking networks at different physical sites

C. A and B

D. None of the above

Answer: C. You can use PPTP and L2TP + IPSec to connect remote networks or to allow a client to dial in to a network; the protocols don't care which.

Manage and monitor remote access.

RRAS server management generally is fairly easy, because in most cases, there's not much to manage. You set up the server, it answers calls, and life is good. You'll probably find it necessary to monitor the server's ongoing activity, and you may find it necessary to log activity for accounting or security purposes.

Critical Information

You can monitor your server's activity in several ways, including having the server keep local copies of its logs or having it send logging data to a remote RADIUS server. In addition, you can always monitor the current status of any of the ports on your system. Microsoft's documentation distinguishes between event logging, which records significant events such as startup and shutdown of the RRAS service, and authentication and accounting logging, which tracks events such as when user X logged on and logged off. The settings for both types of logging are intermingled in the RRAS snap-in.

Monitoring Overall Activity

The Server Status node in the RRAS snap-in shows you a summary of all the RRAS servers known to the system. Depending on whether you use the features to manage multiple RRAS servers from one console, you may see only the local server's information here. When you select the Server Status item, the right pane of the MMC lists each known RRAS server; each entry in the list tells you whether the server is up or not, what kind of server it is, how many ports it has, how many ports are currently in use, and how long the server has been up. You can right-click any Windows 2000 RRAS server in this view to start, stop, restart, pause, or resume its RRAS service; disable RRAS on the server; or remove the server's advertisement from Active Directory.

Controlling Remote Access Logging

A regular RRAS installation always logs *some* data locally, but that data is relatively worthless unless you know what gets logged and where it goes. Each RRAS server on your network has its own set of logs, which you manage through the Remote Access Logging folder. Within that folder, you normally see a single item labeled Local File, which is the log file stored on that particular server.

If you don't have Windows accounting or Windows authentication turned on, you won't have a local log file. Depending on whether you're using RADIUS accounting and logging, you may see additional entries.

Setting Server Logging Properties

The first place where you can control server logging is at the server level; you use the Event Logging tab to control what level of detail you want in the server's event log. Bear in mind that these controls regulate *all* logging by RRAS, not just remote access log entries. You have four choices for the level of logged detail:

- The Log Errors Only radio button instructs the server to log errors and nothing else. This option gives you adequate indication of problems *after* they happen, but it doesn't point out potential problems noted by warning messages.

- The Log Errors and Warnings radio button is the default choice. This option forces the server to log error and warning messages to the event log, giving you a nice balance between information content and log volume.

- The Log the Maximum Amount of Information radio button causes the RRAS service to log mass quantities of messages, covering literally everything the server does. Although this voluminous output is useful for troubleshooting (or even for getting a better understanding of how remote access works), it's overkill for everyday use.

- The Disable Event Logging radio button turns off all event logging for RRAS. *Don't use this option without a good reason.* It prevents you from reviewing the service's logs in case of a problem.

- The Enable Point-to-Point Protocol (PPP) Logging check box allows you to turn on logging of all PPP negotiations and connections. This option can provide valuable information when you're trying to figure out what's wrong, but it adds a great deal of unnecessary bulk to your log files. Don't turn it on unless you're trying to pin down a problem.

Setting Log File Properties

You can select an individual log file in the snap-in to control what that log file contains. More precisely, you can control what events should be logged in that file from the time of the change forward. You make these changes by selecting the log file and using the Action ➤ Properties command to open the log file Properties dialog box. This dialog box has two tabs. The Settings tab controls what gets logged in the file, and the Local File tab controls the format of the file itself.

The Settings tab has three check boxes that control what gets logged:

- Log Accounting Requests should always be checked, because it governs whether events related to the accounting service itself (as well as accounting data) are logged.

- Log Authentication Requests also should remain checked; it specifies whether successful and failed logon requests are logged.

- Log Periodic Status normally should remain off; it controls whether interim accounting packets are permanently stored on disk.

The Local File tab controls how the log file is written to disk. You use this tab to designate three things:

- The Log File Format field determines the format of the log file. By default, RRAS uses the old-school Internet Authentication Service (IAS) format, which was originally used by the IAS component included in the Windows NT Option Pack. You can instead choose to use the database-compatible file format, which is available only in Windows 2000. This format makes it easy for you to store log data in a database, enabling more sophisticated post-processing for things such as billing and chargebacks.

- The New Log Time Period field controls how often new log files are created. Some administrators prefer to get a new log file each week or each month; others are content to let the log file grow without end. You can choose to have RRAS start new log files each day, each week, each month, or when the log file reaches a certain size.

- The Log File Directory field shows where the log file is stored. By default, each server logs its data in %systemroot%\system32\

LogFiles\iasLog.log. By using the Log File Directory field, you can change this location.

Reviewing the Remote Access Event Log

You use the Local File tab to find out exactly where the log file lives, but then what? Windows 2000 online help has an exhaustive list of all the fields logged for each connection attempt and accounting record; you don't need to have all those fields memorized, and you don't have to know how to make sense of the log entries. The Windows 2000 Resource Kit includes a handy utility called iasparse that digests an RRAS log in IAS or database formats and then produces a readable summary.

This log is a good way to identify problems with policies, because multiple policies sometimes combine to have an effect that you didn't expect. Furthermore, if doing so is desirable in your environment, you can use the logged data to generate accounting reports to tell you things such as the average use of your dial-in ports, the top 10 users of dial-in connect time, and how much online time accounts in a certain Windows group used.

Monitoring Ports and Port Activity

You can monitor port status and activity from the RRAS snap-in. The Ports folder below the server contains one entry for each defined port; when you select the Ports folder, you see a list of the ports and their current status. The list indicates whether each port is a dial-in or VPN port and whether it's active, so you can get a summary of your server's workload at any time.

Double-clicking an individual port displays the Port Status dialog box. This dialog box shows you essentially everything that you care to know about an individual port, including its line speed, the amount of transmitted and received data, and the network addresses for each protocol being carried on the port. This tool is useful for verifying whether a port is in active use. The Errors control group gives you a count of the number of transmission and reception errors on the port.

Necessary Procedures

Monitoring remote access is done with logging, and it is important for you to practice changing your logging settings.

Changing Remote Access Logging Settings

Having correct accounting and authorization data is critical to maintaining a good level of security. Follow these steps to change your RRAS logging settings:

1. Open the RRAS MMC snap-in (Start ➤ Programs ➤ Administrative Tools ➤ Routing and Remote Access).

2. Navigate to the server whose logging settings you want to change. Expand the target server; then select the Remote Access Logging node. The right MMC pane lists the log files on that server.

3. Locate the log file named Local Log File; then open its Properties dialog box by right-clicking it and choosing the Properties command. The Local File Properties dialog box appears.

4. Make sure that the Log Accounting Requests and Log Authentication Requests check boxes are checked.

5. Switch to the Local File tab. Select an appropriate time period for log rollover by choosing one of the radio buttons in the New Log Time Period control group.

6. Click the OK button.

Exam Essentials

Know the different ways of monitoring your server. Understand how local logs and RADIUS servers keep logging data, as well as how to distinguish between event logging and authentication and accounting logging.

Know the different types of RRAS logging. Understand that all logging is RRAS logging and that it logs *all* RRAS activity, including the router traffic that you will read about in Chapter 6.

Know about log file properties and how to set them. Understand the Log Accounting Requests, Log Authentication Requests, Log Periodic Status, Log File Format, New Log Time Period, and Log File Directory fields.

Know that the logs show which remote access policy was applied with recorded actions. Understand that remote access policies work only in native Windows 2000 environments.

Know that you can monitor port status and activity from the RRAS snap-in. Understand that you can monitor activity port by port.

Key Terms and Concepts

iasparse A utility (included in the Windows 2000 Resource Kit) that digests an RRAS log in IAS or database formats and then produces a readable summary.

Sample Questions

1. Julia's management has asked her to configure a remote access server so that it restricts what times of day users can dial in. She creates a remote access policy that contains time-of-day restrictions, but it doesn't work. What is the most likely cause of the problem, and how could she check the policy?

   A. The time-of-day policy hasn't been replicated throughout the domain. She can check it in the domain's properties.

   B. The time-of-day policy doesn't have a high-enough priority. She can see policies implemented with actions on the log.

   C. The time-of-day policy has a priority that's too high. She could look for lower-priority policies that superceded its implementation.

D. The time-of-day policy is not linked to an active remote access profile and thus was not implemented. She could check it by making such a linkage.

Answer: B. Policies are evaluated in order, so if the time-of-day restrictions have too low a priority, another policy may allow the connection to proceed instead of stopping it. A log would show the authentication and policies that were implemented at that time of day.

2. Bud's employer wants to implement billing and chargebacks for remote access across all its sites. What is the easiest way for him to accomplish this task?

A. He can configure his RRAS servers to use the Windows Accounting provider and then write a custom set of scripts to extract the log data.

B. He can configure his RRAS servers to use RADIUS as the accounting provider, plus a third-party accounting package.

C. He can configure his RRAS server to use RADIUS as the accounting provider; no external package is necessary.

D. He can configure his RRAS servers to use the Windows Accounting provider with the Windows 2000 License Manager.

Answer: B. This answer may be a matter of opinion, but RADIUS is designed to support centralized accounting for large sites, and a third-party package would be required to analyze the RADIUS logs and generate bills from them.

Configure remote access security.

- **Configure authentication protocols.**
- **Configure encryption protocols.**
- **Create a remote access policy.**

Remote access security is a touchy topic in some quarters, probably because no one wants to admit not having it. Several aspects are involved with remote access security configuration, the most fundamental of which involves configuring the types of authentication and encryption the server uses when accepting client requests.

Critical Information

The Security tab of the server's Properties dialog box allows you to specify which authentication and accounting methods RRAS uses.

You can choose one of two authentication providers by using the Authentication Provider drop-down list. Your choices include the following:

- Windows Authentication, which is what Microsoft calls the built-in authentication suite included with Windows 2000.

- RADIUS Authentication, which allows you to send all authentication requests heard by your server to a RADIUS server for approval or denial.

As a bonus, you can use the Accounting Provider drop-down list in the Security tab to choose between Microsoft-style accounting, in which connection requests are maintained in the event log, and RADIUS accounting, in which all accounting events are sent to a RADIUS server for action.

What if you want to change the set of authentication methods that a particular server allows? You may think that you'd accomplish this task by clicking the Configure button next to the Authentication Provider drop-down menu, but that button actually is used to set up communications with RADIUS servers when using RADIUS authentication. To configure the server by telling it which authentication methods you want it to use, you have to use the Authentication Methods button, which displays the Authentication Methods dialog box. If you look back over the list of authentication protocols earlier in the chapter, you'll find that each one has a corresponding check box in this dialog box: EAP, MS-CHAP v2, MS-CHAP, CHAP, SPAP, and PAP are all represented. If you're feeling *really* adventurous, you can turn on totally unauthenticated access by checking the Allow Remote Systems to Connect Without Authentication check box—but that's a really, really bad idea, because it allows literally anyone to connect to, and use, your server (and thus, by extension, your network).

Using CHAP involves a special set of requirements, because it requires access to each user's encrypted password. Windows 2000 normally doesn't store user passwords in a format that CHAP can use, so you have to take some additional steps if you want to use CHAP. First, enable CHAP at the server and policy levels. Next, you need to edit the default domain GPO's Password Policy object to turn on the Store Password Using Reversible Encryption for All users policy setting. After you've done that, each user's password must be either reset or changed, which forces Windows 2000 to store the password in reversibly-encrypted form. After these steps are completed for an account, that account can be used with CHAP. These steps aren't required for MS-CHAP or MS-CHAP v2; for those protocols, you just enable the desired version of MS-CHAP at the server and policy levels.

Controlling Security at the Policy Level

You can apply authentication restrictions at the policy level, too. As you saw in the preceding sections, policy-level settings don't exactly override the server settings. You could configure your server to allow CHAP, MS-CHAP, and MS-CHAP v2, and then set up a policy that prevents some users from using CHAP. On the other hand, if you disable CHAP at the server level, you can't build a policy that magically allows it.

Having said that, the trick to remember is to configure your server with the *sum* of the authentication methods you want to be able to use, and then create specific policies that limit which authentication methods (and other settings, particularly dial-in constraints) individuals or groups can use on that server.

Providing Connection Security

You can use some additional features to provide connection-level security for your remote access clients. The Callback Control Protocol

(CBCP) allows your RRAS servers or clients to negotiate a callback with the other end. When CBCP is enabled, either the client or the server can ask the server to call the client back at a number supplied by the client or at a prearranged number stored on the server.

Another nifty option is that the RRAS server can be programmed to accept or reject calls based on the Caller ID or Automatic Number Identification (ANI) information transmitted by the phone company. You can instruct your primary RRAS server to accept calls from only your home analog line; although this setting keeps you from calling the server when you're on the road, it also keeps the server from talking to strangers.

Finally, you can specify various levels of encryption to protect your connection from interception or tampering; the exact type and kind of encryption used vary according to the options you specify.

Providing Access Control

Apart from the connection-level tricks you can use to prohibit outside callers from talking to your servers, you can restrict which users can make remote connections in several ways. First, you can allow or disallow remote access from individual user accounts. This function is the same limited control that you have in Windows NT, but it's just the start in Windows 2000.

Remote Access Policies

Besides turning dial-in access on or off for a single user, you can use *remote access policies* to control whether users can get access. Like group policies, *remote access policies* give you an easy way to apply a consistent set of policies to groups of users. The policy mechanism is a little different, however: you create rules in the policy that include or exclude users. Unlike group policies, remote access policies are available only in native Windows 2000 domains (that is, in domains where no Windows NT domain controllers are present). As a result, you may not have the option to use remote access policies until your Windows 2000 deployment is farther along.

Creating a New Policy

To create a policy, right-click the Remote Access Policies folder or in the list of policies; then choose the New Remote Access Policy command. This command starts the Add Remote Access Policy wizard, which uses a series of steps to help you define the policy. First stop: the Policy Name page, in which you define a friendly name for the policy. This name appears in the snap-in's policy list.

Next, you see a page listing the conditions for this policy. Because you're just defining the policy, this page initially is blank. Because a blank page isn't very helpful, you need to click the Add button to create a condition for the policy. Clicking the Add button displays the Select Attribute dialog box, which is much more interesting.

The Select Attribute dialog box lists all the attributes that you can evaluate in a policy. These attributes are drawn from the RADIUS standards, so you can intermix your Windows 2000 RRAS servers with RADIUS servers. When you choose an attribute and click the Add button, another dialog box appears; you use this dialog box to edit the value of the attribute. The Day-and-Time-Restrictions attribute, for example, pops up a calendar grid that allows you to select which days and times are available for logging on. Each attribute has its own unique editor, which makes sense when you consider the wide range of attribute values. After you select an attribute and give it a value, you can add more attributes or move on to the next wizard step by clicking the Next button.

TIP If you want to restrict dial-in access based on an account's group membership, check out the Windows Groups attribute.

The Permissions page of the wizard has only two radio buttons, but they're important because they specify whether the policy you create allows or prevents users from connecting. The two buttons—Grant Remote Access Permissions and Deny Remote Access Permissions— do what their names imply. When you choose a permission and click

the Next button, the User Profile page appears. The primary charac-
teristic of this page is the Edit Profile button, which you use to edit the
user profile attached to the policy. You don't have to edit the profile
when you create the policy; you can always come back to it later.
After you create the policy, it appears in the snap-in, and you can
manage it independently of the other policies.

Working with Existing Policies

You can consider some additional policy-management features. To
begin with, you can reorder policies by right-clicking a policy in the
MMC window and then choosing the Move Up and Move Down
commands. Because policies are evaluated in the order of their
appearance in the snap-in, and because all conditions of all policies
must match for a user to get access, this method is a good way to
establish a set of policies that filters out some users. You could create
one policy that allows only members of the marketing department to
dial in between 8 a.m. and 5 p.m., for example, and then add another
that allows engineers free rein to dial in any time.

In addition, when you open the policy's Properties dialog box, you
can add and remove policy conditions, change the policy's name, or
specify whether a user whose connection matches the policy's conditions is granted or denied access.

You can always delete a policy that you no longer need by right-
clicking it and choosing the Delete command; the snap-in prompts
you for confirmation before it removes the policy.

Using Remote Access Profiles

Remote access profiles are an integral part of remote access policies.
Each policy has a profile associated with it; the profile determines
what settings are applied to connections that meet the conditions
stated in the policy. You can create one profile for each policy, either
when you create the policy or later (by using the Edit Profile button
in the policy's Properties dialog box). The profile contains settings
that fit into six distinct areas; each area has its own tab in the profile
Properties dialog box. These tabs include Dial-in Constraints, IP,
Multilink, Authentication, Encryption, and Advanced.

The Dial-In Constraints Tab

The Dial-in Constraints tab has most of the settings that you think of when you consider dial-in access controls. These controls allow you to adjust how long the connection can be idle before it gets dropped, how long it can be up, what dates and times the connection can be established, and what dial-in port and medium can be used to connect.

The IP Tab

The IP tab gives you control of the IP-related settings associated with an incoming call. If you think back to the server-specific settings covered earlier in the chapter, you'll remember that the server preferences include settings for other protocols besides IP; this is not so in the remote access profile. In the remote access profile, you can specify where the client gets its IP address. As a bonus, you can define IP packet filters that screen out particular types of traffic to and from the client.

The Multilink Tab

The profile mechanism also gives you a degree of control of how the server handles multilink calls; you exert this control through the Multilink tab of the profile Properties dialog box. Your first choice is to decide whether to allow these calls at all and, if so, how many ports you want to allow a single client to use at the same time. Normally, this setting is configured so that the server-specific settings take precedence, but you can override them.

The Bandwidth Allocation Protocol (BAP) Settings control group gives you a way to control what happens during a multilink call when bandwidth use drops below a certain threshold. The settings that you specify in the Multilink tab are ignored unless you have multilink and BAP/BACP enabled on the server.

The Authentication Tab

The Authentication tab allows you to specify which authentication methods you're willing to allow on this specific policy. Notice that these settings, like the other policy settings, are useful only if the server's settings match. If you turn EAP authentication off in the server Properties dialog box, for example, turning it on in the Authentication tab of the profile Properties dialog box has no effect.

Speaking of EAP authentication (as well as CHAP, MS-CHAP, and PAP/SPAP), each authentication method has a check box. Check the appropriate check boxes to control the protocols that you want this profile to use. If you enable EAP, you also can choose which EAP type you want the profile to support. Or you can choose to allow totally unauthenticated access; fortunately, this option is off by default

The Encryption Tab

The Encryption tab controls what type of encryption you want your remote users to be able to access.

Unfortunately, instead of labeling the tab's check boxes with algorithm names and key lengths, Microsoft labels them with the following adjectives:

- The No Encryption check box means what it says. When this box is checked, users can connect using no encryption at all; when the box is unchecked, a remote connection must be encrypted, or it'll be rejected.

- The Basic check box means single DES for IPSec or 40-bit Microsoft Point-to-Point Encryption (MPPE) for PPTP.

- The Strong check box means 56-bit encryption (single DES for IPSec, 56-bit MPPE for PPTP).

- The Strongest check box means triple DES for IPSec or 128-bit MPPE for PPTP connections. This option is available for Windows 2000 installations that use the full-strength High Encryption Pack.

The Advanced Tab

The Advanced tab is useful primarily if you want your RRAS server to interoperate with RADIUS equipment from other vendors. You use the tab to specify additional attributes that you want to incorporate into the profile. When you first open the tab, you see only two attributes specified: a Service-Type of Framed and a Framed-Protocol of PPP. That combination allows the RRAS server to tell its peers that it's handling a framed PPP connection. You can access several dozen additional attributes by clicking the Add button. Some of these attributes are defined in the RADIUS standard; others are specific to particular vendors. It's not necessary to know what attributes are in this list, only that you use the Advanced tab to add attributes when combining RRAS with third-party RADIUS-based solutions.

Necessary Procedures

In these procedures, you get practice in configuring encryption and authentication protocols and in creating a remote access policy:

Configuring Encryption

In this exercise, you force all connections to your server to use encryption. Any client that can't use encryption is dropped; accordingly, don't do this on your production RRAS server unless you're sure that of your clients are encryption-capable. Follow these steps:

1. Open the RRAS snap-in (Start ➤ Programs ➤ Administrative Tools ➤ Routing and Remote Access).

2. In the left pane of the MMC, expand the server that you want to configure.

3. 3. Select the Remote Access Policies folder. The right pane of the MMC displays the policies defined for this server. Select the Allow Access If Dial-in Permission is Enabled policy.

4. Choose the Action ➤ Properties command. The policy Properties dialog box appears.

5. Click the Edit Profile button. The Edit Dial-in Profile dialog box appears.

6. Switch to the Encryption tab.

7. Uncheck the No Encryption check box. Make sure that the Basic, Strong, and Strongest (if present) check boxes are all checked.

8. Click the OK button. When the policy Properties dialog box reappears, click its OK button.

Configuring Authentication Protocols

In this exercise, you configure your RRAS server so that it accepts only inbound calls that use the IP protocol. You may have to skip some steps (as noted) if you don't have all the four network protocols loaded. Follow these steps:

1. Open the RRAS MMC snap-in (Start ➤ Programs ➤ Administrative Tools ➤ Routing and Remote Access).

2. Navigate to the server whose authentication support you want to change. Select the server; then choose the Action ➤ Properties command to open the server Properties dialog box.

3. Switch to the Security tab. Make sure that Windows Authentication is selected in the Authentication Provider drop-down menu.

4. Click the Authentication Methods button. The Authentication Methods dialog box appears.

5. Check the Extensible Authentication Protocol (EAP) check box.

6. Check the two MS-CHAP check boxes.

7. Check the CHAP check box.

8. Clear the SPAP and PAP check boxes.

9. Clear the Allow Remote Systems to Connect Without Authentication check box.

10. Click the OK button. When the server Properties dialog box reappears, click its OK button.

Creating a Remote Access Policy

In this exercise, you create an adjunct policy that adds time and day restrictions to the default policy. This exercise requires you to be in a native-mode Windows 2000 domain. Follow these steps:

1. Open the RRAS MMC snap-in (Start ➤ Programs ➤ Administrative Tools ➤ Routing and Remote Access).

2. In the left pane of the MMC, expand the server that you want to configure.

3. Select the Remote Access Policies folder. The right pane of the MMC displays a single policy, Allow Access If Dial-in Permission Is Enabled.

4. Choose the Action ➤ New Remote Access Policy command. The Add Remote Access Policy wizard starts.

5. In the Policy Name page, type **Working hours restrictions**; then click the Next button.

6. In the Conditions page, click the Add button. The Select Attributes dialog box appears.

7. Select the Day-and-Time-Restrictions attribute; then click the Add button. The Time of Day Constraints dialog box appears.

8. Use the calendar controls to allow remote access Monday through Saturday for whatever hours you choose; then click the OK button. The Conditions page reappears, this time with the new condition listed.

9. Click the Next button. The User Profile page appears.

10. Click the Finish button.

Exam Essentials

Know how to choose authentication providers in the Security Tab of a server's Properties dialog box. Understand the different authentication protocols you can choose.

Know the techniques and limitations of controlling security at the policy level. Understand that policy security is best used to limit authentication methods and dial-in constraints on your server.

Know other features that you can configure for your remote access security. Understand how to use encryption, how to use Call Back Control Protocol (CBCP), and how to accept or reject calls based on Caller ID.

Know the various RA policy attributes and what they specify.
Understand that these attributes are drawn from the RADIUS standards to allow servers to be intermixed with RADIUS servers. A table of these attributes is available in Sybex's *MCSE: Windows 2000 Network Infrastructure Administration Study Guide* by Paul Robichaux.

Know how to edit a policy's profile and work with the six tabs in the profile Properties dialog box.   Understand the Dial-in Constraints tab, the IP tab, the Multilink tab, the Authentication tab, the Encryption tab, and the Advanced tab.

Key Terms and Concepts

remote access policies   Rules that, like group policies, allow the administrator to control whether users can get access. Unlike group policies, remote access policies are available only in native Windows 2000 domains.

Sample Questions

1. When you apply a remote access policy, under which of the following conditions is the user granted access?

A. Only if the policy specifies that access should be granted

B. Only if the policy does not specify that access should be denied

C. Only if the policy specifies that access should be granted and all the policy's conditions are met

D. Only if all the policy's conditions are met

Answer: C. Policies must explicitly grant access if you want them to be used to grant access, and for the policy to take effect, all of its conditions must match.

2. Kristen wants her remote users to use encryption on their dial-in connections. To achieve this result, what must she do?

   A. Create a new group policy object that specifies which encryption method to use.

   B. Create a remote access policy and edit its profile to turn off the No Encryption option.

   C. Require everyone to use IPSec on their dial-in connections.

   D. Buy a third-party network access server.

   Answer: B. Windows 2000 includes support for encryption. To meet her requirements, Kristen needs to create a policy that allows the desired users to connect and then set its profile to disallow unencrypted calls.

Chapter

4

Installing, Configuring, Managing, Monitoring, and Troubleshooting Network Protocols in a Windows 2000 Network Infrastructure

---

MICROSOFT EXAM OBJECTIVES COVERED IN THIS CHAPTER:

▶ **Install, configure, and troubleshoot network protocols.** *(pages 140 – 167)*

- Install and configure TCP/IP.
- Install the NWLink protocol.
- Configure network bindings.

▶ **Configure TCP/IP packet filters.** *(pages 167 – 173)*

▶ **Configure and troubleshoot network protocol security.** *(pages 173 – 187)*

▶ **Manage and monitor network traffic.** *(pages 187 – 196)*

▶ **Configure and troubleshoot IPSec.** *(pages 197 – 213)*

- Enable IPSec.
- Configure IPSec for transport mode.
- Configure IPSec for tunnel mode.
- Customize IPSec policies and rules.
- Manage and monitor IPSec.

This chapter contains five objectives. Count 'em! There are so many, and although related, they are not that close in content. All five objectives revolve heavily around the theme of the protocol derby winner: TCP/IP. In the first objective, you learn about installing, configuring, and troubleshooting network protocols with the emphasis on TCP/IP and NWLink.

Next, you review configuration of TCP/IP packet filters and then look at configuring and troubleshooting network protocol security with IPSec. Managing and monitoring network traffic is next, with a close look at network monitor. You also take a deeper look at IPSec, seeing both of its modes, examining IPSec policies and rules, and finally focusing on managing and monitoring IPSec.

You won't learn about all the possible protocols, but the skills you learn can be applied to other protocols, and the chapter covers the topics that will be in the exam.

Install, configure, and troubleshoot network protocols.

- **Install and configure TCP/IP.**
- **Install the NWLink protocol.**
- **Configure network bindings.**

The Windows 2000 network infrastructure exam objectives require you to know how to install, configure, and troubleshoot network protocols. The exam itself, however, focuses heavily on two protocols: TCP/IP and the NetWare-compatible *NWLink*. Accordingly, those protocols are the focus of this objective. By the time you finish this objective, you'll know how to install any network protocol Windows 2000 supports, and you'll know how to set basic configuration parameters for TCP/IP and NWLink. You also learn how to configure the bindings that attach protocols to particular NICs. Finally, you learn how to troubleshoot TCP/IP and NWLink problems.

Critical Information

Windows 2000 includes support for the same network protocols that you're accustomed to in Windows NT 4.0. Some of these protocols, such as TCP/IP, have assumed new importance; others, such as NetBIOS, are being quietly rolled out to pasture. The majority, however (including DLC and AppleTalk), survive relatively unchanged.

Windows 2000 supports a wide range of network protocols, both in the set provided with Windows 2000 itself and from third-party vendors. In brief, any vendor that wants to write an NDIS-compatible driver can do so; in theory, any network protocol could have a Windows 2000 version.

In practice, Microsoft ships protocol stacks for TCP/IP, NetBEUI, Novell's IPX/SPX (which Microsoft calls NWLink), AppleTalk, and DLC. You install or remove all these protocols by using the same interface. After you install the protocol, you still have to configure it. Because the procedure is fairly simple, you learn how to install NWLink first. Then you move on to the more complicated process of installing and configuring TCP/IP.

You install network protocols through the Local Area Network Connection Properties dialog box, which lists all the known protocols on your Windows 2000 machine. Protocols marked with a check are bound to the adapter whose properties you're inspecting.

Installing and Configuring NWLink

One of the biggest improvements in Windows 2000 is that you usually can install or remove network protocols without rebooting. That's good, because when you install NWLink, you actually get two protocols: NWLink and NWLink NetBIOS. NWLink NetBIOS allows NWLink traffic to be encapsulated inside NetBIOS traffic. In other words, you can send NWLink traffic between machines running NetBIOS or between a Windows machine running NWLink and a NetWare server running Novell's NetBIOS implementation.

Configuring NWLink is very straightforward. Like NetBIOS, the protocol really is not designed to be configured, so there aren't many settings you can change. When you open the NWLink properties dialog box, it's mostly empty, with the following controls:

- The Internal Network Number field, which allows you to designate a network number (roughly equivalent to a TCP/IP network address) for this NIC. IPX and SPX use network numbers to route traffic for particular services directly to the machines that host them, instead of depending on the Service Advertising Protocol (SAP).

- The Adapter group, which controls what types of network data frames your adapter recognizes as containing NWLink-compatible data. There are four separate and incompatible *frame types*: Ethernet 802.2, Ethernet 802.3, Ethernet II, and Ethernet SNAP. Normally, you want to use the Auto Frame Type Detection radio button, because it allows the NWLink stack to decipher the frame types for you. Choosing the wrong frame type means that you won't be able to communicate with other machines. If necessary, you can tell NWLink that a particular network number is using a particular frame type by choosing the Manual Frame Type Detection radio button and then clicking the Add button to specify the desired frame type and network number.

Installing and Configuring TCP/IP

TCP/IP normally is installed as part of the Windows 2000 setup process. This situation is no accident, because Microsoft would much rather have all its Windows 2000 customers use TCP/IP than NetBIOS. If you need to install TCP/IP manually, you still can. The process for installing it is very similar to the process for installing NWLink.

When you install TCP/IP, it defaults to using DHCP for automatic configuration. Think back to the Obtain an IP Address Automatically button in Chapter 2. If you want to use DHCP for automatic configuration, you certainly can, but it's always useful to know how to configure a TCP/IP connection manually (especially because Microsoft will be asking you to prove that you know how to as part of the exam!). In the following sections, you see what that configuration process entails.

Configuring Basic TCP/IP Settings

If you've bought into the rap that TCP/IP is convoluted and difficult to configure, Windows 2000's basic TCP/IP Properties dialog box may surprise you. TCP/IP requires only two pieces of information to function: the IP address that you want to use for this system and the subnet mask that corresponds to the network subnet the client is on.

You access the TCP/IP Properties dialog box by opening the Local Area Connection icon, selecting the Internet Protocol (TCP/IP) protocol, and clicking the Properties button. If you have multiple network adapters in a single computer, of course, you can set independent TCP/IP properties for each adapter. Depending on what you want to do, you use either the automatic configuration buttons or the text fields.

IF YOU WANT TO USE DHCP

If you're configuring a Windows 2000 Professional machine, chances are good that you're using DHCP with it. In that case, the default TCP/IP settings will work fine for you, because they configure the TCP/IP stack to get configuration parameters from any available *DHCP server*, using the process outlined in Chapter 2. Remember that you can mix and match DHCP and non-DHCP machines; on a single client, you can use DHCP to get everything except DNS server addresses if you want. You have two basic choices:

- To configure a client to get its TCP/IP configuration information from a DHCP server, leave the Obtain an IP Address Automatically radio button selected.

- If you're using DHCP for basic IP addressing and want to accept DNS server addresses from the DHCP server, leave the Obtain DNS Server Address Automatically radio button selected.

IF YOU DON'T WANT TO USE DHCP

Some people recommend against using DHCP on servers, because they're not nearly as dynamic as clients. Ideally, you won't reboot servers unless they need rebooting, and you won't be moving them around. Therefore, the "dynamic" in DHCP really isn't useful, and its other benefits are outweighed by the comfort that comes from knowing that your server has a correct and unchanging IP configuration. If you want to configure the TCP/IP settings yourself, start by selecting the Use the Following IP Address radio button. Then fill in the additional fields as follows:

- In the IP Address field, enter the IP address that you want to use for this machine. Remember that Windows 2000 won't do any kind of sanity checking. The most common mistake people make in this field is entering an address that doesn't match the address range they're using for their network.

- In the Subnet Mask field, enter the appropriate subnet mask for your network.

- If you want this machine to be able to route packets to other networks, in the Default Gateway field, enter the gateway or router address you want it to use. Windows 2000 slavishly uses whatever address you enter, so make sure that it's right.

- If you're using DNS on your network, in the Preferred DNS Server field, enter the first DNS server to which you want this client to talk. It's critical to get this entry right on a Windows 2000 network, because DNS is required for Active Directory services. If you want to specify another server to use when the preferred server is unavailable or can't resolve a DNS query, enter it in the Alternate DNS Server field.

Configuring Advanced TCP/IP Settings

The Advanced button in the TCP/IP Properties dialog box brings up something that looks more like something you'd expect from

TCP/IP. The Advanced TCP/IP Properties dialog box contains four tabs that allow you to extend and override the settings from the simpler dialog box.

Expanding the Basic Settings

The basic configuration dialog box allows you to enter one IP address, one subnet mask, and one default gateway. For the majority of systems, that information is enough, but what if you want to configure a machine that can communicate on multiple IP addresses? Adding multiple IP addresses is called *multihoming*. You also may want to specify multiple default gateways so that an outbound packet sent by your system can be sent to whichever gateway is "cheapest" (more on what "cheap" means in a minute). The IP Settings tab of the Advanced TCP/IP Properties dialog box allows you to do both of these things.

Your options in the IP Setting tab include the following:

- The IP Addresses control group, which lists the IP addresses currently defined for this network adapter. You can add address bindings, edit existing bindings, or remove addresses by clicking the buttons at the bottom of the control group. When you add an address in this tab and close all open network Properties dialog boxes, any changes you make become effective.

- The Default Gateways control group, which shows the routing gateways that are currently defined *for this computer only*. These gateways are Microsoft-defined gateways that are equivalent to routers functioning at the network level. Each gateway has an IP address and an associated metric, or cost. When deciding where to send packets bound for other networks, Windows 2000 examines its internal TCP/IP routing table to see whether it already "knows" how to get packets to the destination network. If so, Windows 2000 uses that route; if not, it uses the default gateway. If you specify more than one default gateway, the system chooses a gateway by selecting the one that has the lowest cost. If that gateway is down or can't get packets to the destination system, Windows 2000 tries the next-most-expensive gateway. This process repeats until the packets arrive at their destination or until the system runs out of gateways to try.

Expanding DNS and WINS Settings

If all you want to do is configure your clients to use two DNS servers, you can use the Preferred and Alternate Server Configuration fields in the basic TCP/IP Properties dialog box. The DNS tab of the Advanced TCP/IP Properties dialog box allows you to specify more than two servers; in addition, you can control which DNS domain names are appended to search queries when you don't specify a fully qualified domain name.

The DNS Server Addresses, In Order of Use field (and its associated buttons) allows you to specify multiple DNS servers. When the client resolver needs to have an address looked up, it starts by querying the server at the top of this list and working down the list until it finds an answer or runs out of servers to query. Adding servers to this list is a quick way to improve your clients' fault tolerance, because losing the preferred and alternative DNS servers otherwise results in a loss of DNS service to the clients.

Likewise, the WINS tab allows you to specify multiple WINS servers. In fact, the only place where you can specify which WINS servers to use is this tab, because Microsoft is trying to move you away from using WINS (and NetBIOS) to using pure TCP/IP and DNS.

Finally, the Options tab allows you to configure protocol-specific options, including whether the IP Security (IPSec) extensions are used and whether any type of packet filtering is enabled.

Installing NetBEUI

What about NetBEUI? Up to now, you've been reading that Microsoft is trying its darnedest to drive a pointed wooden stake through NetBEUI and replace it with TCP/IP. Although that's a lofty goal, many NetBEUI networks and seats still exist out there in the world, and it's important to know how to install NetBEUI in case you ever need it on a network. The good news is that there's virtually nothing new to learn at this point, because you install NetBEUI by using steps that are almost identical to those for installing NWLink and TCP/IP. In this case, you may need to install three separate pieces:

- The NetBEUI protocol itself, which you install by following the steps outlined in the "Necessary Procedures" section for this objective. Notice that NetBEUI isn't installed by default in any version of Windows 2000.

- The Client for Microsoft Networks client, which allows your client machine to attach to shares and printers on other servers, no matter what transport protocol you're using. This service is actually the Workstation service, which you may recognize from Windows NT 4.0.

- The File and Print Sharing for Microsoft Networks service, which allows your machine to act as a server, sharing resources with other machines just like the Server service in Windows NT 4.0.

NetBEUI is designed to be self-tuning, so there are no properties to set for it. The WINS tab of the Advanced TCP/IP Properties dialog box, however, provides a radio button that you can use to turn off the use of NetBEUI over TCP/IP. As an alternative, you can remove the protocol or selectively unbind it from some or all of your network adapters.

Configuring Network Bindings

A *network binding* links a protocol to an adapter so that the adapter can carry traffic using that protocol. The statement "TCP/IP is bound to the onboard Ethernet port on a laptop" tells you a few things: TCP/IP is installed, the onboard Ethernet port has a driver that supports TCP/IP, and the adapter is configured to send and receive TCP/IP traffic. One benefit of the NDIS driver specification is the ability to bind more than one protocol to a NIC. That's how your Windows 2000 machine can run TCP/IP, NetBEUI, DLC, and AppleTalk at the same time, even if it has only one network card.

Windows 2000 automatically creates bindings when you install a protocol or when you check or uncheck the check boxes in the Properties dialog box of a particular NIC. You can change these bindings manually; it's commonly considered to be good practice to unbind NetBEUI and NWLink from adapters that are connected to, or visible from, the Internet.

The Windows 2000 way of unbinding NetBEUI and NWLink is quite a bit different from the old-school Windows NT 4.0 process. You access the Windows 2000 binding list from the Network and Dial-Up Connections folder. Select a local NIC and then choose the Advanced ➤Advanced Settings command. You see the Advanced Settings dialog box. This dialog box is divided into two distinct areas.

The Connections list at the top of the dialog box shows all the connections available on your computer. The connections are listed in the order in which they'll be used for services. You can change the order in which connections are used by selecting a connection and then clicking the up- and down-arrow buttons to the right of the list.

The Bindings list shows you which protocols and services are bound to the selected connection. Checking and unchecking services has the same effect as checking or unchecking items in the Adapter Properties dialog box.

You can turn individual protocols on or off on a per-service basis. In addition to turning protocols off and on, you can control the order in which the protocols are used. This optimization is valuable, because many protocols have some sort of built-in retry behavior. Changing the bindings so that the most frequently used protocols are at the top of the list for each service means that the services never waste time trying the wrong protocol; instead, they try the most likely choice first, falling back to other protocols only if the first protocol fails.

Troubleshooting Network Protocols

Knowing how to troubleshoot network problems effectively is an essential part of managing even small networks, and Microsoft expects you to understand basic troubleshooting principles and how to apply them in Windows 2000 networking. Fortunately, you probably already know *what* to check; now you'll read about a set of tools that you can use to verify the proper functioning of your network. More important, you learn how to use those tools the right way at the right time.

When someone complains that a network is broken, your first impulse should be to ask "Well, what changed?" The first sign of network trouble usually is fairly obvious: one machine can't talk to another. You often can save yourself unnecessary time and effort in troubleshooting a problem by doing something simple: stopping to think. It's hard to keep your wits about you when something's wrong with your network and users are clamoring for your head on a stick, but if you can clearly identify the problem source, you're well on your way to being able to resolve it without any time-wasting detours.

What Kind of Problem Is It?   Sometimes, identifying the problem is the most frustrating part of troubleshooting. Getting a phone call or a pager message that says "The network is down" doesn't tell you much. Is the problem your connection to the Internet, your e-mail server, or a file server somewhere on your LAN? Without knowing what specific service or connection is unavailable, you won't know what to start fixing.

Some types of problems immediately suggest a solution. If you can, arm yourself with as many details about how the problem is manifesting itself (including exact error messages), when it started, and whether it's consistent before you try to figure out what the problem is. Knowing these things beforehand can guide you to an easy, quick solution if the problem is one that you've seen and fixed before. Knowing which users or computers are affected by a problem is very important, because that information gives you insight into possible causes and helps you select a course of action.

If one user on your network has a problem, more often than not, the problem stems from some change the user made. When you troubleshoot a user problem, your first question always should involve whether the user changed anything on the machine, including changing control-panel settings, installing or removing software, rebooting, or any other action that may have directly or indirectly changed the state of the machine. If you can find out what changed, that information gives you a list of places to start looking.

Do Several Users Report the Same Problem?   Multiuser troubleshooting is, paradoxically, both easier and harder than single-user troubleshooting. Most of the time, one user can't change anything that affects other users on the network, so you generally don't have to worry about that variable. On the other hand, the kinds of changes that can accidentally affect connectivity for many users at the same time are more likely to be things *you've* changed.

The first step in fixing this kind of problem is identifying its scope. Is everyone on the network affected? Are only people in one workgroup or on one floor of a building affected? Is the problem limited to the lack of one key service (such as DNS), or is all network traffic down? Answering this type of question helps you isolate where the problem is occurring so that you can concentrate your efforts on that area.

Do You Have Physical-Layer Connectivity? Physical-layer connectivity is absolutely critical. If you don't have a physical connection to the network you want to talk to, how can you send packets to it? This question may seem to be an obvious one to ask, but the number of times that people forget to ask it and look for a more complex—and an ultimately nonexistent—problem would boggle your mind. When you first notice a network problem, be sure to verify that all your network cables are connected correctly; that your hub, router, or switch has power; and so on. Look at the activity or "heartbeat" lights on your NIC, hub, or switch to see whether the physical layer is reporting any type of activity.

Using *ipconfig* to See What's What

Windows 2000 includes a useful tool called `ipconfig`. As its name implies, this tool is used to configure, and to see the configuration of, TCP/IP interfaces on your local machine. You learned how to use `ipconfig` to release and renew DHCP configurations in Chapter 2. This tool also has a more fundamental troubleshooting use. Typing **ipconfig** in a Windows 2000 command-prompt window presents a neat summary of your current IP configuration, including the local DNS name, the IP addresses, and the subnet masks configured for all adapters on the computer. You can use `ipconfig` in this mode to get a snapshot of its IP configuration, even if it's using DHCP.

In addition to the DHCP-related switches discussed in Chapter 2, another switch is of interest to troubleshooters: /all. As you might expect, adding the /all switch causes `ipconfig` to spill its guts and display everything it knows about the current IP configuration on all installed adapters. In addition to the DNS information and IP address that the switch ordinarily displays, you get the MAC address of each NIC, the present WINS configuration, and the IP addresses being used for the preferred and alternative DNS servers.

What can you do with all this information? It depends. If you're familiar enough with your network to know what IP address configurations should look like, a quick check with ipconfig often tells you where the problem lies. You may notice, for example, that an adapter that should be DHCP-enabled isn't, or vice versa. Even if you're not familiar with the details of your network, though, knowing how to find the IP addresses and subnet masks in use on your computers can be very valuable.

Tracing Packets

The next step up from physical-layer troubleshooting is tracing the route that packets take, or are attempting to take, between the source and destination. When you've verified that all the physical connections are in good shape, the next step is to see whether you can send *any* type of packet between points A and B.

TCP/IP includes a protocol called *Internet Control Message Protocol*, or *ICMP*. ICMP is designed to pass control and status information between TCP/IP devices. One type of ICMP packet, popularly known as a *ping* packet, tells the receiving system to send back an ICMP response. This response gives you confirmation of whether the ICMP *ping* packet reached the target, which in turn tells you whether you can get packets from place to place. Because name-resolution and application services depend on lower-level protocols, this sort of "Is this thing on?" test is the next logical step after testing the underlying physical connection. The ping and tracert tools both use ICMP to help sniff out network problems.

USING THE *PING* TOOL

When you ping a remote computer by using the ping utility in its default mode, your computer sends out four ICMP *ping* packets and measures the time required before each packet's corresponding response arrives. When it finishes, ping gives you a helpful summary showing the number of packets sent and received; the minimum, maximum, and average round-trip times; and a percentage indicating how many packets got no response. Following is a sample session that pings the machine at IP address 206.151.234.1:

```
F:\Shared\abi-0.7.8>ping 206.151.234.1

Pinging 206.151.234.1 with 32 bytes of data:

Reply from 206.151.234.1: bytes=32 time=125ms TTL=250
Reply from 206.151.234.1: bytes=32 time=110ms TTL=250
Reply from 206.151.234.1: bytes=32 time=110ms TTL=250
Reply from 206.151.234.1: bytes=32 time=110ms TTL=250

Ping statistics for 206.151.234.1:
    Packets: Sent = 4, Received = 4, Lost = 0 (0% loss),
Approximate round trip times in milli-seconds:
    Minimum = 110ms, Maximum = 125ms, Average = 113ms
```

What does this listing tell you? First, you see that all the packets that you sent arrived, and that there are approximately five hops between this machine and your target. You know the latter because the time to live, or TTL, value is 250. By default, the TTL on the packets that ping sends out is set to 255, and each routing device that routes the packets subtracts one from the TTL value. When a packet's TTL hits zero, it is dropped.

More important, this ping session shows that data is flowing normally between your machine and the target. Because all the *ping* packets got there (notice the 0% loss line near the bottom), you can comfortably say that any network problems on this link aren't the result of a routing problem. Packets are flowing normally between here and there.

How would you identify a problem by using this data? The most obvious way to tell is when ping times out without getting *any* packets back from the remote end. That's a big red flag indicating that either you typed the IP address wrong or that something is blocking traffic between the two ends of the connection. Likewise, high rates of packet loss signal that something may be wrong somewhere along the path between the machines.

USING THE *TRACERT* TOOL

When your plumbing is stopped up, you can tell because your sink, toilet, or shower won't drain—but knowing that it won't drain doesn't tell you where the blockage is. Likewise, the `ping` utility can tell you whether packets are flowing, but it won't necessarily tell you where the problem is. Windows 2000 includes a tool called `tracert` (pronounced "traceroute," after the original Unix version) that takes advantage of the TTL in each IP packet to map out the path that the packets are taking as they flow to a remote system.

Recall that each device that routes a packet decrements its TTL. `tracert` begins by sending one ICMP *ping* packet with a TTL of 1. That means that the first router or gateway to encounter it sends an ICMP response, decrements the *ping* packet's TTL, notices that the TTL is now zero, and drops the packet. At that point, `tracert` sends a second packet with a TTL of 2. The first device responds, decrements the TTL, and then routes the packet to the next hop. The next device in the chain responds to the `ping` , decrements the TTL, and drops the original packet. This process continues with `tracert` gradually incrementing the TTL until the packet finally reaches the desired destination host.

As it sends these packets, `tracert` keeps a running log of which hosts along the route have responded and which ones haven't. You can use this information to figure out where the stoppage is. Look at this `tracert` session:

```
F:\>tracert www.microsoft.com

Tracing route to microsoft.com [207.46.131.137]
over a maximum of 30 hops:

  1   <10 ms   <10 ms   <10 ms  ELGRANDE [192.168.0.1]
  2    *        *        *      Request timed out.
  3    *        *        *      Request timed out.
  4    *        *        *      Request timed out.
  5    *        *        *      Request timed out.
```

You can clearly see that the problem lies at the first hop away from your machine—a machine named ELGRANDE, running the Routing and Remote Access Services (RRAS) package. You know this because the trace shows no response from any machine downstream of ELGRANDE. In this case, you can easily fix the problem on your end by restarting the RRAS service on ELGRANDE, but you wouldn't know that you needed to do that unless you did a `tracert`.

Another thing that the `tracert` session shows you is that DNS resolution is working properly. Most of the time, you'll use troubleshooting tools such as `ping` and `tracert` with IP addresses, because you frequently need to verify that packets can be moved at the IP level before trying to use higher-level services such as DNS. Name resolution is important to Windows 2000 because of the way it uses DNS service records to locate network resources.

The `nslookup` tool allows you to query a DNS server to see what information it holds for a host record. You can query for a single piece of information from the command line. If you run `nslookup` with no command-line arguments, it goes into interactive mode, in which you can make several queries in a row:

You can use the `server ipAddress` command to switch resolution to the server at the specified IP address. That feature is very useful when your regular DNS server is down or can't seem to resolve a particular address.

Understanding IPSec

The original specifications for IP (Internet Protocol) made no provisions for any kind of security. That lack wasn't accidental; it stemmed from two completely different causes. One was the expectation that users and administrators would continue to behave fairly well and not make serious attempts to compromise other people's traffic. The other was that the cryptographic technology needed to provide adequate security wasn't widely available, or even widely known about. As the Internet expanded, it became clear that robust authentication and privacy protection were desirable, but version 4 of the IP specification (which is what most of us are using now) didn't include it. As the installed base of IP-capable devices grew, so did the complexity of devising a security protocol that wouldn't screw up all those devices.

Finally, in the late 1990s, vendors began releasing products that incorporated the *IP Security Extensions* (better known as just *IPSec*) to IP version 4.

NOTE   Several major vendors, including Microsoft, Cisco, Nortel, and RSA Security, are shipping IPSec products. The standard itself is still somewhat in flux, however. If you're thinking about implementing IPSec in a mixed-vendor network, make sure that all your devices can talk to one another. Refer to RFC 1825 for additional information on IPSec.

WHAT IPSEC DOES

IPSec has two separate features, but they go together: authentication and encryption. You can use these features together or separately. Each feature has options and parameters that you can tweak to fine-tune security on your network.

Authentication   Authentication protects your network, and the data it carries, from tampering. This tampering might take the form of a malicious attacker sitting between a client and a server, altering the contents of packets (the so-called "man in the middle" attack), or it might take the form of an attacker joining your network and impersonating either a client or a server. IPSec uses an *authentication header (AH)* to digitally sign the entire contents of each packet. This signature provides three separate benefits:

- **Protection against replay attacks.** If an attacker can capture packets, save them until later, and send them again, it can impersonate a machine after that machine's no longer on the network. This form of attack is called a *replay attack*. IPSec's authentication mechanism prevents replay attacks by including the sender's signature on all packets.

- **Protection against tampering.** IPSec's signatures provide data integrity, meaning that an interloper can't selectively change parts of packets to alter their meaning.

- **Protection against spoofing.** Normally, when you hear about authentication, it means the process by which a client or server verifies another machine's identity. IPSec authentication headers provide authentication because each end of a connection can verify the other's identity.

Encryption   Authentication protects your data against tampering, but it doesn't do anything to keep people from seeing it. For that purpose, you need encryption, which actually obscures the payload contents so that a man in the middle can't read the traffic as it goes by. To accomplish this task, IPSec provides the *Encapsulating Security Payload (ESP)*. ESP is used to encrypt the entire payload of an IPSec packet, rendering it undecipherable by anyone other than the intended recipient. ESP provides only confidentiality, but it can be combined with AH to gain maximum security.

IPSEC AND WINDOWS 2000

Windows 2000 implements IPSec, which in and of itself is a big deal because it involves a large number of changes in the TCP/IP stack and its underpinnings. Microsoft's IPSec implementation is actually licensed from, and was written by, Cisco, which guarantees good compatibility with other standards-based IPSec clients.

Some other nifty Windows 2000 features make IPSec more useful. Imagine a large network of computers, some running IPSec. When two computers want to communicate, it would be ideal if they could automatically take advantage of IPSec and if both ends supported it. You'd also want to ensure that the security settings you want to use were applied to all IPSec-capable machines. With Windows NT or most other operating systems, that would mean hand-configuring each IPSec machine to use those settings.

The solution lies in the Windows 2000 Group Policy mechanism. First, you specify the IPSec settings that you want to use on your network. Then, each Windows 2000 machine runs a service called the IPSec Policy Agent. When the system starts, the Policy Agent connects to an Active Directory server, fetches the IPSec policy, and then passes it to the IPSec code.

HOW IPSEC WORKS

IPSec is a fairly complex protocol. In fact, what is referred to as "IPSec" actually is a collage of protocols with different but interrelated functions.

PARTS OF IPSEC

IPSec appears to be a single unitary protocol, but it's implemented in three protocols, as well as several Windows 2000 drivers and services.

The Internet Security Agreement/Key Management Protocol (ISAKMP) and Oakley   ISAKMP provides a way for two computers to agree on security settings and exchange a security key that they can use to communicate securely. In IPSec-speak, a *security association (SA)* provides all the information needed for two computers to communicate securely. The SA contains a policy agreement that controls which algorithms and key lengths the two machines will use ("Let's use 128-bit RC5 and SHA-1"), plus the actual security keys used to securely exchange information. Think of this agreement as being like a contract: it specifies what each party is, and is not, willing to do as part of the agreement.

This process involves two steps. First, the two computers use the ISAKMP to establish a security agreement. This agreement is called the *ISAKMP SA*. To establish the ISAKMP SA, the two computers must agree on the following three things:

- Which encryption algorithm (DES, triple DES, 40-bit DES, or none) they'll use

- Which algorithm they'll use for verifying message integrity (MD5 or SHA-1)

- How connections will be authenticated: via a public-key certificate, a shared secret key, or Kerberos

When the ISAKMP SA is in place, the two machines can use the Oakley protocol to agree securely on a shared master key. This key, called the *ISAKMP master key*, is used along with the algorithms negotiated in the ISAKMP SA to establish a secure connection. After the secure connection is brought up, the two machines start another round of negotiations. These negotiations cover the following:

- Whether the Authentication Header protocol will be used for this connection

- Whether the Encapsulating Security Payload protocol will be used for this connection

- Which encryption algorithm will be used for the ESP protocol

- Which authentication protocol will be used for the AH protocol

After *these* negotiations are finished, the two machines end up with *two* new SAs: one for inbound traffic and another for outbound traffic. These SAs are called *IPSec SAs* to distinguish them from the ISAKMP SA. At this point, Oakley is used again to generate a new set of session keys. The master ISAKMP key is used whenever new SAs are negotiated. When the SA negotiation finishes, though, the communications using that SA are protected via the SA-specific keys.

The Authentication Header (AH)   The AH protocol provides data integrity and authentication, but how? The answer lies in the way that the IPSec packet is constructed. Two features lend AH its security. The first security feature is that the packet signature (which is contained in the AH itself) is computed on the entire packet: payload and headers. This situation means that an attacker can't modify any part of the packet, including the IP or TCP/UDP header. The second security booster is the fact that the AH is placed between the IP header and the TCP or UDP header, adding further tamperproofing.

The Encapsulating Security Payload (ESP)   The ESP protocol is designed to deliver message confidentiality. Look at a sample ESP packet to see how it accomplishes this task. The first thing you'll probably notice is that this packet is more complex in construction than the AH packet, because ESP alone provides authentication, replay-proofing, and integrity checking. It does so by adding three separate components: an ESP header, an ESP trailer, and an ESP authentication block. Each of these components contains some of the data needed to provide the necessary authentication and integrity checking. To prevent tampering, an ESP client has to sign the ESP header, application data, and ESP trailer into one unit; ESP is used to encrypt the application data and the ESP trailer to provide confidentiality. The combination of this overlapping signature and encryption operation provides good security.

Understanding the Process: How Harry Meets Sally

Now it's time to tie all this protocol business together by showing you how it works in practice. Suppose that Harry wants to establish a connection to a file server run by Sally. Harry and Sally are members of the same Windows 2000 domain, so they can use the Windows 2000 default of Kerberos authentication. As you read the steps involved, keep in mind that the entire process is utterly transparent to users on both machines, as well as to most intervening routers and network devices. The negotiation and agreement process is transparent both to the users and the applications that they're using.

AT BOOT TIME

When Harry's computer boots, the IPSec Policy Agent service starts. The service connects to Active Directory and downloads the current IPSec policy for the domain. If this connection attempt fails, Harry's machine keeps trying until it successfully gets an IPSec policy, because without one, the IPSec stack doesn't know what to do.

When the policy is retrieved, policy settings are passed to the ISAKMP /Oakley subsystem and to the actual IPSec drivers in the kernel.

WHEN HARRY INITIATES A CONNECTION

When Harry initially attempts to make a connection to any foreign machine, his computer's IPSec driver checks the active IPSec policy to see whether any IP filters are defined. These filters (which are covered in the third exam objective of this chapter) specify destination networks, traffic types, or both; for the destination or traffic type, the filter also specifies whether IPSec is mandatory, optional, or forbidden.

After Harry's IPSec driver determines that it's allowed to use IPSec when talking to machines on Sally's subnet, it uses ISAKMP to establish an ISAKMP SA with Sally's server.

WHEN SALLY RECEIVES THE CONNECTION REQUEST

When Sally's machine sees the incoming ISAKMP request from Harry's workstation, her ISAKMP service replies to the request, and the two machines negotiate an ISAKMP SA as described earlier in this chapter. This SA includes a shared secret key that can be used to establish connection-specific SAs.

THE DANCE BEGINS

Now that an ISAKMP SA has been established, the two machines have everything they need to establish a pair of IPSec SAs, so they do so. When those negotiations are complete, each computer has two IPSec SAs in place: one for outbound traffic and one for inbound.

Harry's request is processed by the IPSec stack on his computer. His IPSec code uses AH and/or ESP to protect the outbound packets and then transfers them to the lower-level parts of the IP stack for delivery to Sally's server. When her server gets the packets, it uses Sally's IPSec stack to decrypt them, verify their authenticity, and pass them up the TCP/IP stack for further processing.

The ability to control network traffic is a key part of system administration. Many organizations want to protect their network traffic from eavesdropping and tampering, but it's been very difficult to do these things because of the obstacles involved. Interoperability is the most obvious hurdle, but many subtle pitfalls are associated with trying to secure network traffic in a robust yet easily managed way.

The Internet Engineering Task Force (IETF) attacked this problem some time ago; the result was the Internet Protocol Security Extensions (IPSec). As the name suggests, IPSec is a set of extensions to the basic Internet Protocol (IP) that we all know and love. The word *extension* suggests that IPSec capability is layered on top of, and cannot be used without, IP, and that's certainly true in this case.

In the third and fifth objectives in this chapter, you learn how to install and configure IPSec and how to use the security policies. You also learn how to define your own security policies and filters to customize the level of protection available to computers on your network.

Necessary Procedures

In this section, you learn to install NWLink and TCP/IP and to configure TCP/IP settings. You also learn to edit network bindings and to check configurations with the ipconfig tool.

Installing NWLink

Follow these steps to install NWLink:

1. Open the Network and Dial-Up Connections folder (Start ➢ Settings ➢ Network and Dial-Up Connections).

2. Right-click the Local Area Connection icon; then choose the Properties command. The Local Area Connection Properties dialog box appears.

3. Click the Install button. The Select Network Component Type dialog box appears. Select Protocol; then click the Add button. The Select Network Protocol dialog box appears.

4. Choose NWLink IPX/SPX-Compatible Transport Protocol; then click the OK button.

5. If prompted, insert your Windows 2000 CD; then click OK.

6. Click the Close button in the Local Area Connection Properties dialog box.

Installing TCP/IP

Follow these steps to install the TCP/IP protocol:

1. Open the Network and Dial-Up Connections folder (Start ➢ Settings ➢ Network and Dial-Up Connections).

2. Right-click the Local Area Connection icon; then choose the Properties command. The Local Area Connection Properties dialog box appears.

3. Click the Install button. The Select Network Component Type dialog box appears. Select Protocol; then click the Add button. The Select Network Protocol dialog box appears.

4. Choose Internet Protocol (TCP/IP); then click the OK button.

5. If prompted, insert your Windows 2000 CD; then click OK.

6. Click the Close button in the Local Area Connection Properties dialog box.

7. Follow these steps to add a second IP address to your existing NIC.

Notice that this exercise assumes that you're not using DHCP on that NIC, because you can't assign additional addresses to a DHCP-enabled NIC.

Configuring TCP/IP Settings

To configure TCP/IP settings, follow these steps:

1. Choose an IP address on your network that's not currently in use by another device. Make sure that you know the correct subnet mask to use with that IP address.

2. Open the Network and Dial-Up Connections folder (Start ➢ Settings ➢ Network and Dial-Up Connections).

3. Right-click the Local Area Connection icon; then choose the Properties command. The Local Area Connection Properties dialog box appears.

4. Select Internet Protocol (TCP/IP) in the Components list; then click the Properties button. The Internet Protocol (TCP/IP) Properties dialog box appears.

5. Click the Advanced button. The Advanced TCP/IP Properties dialog box appears.

6. Click the Add button in the IP Addresses control group. The TCP/IP Address dialog box appears.

7. Type the IP address and subnet mask you chose in step 1.

8. Click the OK button in the Advanced TCP/IP Settings dialog box.

9. Click the OK button in the Internet Protocol (TCP/IP) Properties dialog box.

10. Click the OK button in the Local Area Connection Properties dialog box.

Editing Network Bindings

Follow these steps to bind IPX/SPX to the File and Printer Sharing service:

1. Open the Network and Dial-Up Connections folder (Start ➢ Settings ➢ Network and Dial-Up Connections).

2. Select the Local Area Connection icon; then choose the Advanced ➢Advanced Settings command. The Advanced Settings dialog box appears.

3. Select Internet Protocol (TCP/IP) in the Components list; then click the Properties button. The Internet Protocol (TCP/IP) Properties dialog box appears.

4. Click the Advanced button. The Advanced TCP/IP Properties dialog box appears.

5. In the Bindings for Local Area Connection list, find the File and Printer Sharing for Microsoft Networks item. Notice that each installed network protocol is listed below the service.

6. In the indented list, if NetBEUI is checked, uncheck it; and if NWLink is unchecked, check it.

7. Click the OK button in the Advanced Settings dialog box.

Checking Configurations with *ipconfig*

Follow these steps to run `ipconfig` and analyze its output:

1. Open a command window (Start ➢ Run; then enter **cmd** in the Run dialog box and click OK).

2. At the command prompt, type **ipconfig** and press the Enter key. You see an abbreviated display containing the machine's connection-specific DNS suffix, its IP address, subnet mask, and default gateway.

3. Type **ipconfig /all** and press the Enter key. Notice that a great deal more information is displayed, including information on multiple adapters (if you have more than one).

Exam Essentials

Know that Microsoft ships protocol stacks for TCP/IP, NetBEUI, Novell's IPX/SPX, AppleTalk, and DLC, and that they are all installed or removed with the same interface. Understand the LAN Connection Properties dialog box and that protocols marked with a check are bound to the adapter. Know that you can install protocols without a reboot.

Know how to install and configure NWLink and TCP/IP. Understand that you can set independent TCP/IP properties for each adapter and that you need to know if you're using DHCP to configure each adapter.

Know the advanced TCP/IP settings, including how to configure multihoming and metric route selection. Understand that you can add any DNS servers over the original two or specify any multiple WINS servers.

Know how to install and remove NetBEUI. Understand that you can use can use the WINS tab in the Advanced TCP/IP Properties dialog box to turn off NetBEUI over TCP/IP (NBP).

Know that network bindings are created automatically when you check a protocol box. Understand that you can control the order in which the protocols are used and the ramifications of that order.

Know how to troubleshoot network protocols. Understand the questions that you need to ask and useful tools—such as ipconfig, ping and tracert—that you can use.

Know about the two separate features included in IPSec: authentication and encryption. Understand IPSec's authentication headers and its function and benefits, along with the Encapsulating Security Payload (ESP) and the encryption that it provides.

Know how the IPSec process works and about ISAKMP Security agreements and subsequent IPSec SAs. Understand that the Oakley protocol is used to come to agreement and that agreements are necessary for inbound and for outbound traffic, respectively.

Know that IPSec is a brainchild of the Internet Engineering Task Force (IETF). Understand that the IPSec is a set of extensions to the basic Internet Protocol (IP) devised by the IETF. This capability is layered on top of, and cannot be used without, IP.

Key Terms and Concepts

authentication header (AH)   A packet portion used to digitally sign the entire contents of each packet.

default gateway   A *TCP/IP* configuration option that specifies the gateway that will be used if the network contains routers.

Encapsulating Security Payload (ESP)   A packet section used to encrypt the entire payload of an IPSec packet, rendering it undecipherable by anyone other than the intended recipient. ESP provides only confidentiality.

frame type   An option that specifies how data is packaged for transmission over the network. This option must be configured to run the *NWLink IPX/SPX/NetBIOS Compatible Transport* protocol on a Windows 2000 computer. By default, the frame type is set to Auto Detect, which attempts to choose a compatible frame type for the network automatically.

Internet Control Messaging Protocol (ICMP)   A protocol designed to pass control and status information between TCP/IP devices.

Internet Security Agreement/Key Management Protocol (ISAKMP)   A protocol that provides a way for two computers to agree on security settings and exchange a security key that they can use to communicate securely with a *security association*.

IP Security Extensions (IPSec)   A process that makes it possible to transfer sensitive information to other hosts across the Internet without fear of compromise. IPSec provides authentication and encryption for transmitted data.

IPSec Policy Agent   A service running on a Windows 2000 machine that connects to an Active Directory server, fetches the IPSec policy, and then passes it to the IPSec code.

multihoming   The process of adding multiple IP addresses on a single physical network connection.

network binding   A program that links a protocol to an adapter so that the adapter can carry traffic using that protocol.

nslookup   A tool that allows you to query a DNS server to see what information it holds for a host record.

NWLINK IPX/SPX/NetBIOS Compatible Transport   An analogous Microsoft implementation of the Novell IPX/SPX protocol stack.

ping   A command used to send an Internet Control Message Protocol (ICMP) echo request and echo reply to verify that a remote computer is available.

security association (SA)   A relationship that defines all the information needed for two computers to communicate securely. The SA contains a policy agreement that controls which algorithms and key lengths the two machines will use, plus the actual security keys used to securely exchange information.

tracert   A tool used to map out the path that the packets are taking as they flow to a remote system.

Sample Questions

1. The `ipconfig/all` command shows you which of the following?

    A. The destination address of a remote host

    B. The MAC address of the nearest router

    C. The domain the current console user is logged into

    D. Local IP addresses and subnet masks

    Answer: D. `Ipconfig/all` shows the local IP addresses and subnet masks.

2. To change network bindings, you must _____.

    A. Use the Advanced Settings command in the Network and Dial-Up Connections window

    B. Edit the Registry manually

    C. Boot into the Windows 2000 recovery console

    D. Remove and reinstall the affected protocols

    Answer: A. The Advanced Settings command is the only supported way to change network bindings in Windows 2000.

Configure TCP/IP packet filters.

One of the most useful and least appreciated features in the Routing and Remote Access Service (RRAS) is its capability to selectively filter TCP/IP packets in both directions. You can construct filters that allow or deny traffic into or out of your network, based on rules that specify source and destination addresses and ports. The basic idea behind packet filtering is simple: You specify filter rules, and incoming packets are measured against those rules. You have two choices: accept all packets except those prohibited by a rule, or drop all packets except those permitted by a rule.

Critical Information

Filters normally are used to block out undesirable traffic. The definition of *undesirable* varies, of course, but in general, the idea is to keep out packets that your machines shouldn't see. You could configure a packet filter, for example, that would block all packets to a Web server except those on TCP ports 80 and 443. On the other hand, you could just as easily create a filter that blocks all outgoing packets on the ports used by the MSN and AOL instant-messaging tools. Another example (and one that is more helpful for the exam) is the use of filters for a PPTP or L2TP server; these filters screen out everything except VPN traffic so that you can expose a Windows 2000 VPN server without fear of compromise.

Filters are associated with a particular interface; the filters assigned to one interface are totally independent of those on all other interfaces, and inbound and outbound filters are likewise separate. You create and remove filters by using the Input Packet Filters and Output Packet Filters buttons in the General tab of the interface's Properties dialog box. The mechanics of working with the filters are identical; you create inbound filters to screen traffic coming to the interface and outbound filters to screen traffic going back out through that interface.

To create a filter, find the interface on which you want to use the filter; then open its Properties dialog box. Click the appropriate packet filter button, and you see a dialog box like the Input Filter dialog box.

This dialog box has the following six salient parts:

- The Receive All Packets Except Those That Meet the Criteria Below and the Drop All Packets Except Those That Meet the Criteria Below radio buttons control what this filter does. To make a filter that excludes only those packets that you specify, choose the Receive All Packets button. To do the opposite, and accept only those packets that meet your rule, choose the Drop All Packets button. Notice that these buttons are inactive until you create a filter rule.

- The Filters list, which initially is empty, shows you which filters are defined on this interface. Each filter's entry in the list shows you the source address and mask; the destination address and mask; and the protocol, port, and traffic type specified in the rule.

- The Add, Edit, and Remove buttons do what you'd expect.

Creating a filter is straightforward: click the Add button, and you see the Add IP Filter dialog box. The conditions that you specify must *all* be true to trigger the rule. If you specify both the source and destination addresses, for example, only traffic from the defined source to the defined destination is filtered.

Follow these steps to fill out the Add IP Filter dialog box:

1. To create a filter that blocks packets by their origin or source address, check the Source Network check box, and supply the IP address and subnet mask for the source that you want to block.

2. To create a filter that blocks according to destination, check the destination network and then fill in the appropriate address and subnet mask.

3. To filter by protocol, choose the protocol that you want to block: Any (which blocks everything), TCP, Established TCP, IP, UDP, ICMP, or Other. For each of these protocols, you have to enter some additional information. If you choose TCP, for example, you have to specify the source or destination port numbers (or both); for Other, you have to enter a protocol number.

After you specify the filter you want to use, click the OK button; you see it in the filter list. Filters go into effect as soon as you close the interface's Properties dialog box; you can always go back and add, edit, or remove filters at any time.

Configuring VPN Packet Filters

Packet filters provide a useful security mechanism for blocking unwanted traffic on particular machines. It's a good idea to use packet filters to keep non-VPN traffic out of your VPN servers. The rules for doing this are fairly straightforward.

PPTP Packet Filters

You need at least two filters to adequately screen out non-PPTP traffic. The first filter allows traffic with a protocol ID of 47 (the Generic Routing Encapsulation, or GRE, protocol) to pass to the destination address of the PPTP interface. The second filter allows inbound traffic bound for TCP port 1723 (the PPTP port) to come to the PPTP interface.

You can add a third filter if the PPTP server also works as a PPTP client; in that case, the third filter needs the interface's destination address, a protocol type of TCP (established), and a source port of 1723.

After you've created these filters, choose the Drop All Packets Except Those That Meet the Criteria Below radio button in the Input Filters dialog box, and close the dialog box. That's not quite all you have to do, though. You have to repeat the process on the output side, creating two or three corresponding output filters that screen out any traffic not originating from the VPN interface and using the correct protocols.

L2TP Packet Filters

To use L2TP packet filters, you have to go through the same basic process, but the filters that you need are slightly different. Four filters are required: two input filters and two output filters. These filters are:

- An input filter with a destination of the VPN interface address and a net mask of 255.255.255.255, filtering UDP with a source and destination port of 500

- An input filter with a destination of the VPN interface address and a net mask of 255.255.255.255, filtering UDP with a source and destination port of 1701

- An output filter with a source of the VPN interface address and a net mask of 255.255.255.255, filtering UDP with a source and destination port of 500

- An output filter with a source of the VPN interface address and a net mask of 255.255.255.255, filtering UDP with a source and destination port of 1701

Necessary Procedures

In this section, you learn to configure PPTP packet filters:

Configure PPTP Packet Filters

In this exercise (which you shouldn't attempt on your production VPN server until you've been successful in trying it on another, less critical machine), you set up RRAS IP packet filters that block everything except PPTP traffic on the specified interface. Follow these steps:

1. Open the RRAS console, and expand the server and IP Routing nodes to expose the General node of the server on which you're working. Select the General node.

2. Right-click the appropriate interface;, then choose the Properties command.

3. In the General tab of the interface Properties dialog box, click the Input Filters button. The Input Filters dialog box appears.

4. Click the Add button. The Add IP Filter dialog box appears.

5. Fill out the Add IP Filter dialog box as follows:

   A. Check the Destination Network check box.

   B. Enter the IP address of the VPN interface in the Destination IP Address field.

   C. Supply a destination subnet mask of 255.255.255.255.

   D. Select a protocol type of TCP; then specify a source port of 0 and a destination port of 1723.

   E. Click the OK button.

6. The Input Filters dialog box reappears, listing the new filter that you created in step 5. Repeat step 5, but this time, specify Other in the Protocol field and fill in a protocol ID of 47. When you're done, click the OK button. You return to the Input Filter dialog box.

7. In the Input Filter dialog box, click the Drop All Packets Except Those That Meet the Criteria Below radio button; then click the OK button.

8. Repeat steps 3-7, but this time create output filters. Make sure that you specify the IP address of the VPN adapter as the source, not the destination.

9. Close the interface Properties dialog box.

Exam Essentials

Know about RRAS's capability to selectively filter TCP/IP packets, both inbound and outbound. Understand that you can accept all packets except those that you exclude through a rule or deny all packets except those that you accept through a rule.

Know how to filter all packets except VPN traffic on a PPTP or L2TP server. Understand this process, including the two filters necessary to screen out non-PPTP traffic and the four filters you need with L2TP.

Key Terms and Concepts

packet filtering   The capability to selectively filter TCP/IP packets in both directions by constructing filters that allow or deny traffic into or out of your network, based on rules that specify source and destination addresses and ports.

Sample Questions

1. When you configure RIP on an interface, you can filter routes based on what?

   A. The originating router or network ID

   B. The origin network ID only

   C. The originating router only

   D. The route source

   Answer: A. RIP routes can be filtered based on the network they cover or on the router that's offering them.

2. When using L2TP packet filters, four filters are required, including two output filters with a source and destination port of:

A. 500

B. 501

C. 1700

D. 1701

E. A and D

F. B and C

Answer: E. An output filter with a source of the VPN interface address and a net mask of 255.255.255.255, filtering UDP with source and destination ports of 500 on one filter and 1701 on the other.

Configure and troubleshoot network protocol security.

Sometimes, it is difficult to collect the information that relates to an objective and segregate it from the material that relates to other exam objectives. This situation probably is more true of this general objective than any other in the exam. To prepare to understand configuring and troubleshooting network protocol security, you need to know most of the material in this chapter.

The material in this objective section involves the general configuration of IPSec, which is continued in the last objective in this chapter. Some of the material also relates to the second subobjective of that IPSec objective: configuring IPSec for transport mode.

Critical Information

You've learned the basic set of IPSec buzzwords. Now it's time to build on that basis by adding some specific terms that you'll encounter while setting up IPSec.

Security Filters A *security filter* ties security protocols to a particular network address. The filter contains the source and destination addresses involved (either for specific hosts or networks, using a net mask), the protocol used, and the source and destination ports allowed for TCP and UDP traffic. IPSec connections have two sides, inbound and outbound. So for each connection, you need to have two filters: one inbound and one outbound. The inbound filter is applied when a remote machine requests security on a connection; the outbound filter is applied before sending traffic to a remote machine.

If any these filters is missing or misconfigured, the IPSec negotiation process fails, and IPSec won't be used. If all filters exist, though, when you try to establish an FTP connection, the outbound filter on your domain fires, and it triggers IPSec to request a security negotiation with the destination's machine. Assuming that everything goes well and that the filters are OK, you end up with two IPSec SAs on your machine, and the connection is secured.

You normally group filters into *filter lists* for ease of management. Because you can stuff any number of individual filters into a filter list, you can easily build rules that enforce complicated behavior and then distribute those rules throughout your network as necessary.

Security Methods Each IPSec connection uses a *security method*, which is a fancy way of saying that each connection uses a prespecified encryption algorithm with a negotiated key length and key lifetime. You can use one of the two predefined security methods (High or Medium), or you can roll your own by specifying which security protocols (AH or ESP), encryption algorithms, and key lifetimes you want to use for a particular connection. When your computer is negotiating with a remote IPSec peer, the ISAKMP service works its way down the list of methods you've specified, trying to use the most secure method first. As soon as your ISAKMP and the one on the other end agree on a method, that method is used.

Security Filter Actions   Filters specify a source and destination, but they also have to specify what action should take place when the criteria specified in the filter match. You can use the following five separate actions in each filter (though you can't combine them in the same filter):

- The Permit action tells the IPSec filter to take no action. It neither accepts nor rejects the connection based on security rules, meaning that it adds zero security. This action is sometimes called the *passthrough action,* because it allows traffic to pass through without modification. In general, you'll use this action for applications such as WINS servers, in which no security-sensitive data is involved.

- The Block action causes the filter to reject communications from the remote system. This action prevents the remote system from making any type of connection, with or without IPSec.

- The Accept Unsecured and Allow Unsecured actions allow you to interoperate with computers that don't speak IPSec. The Accept Unsecured Communication, but Always Respond Using IPSec policy says that it's OK to accept unsecured connections but that your machines will always ask for an IPSec connection before accepting the unsecured request. This policy allows you to handle both unsecured and secured traffic, with a preference for IPSec when it's available. The Allow Unsecured Communication with Non-IPSec Aware Computers action allows your machines to accept insecure connections without attempting to use IPSec. You should not use it in favor of the Accept Unsecured action.

- The Use These Security Settings action allows you to specify which security methods you want to use on connections that trigger this filter. This action allows you to specify custom settings for either individual computers or remote networks.

Security Policies A *security policy* is a set of rules and filters that provides some level of security. Microsoft includes several prebuilt policies, and you can make your own. Three policies are included in Windows 2000:

- Client (Respond Only) specifies that a Windows 2000 IPSec client will negotiate IPSec security with any peer that supports it but won't attempt to initiate security. Don't let the word *client* fool you in this context; it means IPSec clients. Suppose that you apply this policy to a Windows 2000 Server computer. When the server initiates outbound network connections, it won't attempt to use IPSec. When someone opens a connection to it, though, the server accepts IPSec if the remote end asks for it.

- Secure Server (Require Security) specifies that *all* IP communication to, or from, the policy target *must* use IPSec. In this case, *all* really does mean *all*: DNS, WINS, Web requests, and everything else that flows over an IP connection either has to be secured with IPSec or is blocked. This may not be what you want unless you go all-IPSec on your network.

- Server (Request Security) is a mix of the two other policies. In this case, the machine always attempts to use IPSec by requesting it when it connects to a remote machine and by allowing it when an incoming connection requests it. This policy provides the best general balance between security and interoperability.

You assign policies to computers in several ways. The easiest way is to store the policy in Active Directory and have the IPSec Policy Agent take care of applying it to the applicable machines. When an IPSec policy is assigned to a machine through Active Directory, it remains assigned—even after the machine leaves the site, domain, or organizational unit (OU) that gave it the original policy—until another policy is provided. You also can assign policies directly to individual machines. In either case, you can unassign policies manually when you no longer want a policy in place on a specific machine.

Setting General Properties

When you create a new policy by using the IP Security Policy wizard, you still have to customize the policy to make it do anything useful.

To do so, you use the policy Properties dialog box, in which you can add, remove, and manage rules, filter lists, and security actions. The Properties dialog box has two tabs: the General tab, which covers general policy-related settings, such as the policy name; and the Rules tab, which gives you a way to edit the rules associated with the policy.

The General tab allows you to change the policy name and description, which appear in the IPSec snap-in. It's a good idea to use meaningful names for your policies so that you'll remember what each one is supposed to be doing. The Check for Policy Changes Every X Minutes field allows you to change the interval at which clients who use this policy check for updates. The default value—180 minutes—is OK for most applications, because you're unlikely to be changing the policies *that* frequently.

The Advanced button allows you to change the key exchange settings used by this particular policy, via the Key Exchange Settings dialog box. You can use the controls in this dialog box to control how often the policy requires generation of new keys, either after a certain amount of time (eight hours, by default) or a certain number of sessions. The Methods button displays a list of security methods that will be used to protect the key exchange. The method list included when you create a new policy always tries the highest-level security first; then it drops down to less secure methods if the remote end can't handle them.

Managing Rules with the Rules Tab

The Rules tab of the policy Properties dialog box is probably more interesting than the General tab, because it allows you to change the rules included with the IPSec policy.

Here are the most important things to recognize in this tab:

- The tab lists three rules, each of which ties a filter list to a filter action and authentication method. You learn more about these filter lists in the next objective on IPSec. A single policy can contain an arbitrary number of rules; it's common to have several rules that are applied in different situations. It's also common to have many policies defined in a single Active Directory domain or local policy store.

- Each rule has a check box next to it that controls whether the rule is actually applied. You can use these check boxes to turn individual rules on or off within a policy.

- The Add, Edit, and Remove buttons allow to you manipulate the list of rules. Notice that rules aren't evaluated in any particular order, so there's no way to reorder them.

- The Use Add Wizard check box controls whether the Security Rule wizard is used to add a new rule (by default, this box is checked). When the check box is unchecked, you get dumped into the rule's Properties dialog box to set things up by hand.

The Edit Rule Properties dialog box has five tabs, each of which is associated with a rule. You see this dialog box when you select a rule and click the Edit button, or when you create a new rule with the Use Add Wizard check box cleared. All that the wizard does is ask you questions and fill out the tabs for you, so knowing what settings belong with each rule enables you to create them by hand or with the wizard's help. Therefore, instead of going through each step of the wizard, you should know what's in each tab.

The IP Filter List Tab

The IP Filter List tab shows which filter lists are associated with this rule. You manage which filter lists exist by using a separate set of tools. For now, it's enough to know that all the filter lists defined on your server appear in the filter list; you can choose any *one* of them to be applied as a result of this rule. If you like, you can add or remove filter lists in this tab or in the Manage IP Filter Lists and Filter Actions dialog box.

The Filter Action Tab

The Filter Action tab shows all the filter actions defined in the policy; you can apply any filter action to the rule. Remember that you combine one filter list with one filter action to make a single rule, but you can group any number of rules into one policy. The Add, Edit, and

Remove buttons do what you'd expect; the Use Add Wizard check box controls whether adding a new filter action fires up the corresponding wizard or dumps you into the Properties dialog box.

The Authentication Methods Tab

The Authentication Methods tab allows you to define one or more authentication methods that you want a particular rule to use. You can have multiple methods listed; if so, IPSec attempts to use them in the order of their appearance in the list (thus, the Move Up and Move Down buttons). You have the same three choices mentioned earlier in this chapter: Kerberos, certificates, or pre-shared keys.

The Tunnel Setting Tab

The Tunnel Setting tab allows you to specify that this rule forms an IPSec tunnel with another system (or *tunnel endpoint*).

The Connection Type Tab

The Connection Type tab allows you to specify the kinds of connections to which this IPSec rule applies. You may want to specify different rules for dial-up and LAN connections, for example, depending on who your users are, where they're connecting from, and what they do while connected. Your basic choice is simple. Three radio buttons allow you to choose the type of connections to which this rule applies. The All Network Connections button is selected by default, so when you create a new rule, it applies to both LAN and remote access connections. If you want the rule to cover only LAN or RAS connections, just choose the corresponding radio button.

Managing Filter Lists and Actions

Although you can manage IP filter lists and filter actions from the Edit Rule Properties dialog box, it makes more sense to use the management tools provided in the snap-in. Why? Because the filter lists and actions live with the policy, not inside individual rules, the filter lists and actions that you create in one policy scope (say, the default domain policy) are available to all policies within that scope.

You can manage filter lists and filter actions by using the corresponding tabs in the Edit Rule Properties dialog box, but doing so obscures the fact that these items are available to any policy. You can instead choose the Manage IP Filter Lists And Filter Actions command from the context menu (right-click the IP Security Policies item or anywhere in the right pane of the IPSec snap-in). This command displays the Manage IP Filter Lists and Filter Actions dialog box, which has a grand total of two tabs. Most of the items in these tabs are self-explanatory, because they closely resemble the controls that you've already seen. In particular, the functions of the Add, Edit, and Remove buttons (as well as the Use Add Wizard check box) should be evident by this point.

Adding IP Filter Lists and Individual Filters

You get two IP filters for free with Windows 2000: one for all IP traffic and one for all ICMP traffic. Suppose that you're a little more selective, though. Perhaps you want to create an IPSec policy to secure Web traffic between your company and its law firm. You'd first have to open the Manage IP Filter Lists and Filter Actions dialog box, at which point you'd see the Manage IP Filter Lists tab.

Because filter lists aren't used in order, there's no way to reorder items in the list, although you can add, edit, and remove them by using the familiar controls below the list. When you edit or add a filter list, you see the IP Filter List dialog box. This dialog box allows you to name and describe the filter list and then add, remove, or edit the individual filters that make up the list.

When you edit or add an individual filter, you need to know the following pieces of information:

- The source and destination addresses that you want the filter to use. These can be single IP addresses or single DNS names that you can use to indicate the source and destination.

- Whether you want the filter to be mirrored. A *mirrored* filter automatically filters its opposite. If you set up a filter from your IP address to a remote address and configure it to allow only port 80, with mirroring, you also get a filter that allows traffic *from* the remote end back to you on port 80.

- The protocols and ports to which you want the filter to apply. You can choose any protocol type (including TCP, UDP, ICMP, and raw), and you can either select individual source and destination ports or use the Any Port buttons (discussed later in this chapter).

You get these factoids into a filter via the Filter Properties dialog box, naturally. When you click the Add or Edit button in the IP Filter List dialog box, you see the Properties dialog box for the appropriate filter (the new one or whichever one you selected before clicking the Edit button). This dialog box has three tabs: General, Addressing, and Protocol. You can ignore the General tab, because it's used only for naming and describing the filter. That leaves the Addressing and Protocol tabs, which do the following things:

Addressing   The Addressing tab is where you specify the source and destination addresses that you want this filter to match. For the source address, you can choose to use the IP address assigned to the IPSec server, any IP address, a specific DNS domain name or IP address, or a specific IP subnet. Likewise for the destination address, you can choose the IPSec computer's address; any IP address; or a specified DNS name, subnet, or IP address. You use these addresses in combination to specify how you want the filter to trigger. You also can use the Mirrored check box to specify a reciprocal rule. Mirroring makes it easy to set up filters that cover both inbound and outbound traffic.

Protocol   The Protocol tab allows you to match traffic coming from or sent to a particular port, using a specified protocol. This capability is useful, because UDP source port 80 and TCP destination port 80 are entirely different. You use the Select a Protocol Type pull-down menu and the Set the IP Protocol Port control group to specify the protocols and ports you want this filter to match.

Adding a New Filter Action

The Manage Filter Actions tab shows you which filter actions are defined in the current group of IPSec policies; you can add, edit, or remove filter actions to meet your needs. As part of Windows 2000, you get three filter actions—Permit, Request Security (Optional), and

Require Security—that probably will meet most of your needs, but it's still a good idea to know how to create policies yourself instead of depending on Microsoft to do it for you.

The Add button is the most interesting control in the batch, because it allows you to add new filter actions that can be used in any policy you define. The Use Add Wizard check box normally is checked, so by default, you'll get the rule wizard. Instead, this section goes through the property pages associated with a filter action so that you can see what's in one. When you click the Add button with the Use Add Wizard check box off, the first thing you see is the Security Methods tab of the New Filter Action Properties dialog box.

You use this tab to specify which methods you want this filter action to use. In addition to the Permit and Block methods, you can use the Negotiate Security button to build your own custom security methods, choosing whatever AH and ESP algorithms meet your needs. The two check boxes at the bottom of the Security Methods list control what this IPSec computer does when confronted with a connection request from a machine that doesn't speak IPSec. The options include the following:

- The Accept Unsecured Communication, but Always Respond Using IPSec check box configures this action so that incoming connection requests are always answered with an IPSec negotiation message. If the other end doesn't *parlez* IPSec, the computer is allowed to accept the incoming request without any security in place.

- The Allow Unsecured Communication with Non IPSec-aware Computer check box configures the action to allow any computer—IPSec-capable or not—to communicate. Any machine that can't handle IPSec gets a normal, insecure connection. By default, this check box isn't checked; if you check it, you must be certain that your IPSec policies are set up properly; if they're not, some computers that you *think* are using IPSec may connect without security.

Necessary Procedures

You can perform these procedures to familiarize yourself with basic network protocol security.

Managing Network Protocol Security and Enabling IPSec on the Local Computer

Follow these steps to install the IPSec snap-in for managing the local computer's IPSec policy:

1. Use the taskbar's Run command (Start ➤ Run) to launch MMC.exe. An empty MMC console window appears.

2. Select the Console ➤ Add/Remove Snap-In command. When the Add/Remove Snap-In dialog box appears, click the Add button.

3. In the Add Standalone Snap-In dialog box, scroll through the snap-in list until you see the one marked IP Security Policy Management. Select it and then click the Add button. The Select Computer dialog box appears.

4. Select the Local Computer (default setting) radio button; then click the Finish button.

5. Click the Close button in the Add Standalone Snap-In dialog box.

6. Click the OK button in the Add/Remove Snap-In dialog box.

7. Select the IP Security Policies on Local Machine node in the MMC. Notice that the right pane of the MMC lists the three predefined policies discussed earlier in this chapter.

8. Right-click the Server (Request Security) policy; then choose the Assign command.

9. Verify that the entry in the Policy Assigned column for the selected policy has changed to Yes.

This process in and of itself doesn't do much to improve your security posture, because all it does is enable your local computer to accept IPSec connections from other computers. The real payoff comes when you start applying IPSec policies in Active Directory, which you're about to do.

Customizing and Configuring the Local Computer IPSec Policy and Rules for Transport Mode

In the preceding exercise, you assigned the Server (Request Security) policy so that it would always be used. Now it's time to tweak that policy. By default, all IPSec policies you create are transport-mode (as opposed to tunnel-mode) policies. This also is true of the default local computer and domain IPSec policies. In this exercise, you modify the local computer's Server (Request Security) policy settings to improve its interoperability. Follow these steps:

1. Use the Taskbar's Run command (Start ➢ Run) to launch MMC.exe. An empty MMC console window appears.

2. Select the Console ➢ Add/Remove Snap-In command. When the Add/Remove Snap-In dialog box appears, click the Add button.

3. In the Add Standalone Snap-In dialog box, scroll through the snap-in list until you see the one marked IP Security Policy Management. Select it; then click the Add button. The Select Computer dialog box appears.

4. Choose the Local Computer radio button; then click the Finish button.

5. Click the Close button in the Add Standalone Snap-In dialog box; then click the OK button in the Add/Remove Snap-In dialog box.

6. Select the IP Security Policies on Local Machine node in the MMC. In the right pane of the MMC, right-click the Server (Request Security) policy; then choose the Properties command. The Server (Request Security) Properties dialog box appears.

7. Select the All IP Traffic rule; then click the Edit button. The Edit Rule Properties dialog box appears. Read the Description. Click OK.

8. Switch to the Filter Action tab. Select the Request Security (Optional) filter action; then click the Edit button. The filter action's Properties dialog box appears.

9. Click the Add button. When the New Security Method dialog box appears, click the Custom radio button; then click the Settings button.

10. In the Custom Security Method Settings dialog box, check the data and address integrity without encryption (AH); from the drop-down menu, choose SHA1. Using the drop-down menus below (ESP), set Integrity to SHA1 and Encryption to 3DES.

11. First check the Generate a New Key Every check box, and set the key-generation interval to 24,000 Kbytes. (Kbytes must be in the range 20,480 to 2,147,483,647.) Then click the Generate a New Key Every check box and specify a key-generation interval of 1,800 seconds.

12. Click the OK button in the Custom Security Method Settings dialog box; then click OK in the New Security Method dialog box.

13. When the Filter Properties dialog box resurfaces, use the Move Up button to move the custom filter that you just defined to the top of the list.

14. Click the OK button in the Filter Properties dialog box.

15. Click the Close button in the Edit Rule Properties dialog box; then click the Close button in the Server (Request Security) Properties dialog box.

Exam Essentials

Know that security filters tie security protocols to a network address.   Understand that the filter contains source and destination addresses, the protocol used, and the source and destination ports allowed for TCP and UDP traffic.

Know how you group filters in filter lists for ease of management. Understand that because you can put any number of individual filters in a filter list, you can easily build rules that enforce complicated behavior and then distribute those rules throughout your network as necessary.

Know that each IPSec connection negotiates a security method. Understand that the ISAKMP service attempts to use the most secure method it can.

Know different security filter actions, including Permit, Block, Accept Unsecured, Allow Unsecured and Use These Security Settings. Understand that the Permit Action is sometimes called a *passthrough action*, because packets "pass through."

Know Microsoft's three included prebuilt security policies. Understand Client (Respond Only), Secure Server (Require Security), and Server (Request Security).

Know that you edit the rules associated with a security policy in the Rules tab of the Policy Properties dialog box. Understand that a check box implements a rule. Know the functions of all the tabs in the Edit Rule Properties dialog box.

Know the five pieces of information you need to know when you edit or add an individual filter. Understand that you use the Filter Properties dialog box to configure these parameters.

Key Terms and Concepts

filter list   Groups of individual filters that allow you to easily build rules that enforce complicated behavior and then distribute those rules throughout your network as necessary.

mirrored filter   A filter that filters its opposite automatically.

passthrough action   A security filter action that tells the IPSec filter to take no action. It neither accepts nor rejects the connection based on security rules, meaning that it adds zero security. It allows traffic to pass without modification.

security filter   A filter that ties security protocols to a particular network address. For each connection, you must have two filters: one for inbound traffic and one for outbound.

security method   A prespecified encryption algorithm that each connection uses with a negotiated key length and key lifetime.

Sample Questions

1. You can assign _____ filter action(s) and _____ IP filter list(s) to a single policy rule.

A. One; one

B. Any number; any number

C. One; any number

D. Any number; one

Answer: A. You can define multiple rules in a policy but only one filter list and one filter action per rule.

2. A filter action specifies which of the following?

A. Which security methods to use for traffic that matches the associated filter

B. Whether to accept or reject traffic that matches the associated filter

C. A and B

D. None of the above

Answer: C. Filter actions specify whether to accept or reject traffic that matches the filter in question; if the traffic is accepted, the specified action also controls what security methods are used.

▶ Manage and monitor network traffic.

Sometimes, the best way to see what's happening on your network is to watch the traffic as it passes. Because you'd have a really hard time doing that by looking at the lights on your Ethernet hub, Microsoft includes a tool called Network Monitor on the Windows 2000 Server and Advanced Server CDs. This tool is a direct descendant of the Windows NT Network Monitor, which in turn is based on the same-named tool provided with the Systems

Management Server (SMS) product. Network Monitor is an example of a type of program called a network analyzer (or *sniffer*, after the Network General Sniffer toolset). Network analyzers capture raw traffic from the network and then decode it just as the protocol stack would. Because analyzers don't depend on a protocol stack, you can use an analyzer to monitor traffic for protocol types that you don't actually have installed. You could use Network Monitor to capture and decode AppleTalk packets while troubleshooting a Mac connectivity problem, even without having Apple-Talk on your workstation.

Critical Information

Network Monitor comes in two pieces: the application, which you install on Windows 2000 Server or Advanced Server; and the driver, which you install on any Windows 2000 machine. To monitor traffic on a machine, it must have the driver installed (it's installed automatically when you install the application). The driver is required because it puts the network card into *promiscuous mode*, in which the card accepts packets that are not addressed to it—obviously, a requirement for monitoring overall network traffic.

Before you install and use Network Monitor, you need to know about a couple of caveats. First, the Windows 2000 Network Monitor works only with Windows 2000 clients; if you want to use it to monitor Windows NT, 95, or 98 clients, you need the Network Monitor drivers from the SMS product CD. More important, the Windows 2000 version of Network Monitor allows you to watch traffic to and from only the server on which it's installed; the SMS version of Network Monitor supports watching traffic anywhere on your network.

Knowing What Network Monitor Does Network Monitor basically allocates a big chunk of RAM to use as a *capture buffer*. When you tell it to start capturing network packets, it copies every packet it sees on a particular NIC to the buffer, gathering statistical data as it goes. When you stop the capture process, you can analyze the buffered data in a variety of ways, including the ability to apply *capture filters* that screen out packets you're not interested in.

Installing the Network Monitor Driver   If you want to use the Network Monitor to capture packets from a machine that doesn't already have Network Monitor on it, you need to install the Network Monitor driver on the target machine. The "Necessary Procedures" section for this objective explains this process.

Installing the Network Monitor Application   When you've installed the Network Monitor driver on at least one other machine, you can install the Network Monitor application itself and start monitoring. To install Network Monitor, use the Add/Remove Programs Control Panel. Switch to the Add/Remove Windows Components icon; then select the Management and Monitoring Tools item and click the Details button. When the Management and Monitoring Tools dialog box appears, make sure that Network Monitor Tools is checked; then click the OK button. When the installation finishes, you'll find Network Monitor at the bottom of the Administrative Tools group in the Start menu's Program Files group.

Taking a Whirlwind Tour of Network Monitor

There's no way to sugarcoat the fact that Network Monitor is a complicated tool; it's made for complicated tasks, and its interface reflects that purpose. This section doesn't teach you how to troubleshoot subtle network problems with Network Monitor, but it does explain how to use Network Monitor to perform some simple tasks that will give you a good head start on learning to use it well enough to pass the exam (and to solve the occasional problem, too).

TIP   Forget about right-clicking, because Network Monitor doesn't support that function. (It's beginning to show its age!)

When you start Network Monitor, it asks you to choose a network to monitor. The list of networks you see depends on the number of NICs you have installed; if you have only one NIC, Network Monitor selects the correct network for you automatically. When you've done that, you see the Network Monitor window. Although the window may seem to be overwhelming, there's logic to what you see.

The following list explains what you see in the main Network Monitor window (you can turn specific panes on and off with the Window menu):

- The pane in the top-left corner displays bar graphs of current network use (which explains why it's called the Graph pane), including the number of frames, bytes, broadcasts, and multicasts per second. This pane updates only when a capture is in progress.

- The pane in the middle of the left side shows information about connections captured during the current session (the Session Stats pane). This information includes the source and destination network addresses and how many packets have gone in each direction between the two endpoints.

- The entire right side of the window contains the Total Stats pane, which lists a variety of interesting statistics, including the total number of unicast, broadcast, and multicast frames, plus the amount of data currently in the capture buffer. Like the Session Stats pane, this pane's contents are updated continuously during a capture.

- The bottom portion of the window contains the Station Stats frame, which tells you what's been happening on the machine on which you're running Network Monitor.

Capturing Data

When you capture data, you're just filling a big buffer with the packets as they arrive; Network Monitor doesn't attempt to analyze them at that point. To control capture activity, you can use the toolbar buttons (the ones that use the standard start, stop, and pause symbols) or the commands in the Capture menu: Start, Stop, Stop and View, Pause, and Continue. Starting and stopping capture is fairly straightforward, although you may need to adjust the buffer size upward from its default of 1MB by choosing the Capture ➤ Buffer Settings command. When you start the capture, Network Monitor continues working until you've filled the buffer or stopped the capture. At that point, you can view the data or save it to a disk file for later analysis with the File ➤ Save As command.

Viewing Data

After you stop a capture, you can view the accumulated data with the Capture ➢ View Captured Data command. This command opens a new kind of window: the Frame Viewer. This window lists every captured frame, summarizing its source and destination address, the time at which it was captured (relative to the start of the capture operation), the network type, and the protocol in use. Although the display of all this data is certainly interesting, it's hard to pick out much useful detail unless you have *impeccable* timing. It's more likely that you'll need to use Network Monitor's filtering functions to pick out just the data you want.

If you want to see the full contents of an individual frame, just double-click it. This action causes two new panes to appear in the Frame Viewer window: The Detail pane is in the middle, and the Hex pane is at the bottom. This display gives you an easy way to inspect, bit by bit, the contents of any captured frame in the buffer.

Using Filters

You can create two types of filters in Network Monitor. *Capture filters* screen out unwanted packets before they're recorded to the capture buffer, and *display filters* display some packets but not others.

Working with Capture Filters

You create and manage capture filters by choosing the Capture ➢ Filters command, which is available in the standard Network Monitor window. This command displays the Capture Filter dialog box. Don't let the appearance of this dialog box intimidate you; if you understand the following rule, you can build as complex a group of filters as you like.

The rule to remember is that filters are grouped in a tree. The default filter says that any SAP/ETYPE packet(Service Access Point or Ethernet Type; both of these tags mark packets with the protocol they're using) will be captured, because all three conditions below the root of the tree use the *and* modifier. Although you can use *and*, *or*, and *not* for your own filters, you can't remove the original tree branches.

Suppose that you want to create a filter that captures traffic going to port 80 on a particular machine. Capture filters don't care about ports, but you could create a filter based on the address by selecting the SAP/ETYPE branch and using the Edit button to capture only IP packets. Next, edit the Address Pairs item so that you've specified the proper destination address. If you were looking for packets with a particular payload, you could specify a pattern to capture that traffic with the Pattern Matches branch, too. Unfortunately, that's about all you can do with capture filters in the Windows 2000 version of Network Monitor; several additional features work only in the SMS version.

Working with Display Filters

When you've captured some data, you can create display filters that give you much finer control of what you see. This capability is handy, because it's difficult to pick out the few frames you're looking for from a full capture buffer. You create display filters while you're looking at the Frame Viewer window; choose the Display ➤ Filter command to bring up the Display Filter dialog box. The features of this dialog box work just as they do in the Capture Filter dialog box, but you can do some extra things.

Using the Tools Menu

The Tools menu contains four commands that have varying degrees of usefulness:

- Identify Network Monitor Users, which scans the network for other NICs in promiscuous mode. This process becomes a dead giveaway that someone is doing something they're not supposed to, because apart from running a network analyzer, there's no reason why an ordinary user should have their NIC in that mode. When Network Monitor finishes its scan, it displays a dialog box listing all instances of Network Monitor it finds on the network.

TIP Remember the Identify Network Monitor Users command, because it's one of the things that Microsoft *really* wants you to know how to do.

- Find Routers, which doesn't do anything unless you have the version of Network Monitor that comes with SMS; in that case, it does a tracert-like repetitive *ping* to find routers on the network.

- Resolve Addresses from Name, which does the equivalent of a reverse lookup for non-DNS names—if you have the SMS version of Network Monitor; if you don't, it does nothing.

- Performance Monitor, which opens the System Performance snap-in.

Necessary Procedures

In this procedure, you install the Network Monitor driver. Be forewarned that many organizations watch their networks very closely for signs of network analyzer use, so completing this exercise may bring you a visit from the Men in Black. You may be prompted for the Windows 2000 CD, too, so have it handy.

Installing the Network Monitor Driver

Before you can practice with Network Monitor, you must install it. Follow these steps:

1. Open the Network and Dial-Up Connections folder (Start ➢ Settings ➢ Network and Dial-Up Connections).

2. Find the LAN interface that you want to enable Network Monitor to monitor, right-click it, and choose the Properties command. The Properties dialog box appears.

3. Click the Install button. The Select Network Component Type dialog box appears.

4. Click Protocol in the Component list; then click the Add button. The Select Network Protocol dialog box appears.

5. Select Network Monitor Driver; then click the OK button. When the driver is installed, the Properties dialog box reappears.

6. Click the Close button.

Capturing Data with Network Monitor

In this procedure, you use Network Monitor to gather a full capture buffer so that you can experiment with display filters in the following exercise. Follow these steps:

1. Install Network Monitor as described in the preceding exercise.

2. Choose the Capture ➤ Buffer Settings command to increase the capture buffer size to 2MB. This setting gives you room for 4,096 frames of data.

3. Start a capture by choosing the Capture ➤ Start command. While the capture is going, use a Web browser to request a Web page from the machine on which you're running Network Monitor. (This step is necessary for the following exercise.)

4. Let the command run until the buffer is full; you can tell by watching the # Frames in Buffer line in the Total Stats pane.

5. Save the capture buffer to disk by choosing the File ➤ Save As command. You'll need this buffer for the following exercise.

Creating a Display Filter

Using the capture buffer from the preceding procedure, you can create a display filter to limit what appears in the Frame Viewer. Follow these steps:

1. If you quit Network Monitor since the preceding exercise, reopen the capture buffer that you saved by choosing the File ➤ Open command.

2. When the Frame Viewer window appears, choose the Display ➤ Filters command to open the Display Filter dialog box.

3. Select the Protocol = Any line; then click the Edit Expression button. You see the Protocol tab of the Expression dialog box.

4. Click the Disable All button to remove all the protocols. Any protocol that's disabled is screened out by the filter.

5. Select HTTP in the Disabled Protocols list; then click the Enable button. HTTP should be the only enabled protocol. Click the OK button.

6. Optionally, select the ANY <--> ANY filter and use the Edit Expression button to add an address rule to the filter. Normally, you don't need to perform this step, because the Windows 2000 version of Network Monitor monitors only traffic between your computer and one other at a time.

7. When you're done, click the OK button in the Display Filter dialog box. The Frame Viewer window reappears. Notice that the frame numbers (in the leftmost column) are no longer consecutive; the filter is screening out any traffic that doesn't match its criteria.

8. Double-click a frame to see its contents. Because you're looking at unencrypted HTTP packets, you can clearly see the requests and responses.

Exam Essentials

Know what promiscuous mode is and how it facilitates the Network Monitor functionality.   Understand that the Windows 2000 version of Network Monitor works only with Windows 2000 clients and allows you to see only traffic to and from the server on which it is installed.

Know how Network Monitor captures packets in a capture buffer and then analyzes those packets with capture filters.   Understand the two types of filters in Network Monitor: capture filters and display filters.

Know that the Network Monitor Tools menu has four commands you can use.   Understand the Identify Network Monitor Users command, which might show up on an exam.

Key Terms and Concepts

capture buffer   A big chunk of RAM that is used when you tell Network Monitor to start capturing network packets. This buffer copies every packet it sees on a particular NIC to the buffer, gathering statistical data as it goes.

capture filter A Network Monitor process that screens out packets you're not interested in.

promiscuous mode A situation in which a network card accepts packets that are not addressed to it—a requirement for monitoring overall network traffic.

Sample Questions

1. Julia wants to know whether anyone else on her network is using Network Monitor, because she's the only person with permission to do so. To accomplish this task, what should she do?

   A. Perform a port scan on her network for port 2112

   B. Choose the Tools ➢ Identify Network Monitor Users command in Network Monitor

   C. Use the Computer Management snap-in to look for instances of the Network Monitor service

   D. Use the Network Monitoring snap-in to look for instances of the Network Monitor application

   Answer: B. Port 2112 has nothing to do with Network Monitor, and the Network Monitor service is present on machines that are being monitored, not just those running the service. There is no Network Monitoring snap-in. The correct answer is to use the built-in function for spotting Network Monitor on the network: the Tools ➢ Identify Network Monitor Users command.

2. If you want to use Network Monitor to grab some packets on your network, where do you first hold the packets?

   A. Capture filter

   B. Capture buffer

   C. Monitor picker

   D. Monitor queue

   Answer: B. The capture buffer is where packets are held in RAM.

Configure and troubleshoot IPSec.

- **Enable IPSec.**
- **Configure IPSec for transport mode.**
- **Configure IPSec for tunnel mode.**
- **Customize IPSec policies and rules.**
- **Manage and monitor IPSec.**

In the first objective section of this chapter, you learned the fundamentals of how IPSec uses the Authentication Header (AH) and Encapsulating Security Payload (ESP) protocols to protect your network communications from tampering or spying. In the third objective section, you looked at general network protocol security. Now it's time to delve a little deeper into the mysterious world of IPSec so that you'll better understand how to manage it.

Critical Information

The whole idea behind IPSec is that it operates at the network layer; users and applications never need to be aware of whether their traffic is being carried over a secure connection. In IPSec parlance, there are clients and servers, but this terminology is a little misleading. Any Windows 2000 machine may be an IPSec client or server. An *IPSec client* is the computer that attempts to establish a connection to another machine, and an *IPSec server* is the target of that connection. By choosing appropriate client and server settings, you can fine-tune which computers use IPSec to talk to each other.

IPSec provides two primary services: a way for computers to decide whether they trust each other (*authentication*) and a way to keep network data private (*encryption*). The IPSec process calls for two computers to authenticate each other before beginning an encrypted connection. At that point, the two machines can use the Internet Key Exchange (IKE) protocol to agree on a secret key to use for encrypting the traffic between them. This process takes place in the context of IPSec security associations (SAs).

> **NOTE** If you're really interested in the guts of IKE, check out RFC 2409.

As if that weren't enough, the Windows 2000 implementation of IPSec explicitly supports the idea of policy-based security. Instead of running around changing security settings on every machine in a domain, you can set policies that configure individual machines, groups of machines within an organizational unit or domain, or every Windows 2000 machine in your network.

When you use IPSec to encrypt or authenticate connections between two machines, that's called *end-to-end mode*, because network traffic is protected before it leaves the originating machine and remains secured until the receiving machine gets it and decrypts it. (This mode also is called *transport mode*.) A second application is using IPSec to secure traffic that's being passed over someone else's wires. This use of IPSec usually is called *tunnel mode*, because it's used to encrypt traffic to pass over (or through) a tunnel—either one established by L2TP or an imaginary one established over someone else's network circuits.

> **NOTE** In this chapter and on the exam, when you see the phrase *IPSec tunnel mode*, assume that it means the use of IPSec for tunneling, not for VPN traffic. When you see *L2TP* mentioned, you can safely assume that it really means L2TP + IPSec.

Understanding IPSec Authentication

IPSec supports three separate authentication methods; which ones you'll use depend on what kind of network you have and what computers you're talking to. Because the first thing an IPSec client and server want to do is authenticate each other, they need some way to agree on a set of credentials to use. The Windows 2000 version of IPSec supports three authentication methods; these methods are used only during the initial authentication phase of building the SAs, not for generating encryption keys. The methods supported are:

- *Kerberos*, which is the authentication system used by Windows 2000 clients and servers in lieu of the older, and less secure, NT LAN Manager authentication scheme. Kerberos is a widely supported open standard that offers good security and a great deal of flexibility. Because it's natively supported in Windows 2000, it's the default authentication method; many third-party IPSec products include Kerberos support.

- *Certificates*, which use public-key certificates (see Chapter 8) for authentication. When you use certificate-based authentication, each end of the connection can use the other's public certificate to verify a digitally signed message. This system provides great security, with some added overhead and infrastructure requirements. As you add machines to a domain in Windows 2000, they're automatically issued *machine certificates* that can be used for authentication. If you want to allow users and computers from other domains or organizations to connect to your IPSec machines, you need to explore certificate solutions that allow cross-organization certification.

- *Pre-shared keys*, which basically are just reusable passwords. The pre-shared key itself is just a word, code, or phrase that both computers know. The two machines use this password to establish a trust, but they don't send the plain-text phrase over the network. The unencrypted key is stored in Active Directory, however, so Microsoft recommends against using it in production. (because anyone who can get the key can impersonate you or the remote computer). Most of the time, you use this mode only when you need to talk to a third-party IPSec product that doesn't yet support certificate or Kerberos authentication.

Installing IPSec

The components necessary for a Windows 2000 machine to act as an IPSec client are installed by default when you install Windows 2000 Professional, Server, or Advanced Server. But—also by default—no policy requires the use of IPSec, so the default behavior for Windows 2000 machines is not to use it. The good news is that you don't really have to install IPSec; you just have to install the tool that you use to manage it and then start assigning policies and filters to get the desired effect.

IPSec is managed through the IP Security Policy Management snap-in. Interestingly, no prebuilt MMC console includes this snap-in, so you have to create one by opening a console and adding the snap-in to it. One thing about this snap-in is slightly different from the normal routine: when you install it, you must choose whether you want to use it to manage a local IPSec policy, the default policy for the domain your computer is in, the default policy for another domain, or the local policy on another computer. This arrangement gives you an effective way to delegate control of IPSec policies, should you choose to do so.

Configuring IPSec by Managing Policies

You can configure IPSec by modifying the default policies, creating your own policies that embody the rules and filters you want to use, and by controlling how policies are applied to computers in your management scope. Because group policy management is outside the range of this book, the following sections instead focus on how you customize and control the IPSec settings themselves.

You manage policies at a variety of levels, depending on where you want them to be applied. You always use the IPSec snap-in to manage them, however, and the tools that you use to create new policies or edit existing ones are the same whether you're using local or Active Directory policy storage.

Creating a New Policy

You create new policies by right-clicking the IP Security Policies folder in the snap-in and then choosing the New IP Security Policy command. That command activates the IP Security Policy wizard, which allows you to create a new policy. In fact, that's *all* the wizard does; you still have to edit the policy settings manually after it's created. The first two pages of the wizard are fairly innocuous; the first page tells you what the wizard does, and the second page allows you to enter a name and description for the policy. After that, things get slightly more interesting.

SETTING THE DEFAULT RESPONSE RULE

The next wizard page asks you whether you want to use the *default response rule*. Because this book hasn't talked about this rule before, this section is a good place to explain it. The default rule is what governs security when no other filter rule applies. When your server gets an incoming IPSec request, you'd probably expect IPSec to reject the connection—and it does, unless you leave the default response rule turned on. That rule basically says, "Accept anyone who requests a secure connection." Paradoxically, for maximum security, you may want to turn it off so that you accept IPSec connections only from known hosts. You can customize the settings associated with the default rule, however; that's the wizard's primary purpose.

NOTE   If you choose not to use the default response rule, the wizard skips the steps described in the following section and takes you directly to the completion page.

CHOOSING AN AUTHENTICATION METHOD FOR THE DEFAULT RESPONSE RULE

If you choose to use the default response rule, you still have to configure an authentication method for it. To do so, you use the Default Response Rule Authentication Method page. You can choose one of the three authentication methods mentioned earlier in this chapter. By default, Kerberos is selected, but you can choose a certificate authority or a pre-shared key instead. (If you choose to use a preshared key, make sure that you enter the same key on both ends of the connection.)

FINISHING THE POLICY WIZARD

When you complete the IP Security Policy wizard, the completion page contains a check box labeled Edit Properties. This check box is the most interesting part of the wizard, because it gives you access to the actual settings embedded within the policy.

Storing Policies in Active Directory

So far, you've read only about managing policies that apply to the local computer. You also can use the IPSec snap-in to create and manage policies that are stored in Active Directory, from which they can be applied to any computer or group of computers in the domain. You accomplish this application by completing these three separate, but related, steps:

1. You target the IPSec snap-in at Active Directory and then open it while logged in with a privileged account.

2. You edit or create the policy that you want to apply, using the tools in the snap-in.

3. You use the Group Policy snap-in to attach the policy to a site, domain, or organizational unit.

The first two steps are discussed throughout this chapter, but you should first take a minute to read about the third step. Because you can assign group policies to any site, domain, or organizational unit, you have the ability to fine-tune IPSec policy throughout your entire organization by using an appropriately targeted policy.

You don't actually use the IPSec snap-in to assign policies; you use it to configure them and to create policies that live in Active Directory. When you want to apply a policy to some group in the directory, you use the group policy snap-in itself.

Assigning and Unassigning Policies

Whether you're defining policies that affect one computer or a multinational enterprise network, you assign and unassign IPSec policies in the same way—by right-clicking the policy in question and then choosing the Assign and Un-assign commands. Assigning a policy makes it take effect the next time IPSec policies are refreshed. You may remember that the IPSec Policy Agent downloads the policy information for a computer when the computer is restarted. If you're using Group Policy to distribute your IPSec settings, you can force a policy update by using the Group Policy snap-in.

Using Other Helpful Policy Tricks

If you know how to create new policies, assign them, and set their properties, you already know almost everything that you need to know to manage IPSec. A few additional tricks may be useful in your IPSec implementation, however.

Forcing a Policy Update

If you want to force one machine to update its IPSec policy, just stop and restart the IPSec Policy Agent service on that machine. When the service starts, it attempts to retrieve the newest available policy from Active Directory or the local policy store. When the policy has been loaded, it's applied immediately. Restarting the policy agent forces it to refetch and reapply the correct policy; this feature can be useful when you're trying to troubleshoot a policy problem or when you want to be sure that the desired policy has been applied. By default, the IPSec Policy Agent refetches policies every 180 minutes anyway, although you can change that setting.

Wrangling with the Context Menu

You can do some other nifty things with your IPSec policies by right-clicking them; the context menu that appears allows you to rename them, delete them, or import and export them. The latter commands may seem to be unnecessary, but they occasionally come in handy if you're not using Active Directory. Suppose that you have a small network of computers using Windows 2000 Professional. You can create local IPSec policies on one machine and then export and import them on the remaining machines. This procedure ensures that you have a consistent set of IPSec policies without having an Active Directory domain controller present.

Configuring IPSec for Tunnel Mode

You can use IPSec tunnels to do several useful and interesting things. You can, for example, establish a tunnel between two subnets, effectively linking them into an internetwork, without having to have a private connection between them. IPSec tunneling isn't intended as a way for clients to establish remote access VPN connections; instead, it's what you use to connect your Windows 2000 network to a remote device (such as a Cisco PIX) that doesn't support L2TP+IPSec or PPTP. You also can build a tunnel that connects two IP addresses directly.

Either way, you establish the tunnel by building a filter that matches the source and destination IP addresses, just as you would for an ordinary transport mode. You can use ESP and AH on the tunnel to give you an authenticated tunnel (AH only), an encrypted tunnel (ESP only), or a combination of the two. You control this behavior by specifying a filter action and security method. When you build a tunnel, however, you can't filter by port or protocol; the Windows 2000 IPSec stack doesn't support it.

To construct a tunnel properly, you need two rules at each end: one for inbound traffic and one for outbound traffic. Microsoft warns against using mirroring on tunnel rules; instead, if you want to link two networks, you need to specify settings. Each side's rule has two filter lists. The filter lists on one side specify a filter for outgoing traffic that has the other side's router as a tunnel endpoint and then another filter for incoming traffic from any IP subnet that points back to the tunnel endpoint. In conjunction with these filter lists, of course, you specify a filter action that provides whatever type of security is appropriate for the connection.

You specify whether a connection is tunneled on a per-rule basis by using the Tunnel Settings tab of the Edit Rule Properties dialog box. The two radio buttons specify whether this rule establishes a tunnel or not. The default button, This Rule Does Not Specify an IPSec Tunnel, is self-explanatory. To enable tunneling with this rule, select the other button, The Tunnel Endpoint Is Specified by This IP Address; then fill in the IP address of the remote endpoint.

Managing IPSec

Now that you know how to configure IPSec, it's time to learn how to manage it. The management aspects of IPSec are relatively simple, because about 90 percent of your workload is building filter lists, rules, and filter actions that correctly specify the traffic and hosts you want to protect. The other 10 percent falls under the general rubric "Watch it and fix it if it breaks."

Monitoring IPSec

You can monitor IPSec traffic on your computers in several ways, but the two most useful methods are viewing the security associations and traffic flowing between specific computers and checking the event log for IPSec-related events.

Using the IP Security Monitor Tool

Microsoft was thoughtful enough to include a monitoring tool specific to IPSec. This feature may not seem to be a big deal until you consider that encrypted IPSec traffic is awfully hard to read with a conventional network-monitoring tool. The `ipsecmon.exe` tool provides an easy-to-understand summary of the current state of your computer's IPSec connections.

The list at the top of the `ipsecmon` window lists each policy that is currently in use, along with any filters applied, the source and destination addresses, and the protocols and ports in the filter. When you use a policy that makes IPSec optional, it's normal to see a mix of secure and insecure connections, because not every machine that you talk to uses IPSec. The IPSec Statistics and ISAKMP/Oakley Statistics areas also give you some interesting data, including the number of bytes sent and received via the AH and ESP protocols (these totals match if your policies specify that both should be used together).

The only option you have in `ipsecmon` is to change its refresh interval; clicking the Options button allows you to adjust it from its 15-second default to whatever value is appropriate. Oddly, there's no manual refresh command, so you're at the mercy of the update interval.

Using Event Logging

If you turn on auditing for logon events and object access, you get a wealth of logged information that can be very useful when you're trying to troubleshoot a problem. In particular, IPSec logs events when it establishes a security association. Those event messages tell you what policy, filter, and filter actions were used, as well as which security methods were active on the connection. Table 4.1 lists the most common event log messages and describes their meanings.

TABLE 4.1: Interesting IPSec Event Log Messages

Event ID	Appears in	What it means
279	System log	Generated by the IPSec Policy Agent; shows which policy was installed and where it came from.
284	System log	Generated by the IPSec Policy Agent; appears when the agent can't fetch a policy.
541	Security log	An IPSec SA was established.
542	Security log	An IPSec SA was closed. This happens when you terminate a connection to a remote machine. (This error also may appear as event 543, depending on the type of SA.)
547	Security log	IPSec SA negotiation failed, so no SA could be established.

Troubleshooting

Troubleshooting IPSec can be tricky. Microsoft's online help system does a good job of explaining the various ins and outs, but the basic principles aren't hard to understand. First, of course, you need to verify that you have basic, unsecured TCP/IP connectivity to the remote system. Because IPSec operates atop IP and UDP, if you can't get regular IP datagrams to the destination, you won't be able to get

IPSec packets there, either. Consequently, you need to perform all the standard connectivity and name-resolution tests (including making sure that the network cable's plugged in) before you dive into IPSec troubleshooting.

Testing Policy Integrity

You can check policy integrity at any time by right-clicking a policy folder (such as the IP Security Policies on Local Machine item) and then choosing the All Tasks ➤ Check Policy Integrity command. The integrity checker makes sure that there are no errors or missing pieces in the policies, their filter lists, or their filter actions and reports any errors that it finds. Normally, though, you see only a dialog box that displays "Integrity Verified" when the test is complete.

Verifying That the Right Policy Is Assigned

If you don't have an IPSec policy assigned, or if you have the wrong one in place, your communication efforts may fail. You have several ways to check the policy to see whether it's the right one. These checks include the following:

- Use ipsecmon, because it tells you which policy is being used for the association with each machine.

- Check the event log for event ID 279; that's the IPSec Policy Agent's way of telling you what policy it has applied.

- Look at the Options tab of the Advanced TCP/IP Settings dialog box, which you access from the TCP/IP Properties dialog box. The Options tab has a list of features that includes IPSec; select it and then click the Properties button to see the next dialog box.

- Look in the appropriate group policy object (including the local computer policy) to see whether an IPSec policy is assigned. The IPSec snap-in warns you that a group policy-based IPSec policy is assigned when you try to edit local policies on a computer.

You also can test to see which policy is in effect by using the ping command to send packets to the target computer. By watching the ipsecmon window, you can see whether a hard or soft SA is established when you connect, as well as what policy is in use for that SA.

Checking for Policy Mismatches

If you have policies applied at each end but still can't establish a connection, the policies may not match. To verify whether this is the case, review the event log and look for event ID 547. If you find this event, read the descriptive text carefully, because it can give you great clues. Make sure that the authentication and security methods used in the two policies have at least one setting in common.

Necessary Procedures

Following are some more necessary procedures to give you essential practice with IPSec.

Enabling IPSec for an Entire Domain

Follow these steps to configure a default IPSec policy for all domain computers (you must have administrative access to the domain):

1. Choose the taskbar's Run command (Start ➤ Run) to launch MMC.exe. An empty MMC console window appears.

2. Choose the Console ➤ Add/Remove Snap-In command. When the Add/Remove Snap-In dialog box appears, click the Add button.

3. In the Add Standalone Snap-In dialog box, scroll through the snap-in list until you see the one marked Group Policy. Select it; then click the Add button. The Select Group Policy Object dialog box appears.

4. Click the Browse button to bring up the Browse for a Group Policy Object dialog box.

5. Select Default Domain Policy; then click the OK button.

6. Click the Finish button in the Select Group Policy Object dialog box.

7. Click the Close button in the Add Standalone Snap-In dialog box; then click the OK button in the Add/Remove Snap-In dialog box.

8. Expand the Default Domain Policy node until you find the IPSec settings (Default Domain Policy ➤ Computer Configuration ➤

Windows Settings ➤ Security Settings ➤ IP Security Policies on Active Directory).

9. Select the IP Security Policies on Active Directory item. The right side of the MMC window lists the available policies, including the three predefined policies and any new ones that you've added by using the IPSec snap-in.

10. Right-click the Server (Request Security) policy; then choose the Assign command. Notice that the Policy Assigned column for that policy now reads Yes.

Configuring a Policy for IPSec Tunnel Mode

This exercise requires you to use two separate machines—A and B—to which you have administrator access. Before you start, you need the IP addresses of both machines, and you need to have their local IPSec policies open in an MMC console.

To configure machine A, follow these steps:

1. Right-click the IP Security Policies on Local Machine node; then choose the Create IP Security Policy command. The IP Security Policy wizard appears. Click Next.

2. In the first wizard page, name your policy Tunnel to B; then click the Next button.

3. In the Requests for Secure Communication page, uncheck the Activate Default Response Rule check box; then click the Next button.

4. When the summary page for the wizard appears, make sure that the Edit Properties check box is checked; then click Finish. The Tunnel to B Properties dialog box appears.

5. Click the Add button in the Rules tab; then click Next.

6. In the Tunnel Endpoint dialog box, select The Tunnel Endpoint Is Specified by This IP Address, and enter the IP address of machine B. Click Next.

7. In the Network Type dialog box, select Local Area Network (LAN); then click Next.

8. In the Authentication Method dialog box, select Windows 2000 Default (Kerberos V5 Protocol); then click Next.

9. Select All IP Traffic; then click Next.

10. Select Request Security (Optional) in the Filter Action page; then click Next.

11. Click the Finish, OK, and Close buttons.

12. Repeat steps 1-11 on machine B, creating rules using the appropriate IP addresses and names (such as Tunnel to A) in steps 2-5.

Monitoring IPSec Logon Activity

In this exercise, you turn on auditing for logon events and object access. To see anything in the log, you need at least two IPSec-capable machines that can talk to each other. It doesn't matter which one you use for this exercise, provided that you have administrative access to it. Follow these steps:

1. Use the Taskbar's Run command (Start ➤ Run) to launch MMC.exe. An empty MMC console window appears.

2. Select the Console ➤ Add/Remove Snap-In command. When the Add/Remove Snap-In dialog box appears, click the Add button.

3. In the Add Standalone Snap-In dialog box, scroll through the snap-in list until you see the one marked Group Policy. Select it; then click the Add button. The Select Group Policy Object dialog box appears.

4. Leave Local Computer set as the focus; then click the Finish button.

5. Click the Close button in the Add Standalone Snap-In dialog box; then click the OK button in the Add/Remove Snap-In dialog box.

6. Find and select the Audit Policy folder (Local Computer Policy ➤ Computer Configuration ➤ Windows Settings ➤ Security Settings ➤ Local Policies ➤ Audit Policy).

7. Double-click the Audit Logon Events entry. When the Local Security Policy Setting dialog box appears, check the Success and Failure check boxes; then click the OK button.

8. Double-click the Audit Object Access entry. When the Local Security Policy Setting dialog box appears, check the Success and Failure check boxes; then click the OK button.

9. Establish an IPSec connection from the *other* machine to the one whose local security policy you just modified.

10. Examine the event log and ascertain whether the IPSec negotiation succeeded or failed.

Exam Essentials

Know that any Windows 2000 machine can be a client or server. Understand that the machine that initiates an attempted connection is always the client.

Know that IPSec implemented between two machines is known as *end-to-end mode,* because it protects the traffic between the two machines. Understand that this mode also is referred to as *transport mode*, in contrast with IPSec's tunnel mode.

Know the three authentication methods supported by IPSec. Understand that these methods include Kerberos, certificates (discussed in Chapter 8), and pre-shared keys (reusable passwords).

Know how to create a new IPSec policy with or without the default response rule. Understand how to store policies in Active Directory, and have a general understanding of how policies at different places in the hierarchy interact and override one another.

Know how to use the *ipsecmon.exe* tool to monitor and manage IPSec on your network. Understand the refresh rate that you can change and common event-log messages.

Know how to troubleshoot IPSec. Understand how to find problems by first troubleshooting connectivity issues and then performing tasks such as checking policy integrity and checking for policy mismatches.

Key Terms and Concepts

default response rule   An IP filtering rule that governs what the IP filtering stack does when no more explicit filter rule applies.

encryption   The process of translating data into code that is not easily accessible to increase security. When data has been encrypted, a user must have a password or key to decrypt the data.

end-to-end mode   A process in which you use IPSec to encrypt or authenticate connections between two machines so that network traffic is protected before it leaves the originating machine and remains secured until the receiving machine gets and decrypts it.

IPSec client   The computer that attempts to establish a connection to another machine. See also *IPSec server*.

IPSec Policy Agent   A service running on a Windows 2000 machine that connects to an Active Directory server, fetches the IPSec policy, and then passes it to the IPSec code.

IPSec server   The target of an IPSec client's attempts.

Kerberos   A standard mechanism for authenticating a user or system.

mirrored filter rule   A rule that creates two separate rules with opposite effects. An inbound filter rule that allows traffic from any address to TCP port 80 will, when mirrored, create a rule that allows traffic to any address on TCP port 80.

pre-shared key   A code or phrase that both computers know. The two machines use this password to establish a trust, but they don't send the plain-text phrase over the network.

security association (SA)   A relationship that provides all the information needed for two computers to communicate securely. The SA contains a policy agreement that controls which algorithms and key lengths the two machines use, as well as the actual security keys used to exchange information securely.

transport mode   Another name for *end-to-end mode*, in which IPSec is used to encrypt data before it is sent and decrypt the data at the other end, while the data is protected during transport.

tunnel endpoint   The systems at the end of a two-way IPSec tunnel.

tunnel mode   The method of using IPSec to secure traffic that's being passed over someone else's wire.

Sample Questions

1. What is the IPSec Policy Agent?

   A. An optional component that's required when using IPSec *with* Active Directory

   B. An optional component that's required when using IPSec *without* Active Directory

   C. An optional component that's required when using IPSec with L2TP

   D. A mandatory component for using IPSec.

   Answer: D. The IPSec Policy Agent is the component that downloads IPSec policy settings from the local computer or Active Directory. Accordingly, its presence is required for IPSec to function.

2. Jamie is trying to isolate an IPSec negotiation failure on an otherwise-working network. He checks the event log and finds event ID 547, recording the negotiation failure. From this log, Jamie can establish which probable cause?

   A. Negotiation has failed because there is a policy mismatch between the two computers.

   B. Negotiation has failed because one endpoint has the wrong key material.

   C. Negotiation has failed because one side has an incorrect tunnel endpoint.

   D. Negotiation has failed for an unknown reason.

   Answer: A. The presence of event ID 547 indicates that negotiation failed.

Chapter

5

Installing, Configuring, Managing, Monitoring, and Troubleshooting WINS in a Windows 2000 Network Infrastructure

MICROSOFT EXAM OBJECTIVES COVERED IN THIS CHAPTER:

▶ **Install, configure, and troubleshoot WINS.** *(pages 217 – 225)*

▶ **Configure WINS replication.** *(pages 225 – 235)*

▶ **Configure NetBIOS name resolution.** *(pages 236 – 245)*

▶ **Manage and monitor WINS.** *(pages 246 – 249)*

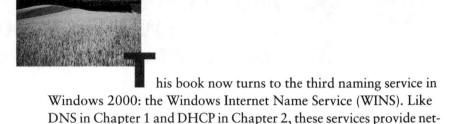

his book now turns to the third naming service in Windows 2000: the Windows Internet Name Service (WINS). Like DNS in Chapter 1 and DHCP in Chapter 2, these services provide network name and address information to applications that request it.

All three of these naming services are open Internet standards, defined by documents called Internet Requests for Comments (RFCs). *RFCs* define the function and form of network protocols and services, and act as standards that any vendor can follow to implement a service that will interoperate with other vendors.

In this chapter, you learn how the WINS protocol works and what services it provides. You discover how to install, configure, and manage WINS services under Windows 2000. The WINS service is largely unchanged from its Windows NT predecessor, although it sports a spiffy new Microsoft Management Console (MMC)–based interface.

Parallel with the exam objectives, you learn how to install and configure the WINS service by using the snap-in; you also learn how to plan and troubleshoot WINS installations effectively. Don't assume that you can neglect this material because Microsoft would like to see WINS disappear—it's still an important part of the exam objectives.

You also learn to configure WINS replication and NetBIOS name resolution in this Chapter. Finally, the chapter covers topics that relate to the last objective: managing and monitoring WINS.

As you may know, NetBIOS works by broadcasting tons of network resource information—such as which shares a server offers and where the domain master browser is—so that any client can hear what its peers have to offer. Broadcasts work for smaller networks, but they generate a great deal of unnecessary and undesirable clutter in larger networks. Because NetBIOS packets aren't routable, the problem becomes even worse. All those broadcasts not only clutter the network, but also don't even do any good, because only machines on the local subnet can hear them.

Microsoft solved the routability problem by offering NetBEUI over TCP/IP, or NBT. NBT still sends out broadcasts, however. Although NBT broadcasts do allow NetBIOS-style name resolution on TCP/IP networks, Microsoft's designers realized that it was possible to come up with a better solution, and the Windows Internet Name Service (WINS) was born.

NOTE   WINS is documented in RFCs 1001 and 1002.

Install, configure, and troubleshoot WINS.

This section examines WINS installation, configuration and troubleshooting. You see how to configure replication and NetBIOS name resolution, and how to manage and monitor WINS. Once again, managing and monitoring WINS blur with troubleshooting WINS.

Before seeing the installation procedure, you review how WINS works.

Critical Information

WINS listens to NBT broadcasts and collates them in a central source. In this role, it effectively serves as a clearinghouse for NetBIOS naming information. When you consider how NBT works, this arrangement makes a great deal of sense. A pure NetBIOS network can use NetBIOS addresses. When one machine wants to communicate with another, it can use information broadcast by its local master browser to find the address of the target machine. That approach doesn't work as well in TCP/IP, because the source machine has to know the target's IP address to be talking to it.

Think back to what you know about DNS. When a TCP/IP application needs an address, it calls the resolver, which uses the DNS query mechanism to obtain an IP address. The application then uses the address to open a communication channel. If you apply the same model to the crusty old NBT protocol, you'll see how WINS works: by providing a service that maps NetBIOS names to IP addresses. This service works in three simple steps:

1. Each time a WINS client (a machine that's been given the address of a WINS server) starts, it registers its NetBIOS name and IP address with the WINS server.

2. When a WINS client wants to talk to another computer, the resulting NBT name query is sent directly to the WINS server instead of being broadcast all over the local network.

3. If the WINS server finds the destination host's NetBIOS name and IP address in its database, it returns this information directly to the WINS client. If it doesn't find the information, the WINS server can make a standard NBT broadcast to hunt down the necessary address.

Because the WINS server receives updates from each WINS client as it starts up, its database entries are always current. You can set up multiple WINS servers on a network so that queries and answers are distributed; the servers can replicate their database entries according to the method and schedule you specify.

Using WINS and Windows 2000

The WINS implementation in Windows 2000 is largely unchanged from what Microsoft shipped with Windows NT 4.0. The biggest difference is that Microsoft is pushing DNS and TCP/IP as the linchpins of Active Directory-based networks, so WINS is being shoved off to the side (like campaign finance reform). Don't let that stop you from learning the interesting Windows 2000 features with WINS.

First, WINS is integrated with DNS, which means that DNS-capable clients such as Web browsers can take advantage of WINS resolution transparently (provided that you turned on this integration). You can fetch a Web page or other resource from a machine when all you know is its NetBIOS name. Your application uses the resolver, which makes a DNS query; the DNS server can ask the WINS server for the address after it fails to find it in its local zone.

Understanding How WINS Works

When a WINS client starts, the client exchanges WINS messages with its designated WINS server. Each client can actually hold addresses for a *primary* and a *secondary WINS server*; the secondary is used if the primary doesn't answer. The purpose of these messages is to allow the client to register its address with the server without allowing name or address duplication. This message exchange occurs in four phases, which can be called the four Rs: *name registration, name renewal, name release*, and *name resolution*. The following sections explain what those steps entail.

Name Registration

When a client starts in a WINS network, it is required to register its name and IP address with its designated WINS server. When the WINS server gets a *name registration request*, it has to evaluate that request by asking two questions:

Is the Name Unique?   Duplicate names are undesirable, because they make it impossible to tell which computer *really* has a particular name. If the WINS server receives a request to register a name that already appears in its database, it sends a challenge to the currently registered owner of the disputed name.

When the client happens to be a multihomed system, the WINS server sends challenge and confirmation messages to each of the client's IP addresses in sequence, until the server either receives a reply or tries each address three times.

Is the Name Valid?   NetBIOS names have restrictions: they must be 15 or fewer characters long, and they can't contain certain characters. The WINS server rejects any registration request for an invalid name.

Assuming that the WINS server gets a request for a unique, valid name, it registers the name in its database and returns a message confirming the registration. This confirmation includes a time to live (TTL) for the WINS record; this TTL functions exactly like the TTL for a DNS record.

Name Renewal

Earlier in this chapter, you learned how DHCP leases are offered and renewed. Guess what? WINS clients have to renew their names with the server every so often. With WINS, the client has to notify the server that it wants to continue using its registered name so that the server will reset the TTL.

When the TTL has reached 50 percent of its original value, the WINS client sends a name-renewal message to the primary WINS server. This message contains the client's name, the source, and the destination IP addresses for the client and the server. If there's no response, the message is sent once more when one-eighth of the original TTL remains. If there's still no response from the primary server, the client attempts renewal through the secondary WINS server, if one is configured. If the effort is successful, the WINS client attempts to register with the secondary server as though it were the first attempt. If, after three attempts, the WINS client fails to contact the secondary WINS server, it switches back to the primary one.

When successful contact is made, either the primary or secondary WINS server responds by sending the client a new TTL period. This process continues as long as the client computer is powered on and as long as it remains a WINS client.

Name Release

A WINS client can relinquish ownership of its name at any time by sending a *name-release* message, which contains its IP address and name. If the IP address and name sent by the client don't match the WINS database, the WINS server returns a negative release message. If the client doesn't get either a positive or negative release message, it sends up to three B-node broadcasts, notifying all other systems (including non-WINS clients) to remove the now-invalid name from their NetBIOS name caches.

The extinction interval (four days, by default) controls how long a released WINS record remains marked as "released" before it's marked as "extinct." The extinction timeout (six days, by default) controls how long an extinct record can remain in the database before it's removed.

Name Resolution

So far, you've learned about the communications only between a WINS-enabled computer and a WINS server. How do regular network clients get information from the WINS database? The basic idea is that the client should try to exhaust other methods of resolution before it resorts to blasting out network broadcasts.

The following section covers installing WINS—a direct focus of this objective.

Installing WINS

As it was in Windows NT, WINS remains a stand-alone service that you manage and install like any other network service. In this case, you use the Windows Components wizard to install the service, and it begins running immediately after you install it. You follow the steps in the "Necessary Procedures" section later in this chapter.

Troubleshooting WINS

Troubleshooting WINS problems usually is fairly easy, because neither the protocol nor the service is as complicated as DNS. When you have a name-resolution problem, the first step is to determine where it's occurring. The problem is most likely to be at the client side, and you'll most often hear about it when a client can't resolve a particular network name.

In that case, you need to begin by asking the client the following questions:

- Is the TCP/IP configuration correct? In particular, does the client have a WINS server configured?

- Can you use the ping command to ping the IP address of the WINS server? If not, that failure indicates an underlying network-connectivity problem that you'll need to fix.

- Is the client using DNS or WINS to resolve the name? Whichever protocol the client is using, does the desired name exist on the server?

- Is the WINS server running and accepting requests?

If you determine that the problem isn't with the client, you'll want to check some common causes of server misbehavior. First, verify that the WINS server is running and accepting requests. After you double-check and find that everything is OK, the next step normally is to search the database to see whether the name requested by the client exists in the database. If it doesn't, that's the problem! Then, of course, you have to decide what the *real* problem is: the name isn't registered, or the name is registered by its owning server, but the record hasn't been replicated.

If the desired name does show up in the database, the problem may be that the server is returning bogus data because there's an old static mapping in place (in which case you should remove it) or because there's a problem with the database. If the database is, or appears to be, corrupt or damaged, you can run a consistency check on it or just stop the service and remove the database files. When you restart the service after doing so, the server uses its replication partners to get back the data that it formerly owned, as well as any updates from other partners on the network.

Necessary Procedures

In this section, you learn how to install WINS.

Installing the WINS Service

1. Follow these steps to install a WINS server:

2. Open the Add/Remove Programs in Control Panel (Start ➤ Settings ➤ Control Panel ➤ Add/Remove Programs).

3. When the Add/Remove Programs window appears, click the Add/Remove Windows Components icon. This action starts the Windows Components wizard.

4. In the Components list, scroll down until the Networking Services item is visible. Select it; then click the Details button. The Networking Services window appears.

5. Scroll down the Networking Services list until you see Windows Internet Name Service (WINS); then check its check box. Click the OK button. The Windows Components wizard reappears.

6. Click the Next button.

After you install WINS, you can start its snap-in from the Start menu (Start ➤ Programs ➤ Administrative Tools ➤ Windows Internet Name Service).

Exam Essentials

Know how WINS manages broadcasts.   Be aware of why and when WINS communications happen with WINS servers and how broadcast traffic is minimized.

Know how WINS is integrated with DNS.   Understand how communications between DNS and WINS servers allow DNS-aware clients such as Web browsers to access NetBIOS names.

Know how WINS message exchanges occur in four phases.   Know the four Rs: registration, renewal, release, and resolution of WINS names.

Know how time to live (TTL) affects WINS client-server communications.   Be clear about what effect changing these values would have on your network.

Know the troubleshooting questions you must ask and answer. Because WINS naming concerns names and requests for names, follow the name.

Know how to install WINS.   Understand that this process involves selecting WINS in the Add/Remove Windows Components window in the Add/Remove Programs Control Panel window.

Key Terms and Concepts

database verification   The process that allows you to adjust the interval at which the consistency and integrity of a WINS or DHCP database is verified.

extinction interval   The period (four days, by default) that controls how long a released WINS record remains marked as "released" before it's marked as "extinct." The extinction timeout (six days, by default), controls how long an extinct record can stay in the database before it's removed.

Requests for Comments (RFCs)   The set of standards defining the Internet protocols, as determined by the Internet Engineering Task Force and available in the public domain on the Internet. RFCs define the functions and services provided by each of the many Internet protocols. Compliance with the RFCs guarantees cross-vendor compatibility.

Windows Internet Name Service (WINS)   A network service for Microsoft networks that provides Windows computers Internet numbers for specified NetBIOS computer names, facilitating browsing and intercommunication over TCP/IP networks.

WINS name registration   A request sent by the client to the designated WINS server to register its name and IP address.

WINS name release   A request sent by the client to relinquish ownership of its name.

WINS name request   A request for a NetBIOS name on the network that may go to the primary or secondary WINS servers for resolution.

WINS name resolution   The process occurring when the NetBIOS name is registered on the network through WINS.

WINS server   The server that runs WINS and is used to resolve NetBIOS names to IP addresses.

Sample Questions

1. WINS is used primarily for which of the following purposes?

A. Mapping NetBIOS names to IP addresses

B. Mapping domain names to MAC addresses

C. Mapping IP addresses to MAC addresses

D. Mapping NetBIOS names to MAC addresses

Answer: A. WINS is designed to allow DNS-style name resolution without requiring DNS.

2. A WINS client can relinquish ownership of its name:

A. Only after it is reconciled

B. After a primary WINS server has mapped its NetBIOS name correctly

C. Any time it wants to

D. After its time to live is half-expired

Answer: C. A WINS client can relinquish ownership of its name at any time by sending a *name-release* message, which contains its IP address and name.

Configure WINS replication.

Microsoft expects you to know how to configure and control replication traffic between WINS servers. First, though, you'll probably find it helpful to understand what gets replicated and why. The preceding sections discussed how WINS works but purposely didn't talk about how WINS replication functions, because replication is independent of the WINS protocol itself.

Critical Information

Replication is a service that makes the WINS data stored on your servers more useful by making it available across subnets. For this objective, you need to understand how replication works.

WINS and Replication

Consider a network with two subnets and one WINS server on each. Normally, each WINS server collects name-resolution information about the hosts on its subnet; with proper use of the WINS proxy agent, each subnet can query the other subnet's WINS server for names on that subnet. That solution is inefficient, however, because all queries from one subnet for hosts on the other have to travel to the other subnet. Replicating WINS registrations from one server to another provides a way around this problem. Because the registrations are duplicated on both servers, a host on one subnet can get the IP address for a host on the other subnet without having to actually send a resolution request to the other subnet.

For replication to work properly, additional subtleties come into play. One is the concept of *convergence time*. If you think back to the meaning of convergence for IP routing—the state in which every router knows about all its peers—you'll have a good idea of how it applies to WINS. In a network with more than one WINS server, the convergence time for that network is the time that it takes a change from any server to propagate to all other servers. You may think that a very short convergence time would be desirable, but it's actually the opposite. Short convergence times mean that every little change is replicated everywhere. WINS registrations, though, tend to be ephemeral, because machines release their reservations when they shut down or reboot. Longer convergence times reduce overall replication loads by not replicating changes—such as name releases—that will just be rendered obsolete before the convergence interval has been reached.

NOTE   WINS releases aren't always guaranteed to happen, either— because they happen at normal shutdown, an abnormal shutdown leaves a dangling registration. Eventually, the server purges this record, but a WINS registration doesn't carry the same authority as, say, a DNS or DHCP record.

Push and Pull

The relationship between two servers that replicate data back and forth usually is described as a partnership, and the servers are called *replication partners*. A single server can be involved with any number of replication partners; in fact, in large networks it's common for a single server to replicate to most of its peers.

WINS servers use two different types of replication partners: *pull partners* and *push partners*. Both provide the same result: data from one server is copied to another. These servers are always paired, so that in any partnership, one server pulls while the other pushes. The method of initiating the replication differs, however, and you can set different values for the parameters that govern when and how replication works for each set of partners.

Push Partners   A push replication partner sends its partner a notice that says, "I have new data, so ask me if you want it." This exchange happens when the WINS server starts, and you can configure it to take place when a registered client's IP address changes or when a certain number of replicated changes have arrived from other partners.

This "I have new data" message is called a *push replication trigger*, and it signals the receiving server to request the changed data.

Pull Partners   A pull partner sends its partner a request for new data by sending a record number and asking for any records that are newer. This message is called a *pull replication trigger*. When the partner receives this request, it sends back the requested data. A pull trigger can be sent either on its own or in response to a push trigger received from a partner.

Pull requests are sent to a server's partners when the server starts and when the specified replication interval expires. You also can send a pull replication trigger to a partner manually at any time, as you'll see later in this chapter.

To further muddy the waters, Microsoft's WINS implementation allows a single pair of servers to be each other's push and pull partners. For servers A and B, that arrangement means that A can push or pull to B, and vice versa. These *push/pull partnerships* are often used when you want to pair servers in even groups across a high-speed LAN connection.

Knowing What Is Replicated

WINS data is replicated at record level, which means that as individual records are updated, they can be replicated, but the entire database won't be replicated. Each change to a record held by a server causes that server to increment an internal record called a *version ID*. When a replication partner asks, "What's new?", it's really asking whether the partner's version ID is higher than the one it already has.

How do servers know which version IDs belong to which servers? Each server maintains a table called the *owner-version mapping table*, which keeps track of which WINS server owns (or holds) a particular registration, along with the highest version ID received from that server. When one server sends another a replication trigger, the sending server includes a copy of its owner-version mapping table. This table allows the receiving server to determine what the sending server "knows" about the state of the WINS databases.

Controlling WINS Replication

You control WINS replication at two levels. At the highest level, you can assign settings that apply to all replication partnerships in which the target server participates. Although this is useful, it's equally useful to control replication settings for individual partnerships, and you can do that, too.

SETTING PROPERTIES FOR ALL REPLICATION PARTNERS

When you right-click the Replication Partners node in the WINS snap-in and choose the Properties command, the Replication Partners

Properties dialog box appears. This dialog box has four tabs: the General tab, the Push Replication tab, the Pull Replication tab, and the Advanced tab. The defaults that you set in this dialog box apply to all partners of the current server that don't have their own overriding settings in place; the settings also will apply to all newly added partners.

The General Tab   The General tab has only two settings, one of which is very simple. The other setting takes some explaining. The simple setting, the Replicate Only with Partners check box, controls whether this server chastely confines its replication traffic to its defined partners. When the box is unchecked, the server happily replicates with any server that asks it to do so.

The other check box has a fairly impressive name: Overwrite Unique Static Mappings at This Server (Migrate On). Remember that a WINS administrator can add static NetBIOS-to-IP mappings; these mappings stay in the database, as opposed to normal dynamic WINS records. The mappings normally are used to provide WINS resolution for machines that aren't using NetBIOS, such as Macintoshes and Unix boxes. These static records normally work well, but the check box is included to handle the case in which the same name has both a static and a dynamic mapping attached. This situation can happen as you migrate from systems that are not using WINS to those that do. When the check box is checked, a dynamic WINS registration request (which can be generated only by a real, live WINS client) always trumps a static mapping for the same name.

The Push Replication Tab   The Push Replication tab allows you to control how replication works for push partners of the current server. A push trigger request tells the partner that it needs to send a pull trigger. Because this is its sole function, the controls in this tab are all fairly easy to understand:

- The two Start Push Replication check boxes allow you to specify when this server will send push replication triggers. You can send push triggers when the WINS service starts or when a client registers a new or changed IP address with the server.

- The Number of Changes in Version ID Before Replication control gives you a further measure of control, because it allows you to specify how much drift in the owner-version mapping table you're willing to accept. If you set this value to 50, for example, you're telling your server to accumulate 50 changes before sending a push trigger to its partners. These changes may be changes in registrations owned by the server, or they may be changes received from other replication partners.

The Use Persistent Connections for Push Replication Partners check box is perhaps the exception to the rule that these controls are simple to understand. Normally, WINS servers bring up new connections each time they initiate a replication and tear down the connection when they're done. In some networks, this system can waste bandwidth unnecessarily, because the connection setup and teardown may have to be done several times in fairly rapid succession. To work around this problem, you can specify that you want a partner connection to be persistent, meaning that the two partners maintain an open communication session even when they're not actively replicating data back and forth.

The Pull Replication Tab   You get a separate, and different, set of properties to control for pull partners. Because pull partners actually reach out to their partners to seek updates, you have more options to configure:

- The Start Time controls allow you to regulate when replication starts.

- The Replication Interval controls govern how often the pull partner sends pull triggers to its partners.

- The Number of Retries field specifies how many times you want a pull partner to send pull triggers before it skips a particular partner.

- The Start Pull Replication at Service Startup check box, which is checked by default, gives you a way to control when the first pull trigger is sent by the service.

- The Use Persistent Connections for Pull Replication Partners check box does the same thing as its counterpart in the Push Replication tab.

The Advanced Tab   The Advanced tab of the Replication Partners Properties dialog box has two primary functions; it just so happens that these functions are not related.

The first function allows you to block the replication of records from certain owners. This feature allows your servers to remain willfully (and blissfully) ignorant of replicated data from the owners of those IP addresses specified in the Block Records for These Owners list. This method is an easy way to screen out WINS records offered by rogue servers, or by servers in a test lab, that you don't want polluting your "real" WINS database.

Automatic partner configuration is the reason for the remaining controls in this tab. The Enable Automatic Partner Configuration check box controls whether this server will attempt to buddy up with other servers on the network automatically. When this check box is checked, you can use the multicast interval and TTL controls to configure automatic multicast announcements from this WINS server. Automatic partners are configured as both push and pull partners.

CHOOSING YOUR PARTNERS

When you've configured the settings that you want to apply to all replication partners of a server, you're ready to select the partners themselves. You do so from the Replication Partners node of the server.

NOTE   Changing partnership status for a server requires you to have administrative access to both servers.

TURNING ON AUTOMATIC PARTNER CONFIGURATION

If you want your server to participate in automatic partner configuration with similar servers, use the controls described in "The Advanced Tab" to configure the Advanced tab of the Replication Partners node in the snap-in to advertise to its partners automatically.

LINKING PARTNERS MANUALLY

Adding a partner manually is a trivial procedure: navigate to the server you want to partner up, and right-click its Replication Partners node. When the context menu appears, choose the New Replication Partner command, and then specify the IP address or name of the server with which you want to partner. This action adds the new server as a push/pull partner, but you can change the replication type to match your needs after the partnership is created.

REMOVING A PARTNERSHIP

If you want to remove a replication partner from a server, open the server's Replication Partners node, right-click the server that you want to whack, and then choose the Delete command. When the confirmation dialog box appears, click the Yes button, and voilà—it disappears.

Controlling Replication for an Individual Partner

Each partner listed in the Replication Partners node has its own list of server settings, all of which you can change. You can change from a pull partner to a push partner or vice versa, and you can set a few of the settings that you just explored at the all-servers level.

When you open the Properties dialog box for a specific replication partner, the General tab doesn't show anything except the NetBIOS name and IP address of the partner server. The Advanced tab, though, is considerably more interesting, because it allows you to change the server's replication-partner type from the pull-down menu. This change is fairly innocuous, because it affects only the way that the server you're managing sends requests to the partner server—it doesn't change anything on the partner server.

TIP Before changing the replication type, you may want to force a replication with the target partner to ensure that you get an up-to-date replication.

Two additional control groups give you some control of pull and push replication with this particular partner. The controls in the Pull

Replication group are a subset of the ones in the Pull Replication tab of the Replication Partners Properties dialog box; you can specify the start time and replication interval, as well as whether you want to use persistent connections. Likewise, the Push Replication control group has a pair of controls that match the Push Replication tab of the Replication Partners Properties dialog box. In both cases, the primary difference is that you can't use the individual server's Properties dialog box to control what happens when the service starts.

Forcing Replication

By right-clicking a replication partner, you can send a replication trigger request directly to that partner. This action allows you to force replication at any time, not just at the scheduled intervals.

Necessary Procedures

In this section, you will learn the process for configuring WINS replication.

Configuring WINS Replication

Follow these steps:

1. Open the WINS snap-in (Start ➢ Administrative Tools ➢ WINS).

2. Choose the WINS server that you want to manage; then expand it so you can see its Replication Partners node.

3. Right-click the Replication Partners node; then choose the Properties command. The Replication Partners Properties dialog box appears.

4. Make sure that the Replicate Only With Partners check box is checked.

5. Switch to the Push Replication tab; then check both Start Push Replication check boxes.

6. Switch to the Pull Replication tab, and check the Start Pull Replication At Service Startup check box.

7. Click the OK button in the Properties dialog box.

Exam Essentials

Know the motivating factors for WINS replication. Understand how resolution requests are eliminated between different subnets.

Know the meaning of WINS convergence. Understand the reasons why longer convergence times reduce the replication loads.

Know the different functions with push and pull partners. You need to understand push/pull partnerships to configure WINS communications.

Know what a version ID is and how owner-version mapping tables keep track of the most up-to-date WINS naming information. The table keeps track of the latest version of names, so the latest numbered version is favored.

Key Terms and Concepts

convergence time The time that it takes a change from any RIP router to propagate to all other routers in the internetwork.

owner-version mapping table A table that keeps track of which WINS server owns (or holds) a particular registration, along with the highest version ID received from that server.

pull partner A network client or server that pulls data from another server.

pull replication trigger A request for new data made by sending a record number and asking for any records that are newer.

push partner A network server or client that pushes data to another server.

push replication trigger A signal sent to the receiving server to request the changed data.

push/pull partnership A partnership in which one server pulls while the other pushes. These partnerships are often used when you want to pair servers in even groups across a high-speed LAN connection.

replication partners   Two servers that replicate data back and forth.

version ID   An internal record used to identify which server in a replication partnership has the more recent version of a registration.

Sample Questions

1. Microsoft's WINS implementation allows a single pair of servers to be each other's push and pull partners. Which of the following statements are true?

   A. For servers A and B, A can push or pull to B, and vice versa.

   B. For servers A and B, only A—the first server registered—can push.

   C. Push/pull partnerships are often used when you want to pair servers in even groups across a high-speed LAN connection.

   D. If server A is the push partner, it has to be the primary WINS server.

   Answer: A, C. Either server in a pair can push or pull. Push/pull partners normally are set up over high-speed connections. Pull partners normally are set up over slow WAN connections. C is true as well.

2. Automatic partner configuration is accomplished by which of the following actions?

   A. Sending push messages

   B. Sending pull messages

   C. Checking the Enable Automatic Partner Configuration check box

   D. Enabling NBT on your network

   Answer: C. This box is checked in the Advanced Tab of the Replication Partners Properties dialog box.

Configure NetBIOS name resolution.

$\mathbf{S}$o far, you've learned about communications only between a WINS-enabled computer and a WINS server. How do regular network clients get information from the WINS database? The basic idea is that the client should try to exhaust other methods of resolution before it resorts to blasting out network broadcasts (although, as you'll see, the process works a little differently in practice).

Critical Information

WINS as a service is fairly simple. As you have seen, its job is to listen for "here I am" broadcasts from NBT clients and then answer queries for NetBIOS-to-IP mappings so that clients can get address data without resorting to those bad old network broadcasts. To understand this objective—configuration of NetBIOS name resolution—you must turn to the WINS snap-in.

Using the WINS Snap-In

As befits a simple service, the WINS snap-in is fairly simple; most of its functionality is tucked into the Properties dialog boxes for the server and its databases. You need to know a few other things to manage WINS effectively, however. You have to be able to manage data replication between WINS servers, for example, because the most efficient way to implement WINS is to use several servers that share data so that broadcasts and requests never have to cross from one TCP/IP subnet to another.

Setting Server Properties

Each individual WINS server has its own group of settings, including settings that govern when the service replicates its data and how often it backs up its database. You control these settings by selecting a server in the WINS snap-in and then opening its associated Properties dialog box. The Properties dialog box has four tabs that allow you to control these settings: the General tab, the Intervals tab, the Database Verification tab, and the Advanced tab.

The General Tab

The General tab controls some useful but generally unremarkable server properties:

- The Automatically Update Statistics Every check box and the associated time controls allow you to govern how often your WINS server parses its logs and databases to gather statistical information (how many registration attempts have succeeded or failed). Although useful in the aggregate, this statistical information generally isn't critical to the success or failure of your WINS implementation, and the default interval of 10 minutes is frequent enough.

- The Database Backup control group allows you to specify a backup location for your WINS database files. The Windows NT WINS server had an unfortunate propensity to corrupt its databases, which is why these backup options are present. The generally accepted best practice is to keep a backup of your WINS databases on a separate physical volume on the same computer. It's a good idea to keep a database backup, although WINS data can always be reloaded from a replication partner if necessary.

- The Back Up Database During Server Shutdown check box is another nice safety feature: it requests that the server make an additional backup of the database when the WINS-server service is shut down. This feature operates in addition to the backup that takes place at scheduled intervals.

The Intervals Tab

Speaking of intervals, the server Properties dialog box also has an Intervals tab. Unfortunately, it has nothing to do with database backups; instead, it controls the intervals at which the WINS server performs maintenance tasks on its databases. Unlike DNS, in which records never expire, and DHCP, in which the server handles database maintenance on its own, the WINS server allows you some measure of control of these tasks—at least to the extent of controlling how often they happen.

This dialog box has four sets of controls, each of which controls a separate maintenance activity:

- The *Renew Interval* setting controls how often a WINS client has to renew its registration. The default value (six days) is fine for most networks. Shorter values increase the load on the WINS server and network, but they also reduce convergence time.

NOTE   The Renew Interval setting influences the values of the other intervals.

- The *Extinction Interval* setting (four days, by default) controls how long a released WINS record remains marked as "released" before it's marked as "extinct."

- The *Extinction Timeout* setting (six days, by default) controls how long an extinct record remains in the database before it's removed.

- The *Verification Interval* setting regulates how long a stale record owned by another server can remain in the database before it's verified to determine whether the registration is still valid. The standard value is 24 hours. Notice that the Database Verification tab controls the actual settings that perform the verification.

- Finally, the Restore Defaults button returns these control values to their original factory values.

The Database Verification Tab

An inconsistent WINS database is bad. Because clients may depend on WINS for all their name resolution, it's desirable to have some way to cross-check database entries for correctness. But that raises the question of what you check and what it gets checked against. After all, comparing two different copies of the same wrong data wouldn't do much good. Microsoft has implemented a mechanism that correlates WINS registrations among multiple servers so that conflicts or incorrect entries can be identified and flagged. Resolving conflicts or problems is still up to you, but at least you can find out where they are.

The Database Verification tab allows you to adjust the interval at which database consistency and integrity are verified. In fact, these controls allow you to specify whether consistency checking is done at all. Here's what you can control:

- The Verify Database Consistency Every check box controls whether verification is turned on. When you turn it on (as it is by default), the interval that you enter in this tab matches the same interval in the Intervals tab; changing it in one place changes it in the other. If you want, you can turn off verification, although doing so is not recommended unless you have a very small network.

- The Begin Verifying At control allows you to specify when the verification pass begins. Normally, this pass begins two hours after the server starts, and the interval actually starts only after that initial pass completes.

- The Maximum Number of Records Verified Each Period control gives you a limited way to throttle back verification. A 30,000-record WINS database is still large, though, and because verification always involves network chatter between the two servers involved, you may benefit from turning this setting down somewhat if your WINS database has more than 1,000 records.

- The Verify Against radio-button group probably is the most interesting feature of this tab. When you are comparing two sets of data to see which version is correct, the choice of source is fairly important. You have two verification choices. The first is to verify registrations with the server that issued them. Think of this process as verifying a driver's license by calling the issuing state's license bureau. This option gives you complete verification, but it may involve calling many places.

The alternative is for you to verify data by checking it against a replication partner. If your server has a single partner, this option may not be useful. Because many WINS implementations use several partners, however, this option picks a partner at random and cross-checks the subject record against it. Using the same partner all the time may lead to a failure to spot a problem record, so the WINS verifier automatically picks a new partner for each record that it verifies.

NOTE You can verify the database manually by right-clicking it and choosing the Verify Database Consistency command.

The Advanced Tab

By now, you're probably starting to figure out that the Advanced tab of a Microsoft Properties dialog box usually is one of two things: a dumping ground for settings that don't belong on other pages in the dialog box, or a potentially dangerous group of things that you shouldn't touch without a good reason. The Advanced tab of the WINS Properties dialog box is a little of both.

The following list describes what's in this tab:

- The Log Detailed Events to Windows Event Log check box allows you to turn on more detailed logging. When you check this box, expect your event log to fill quickly, because the WINS service will begin logging each registration and renewal request, as well as information about the request's success or failure. This option may be useful for the next objective-monitoring WINS.

- The Enable Burst Handling check box and control group give you gross (as opposed to fine) control of how many simultaneous requests your WINS server can accept. If the server is busy, any client that attempts a registration or renewal has to wait until the server can handle it.

   Normally, burst handling is turned on. If you turn this feature off, you limit your server to processing a single request at a time—which can cause a bottleneck. At the same time, you may not want your WINS server to accept a great many requests at the same time, so you can adjust its acceptance with the radio buttons in the control group. Choosing the Custom radio button and providing a number in the attached field specifies a firm limit on how many concurrent requests the server will accept.

- Normally, WINS databases are stored in the system's directory. Microsoft uses %windir% as shorthand for the directory in which Windows 2000 is installed, so the default path for the WINS database appears in the Database Path field as %windir%\system32\wins. You're free to change the path, preferably to someplace where it gets backed up regularly.

- WINS servers use a version ID in their database. This ID, which is incremented when changes occur, can be used to identify which server in a replication partnership has the more recent version of a registration. By changing the value in the Starting Version ID (Hexadecimal) field, you can twiddle the version ID of your database. Normally, you'd do this only if you want your database to appear to be newer than the version on its partner's database (perhaps because it had already replicated some incorrect data).

- The Use Computer Names That Are Compatible With LAN Manager check box instructs the WINS server to register only names that are usable with older computers that are still stuck with LAN Manager. In practice, that limit means names that are fewer than 14 characters long and that contain only letters, numbers, and the underscore (_) character.

Configuring WINS Clients

WINS gets a great deal of bad press, only some of which it deserves. True, WINS is not as flexible or open as the DNS protocol, which is why Microsoft is trying to move away from it. At the same time, though, WINS is deeply entrenched in many networks, and it will be for a long time to come.

Unlike Windows NT, Windows 2000 buries the WINS client configuration options in the Advanced TCP/IP Settings dialog box. The WINS tab offers you a small group of controls for configuring how (if at all) your client uses WINS for name resolution.

First, the WINS Addresses, In Order of Use list and its related controls show you which WINS servers you have defined for this client. By default, this list is empty, so you have to add WINS servers to it manually if you want to use WINS. Realize that in most systems, the WINS server address is supplied by DHCP through the 044 and 046 options. A manual setting here overrides the DHCP setting.

As with DNS, the WINS code sends WINS resolution requests to the servers in this list in the order of their appearance. You add, remove, and change server addresses with the buttons below the list, and you change the ordering of the servers by selecting a server and clicking the up and down arrow buttons along the right side of the list.

The next group, which falls immediately below the WINS address list group, controls whether the old-style *LMHOSTS file* is used as a source for address-resolution information. The Enable LMHOSTS Lookup check box controls whether Windows 2000 will use the IP-to-host-name mappings in the LMHOSTS file before querying a WINS server. When you check this box, LMHOSTS lookups are enabled for all connections that are using TCP/IP, not just the one whose properties you're editing. The Import LMHOSTS button allows you to read the contents of a file into the WINS name cache, which is handy if you want to load a set of name mappings without keeping a file around on disk.

The final controls are the three radio buttons at the bottom of the dialog box. These radio buttons control whether NetBIOS over TCP/IP is active at all. In the olden days of Microsoft networking, NetBEUI was the only transport that could carry NetBIOS traffic, but it wasn't routable and performed poorly in large networks. Microsoft devised a scheme for encapsulating NetBIOS inside TCP/IP (for a while, this scheme was called NBT), and it's been a part of Windows since Windows NT 3.5 or so. In Windows 2000, NBT lives on, even though many observers expect its use to diminish as networks move toward pure TCP/IP. Here's what the buttons do:

- The Enable NetBIOS Over TCP/IP option is selected by default. It allows this client to exchange NetBIOS traffic with servers using TCP/IP as a transport.

- The Disable NetBIOS Over TCP/IP option turns off NBT, which is handy when you want to rid your network of all NetBIOS traffic, even when it's encapsulated.

- The Use NetBIOS Setting from the DHCP Server option forces this particular client to use the DHCP server's setting instead of either of the two preceding settings. If this option is *not* selected, whatever setting is in force overrides the DHCP server's setting.

Necessary Procedures

This section describes how to accomplish NetBIOS name resolution and another subsequent necessary procedure: how to configure a Windows 2000 client to use WINS.

Configuring NetBIOS Name Resolution

Follow these steps to configure NetBIOS name resolution:

1. Install the WINS server as directed in the first chapter objective.

2. Configure a WINS client to point to the WINS server that you just installed. (See the following procedure.)

Configuring a Windows 2000 Client to Use WINS

Follow these steps to enable WINS resolution on a Windows 2000 client:

1. Choose Start ➤ Settings ➤ Network and Dial-Up Connections.

2. Right-click the Local Area Connection icon; then choose the Properties command. If you have more than one LAN adapter, choose the one that you want to configure. The Local Area Connection Properties dialog box appears.

3. Select Internet Protocol (TCP/IP) in the Components Checked Are Used by This Connection list.

4. Click the Properties button. The Internet Protocol (TCP/IP) Properties dialog box appears.

5. Click the Advanced button. The Advanced TCP/IP Settings dialog box appears.

6. Click the WINS tab.

7. Click the Add button. When the TCP/IP WINS Server dialog box appears, enter the IP address for your WINS server; then click the Add button.

8. (Optional) Enter additional WINS server addresses and reorder the servers as necessary.

9. Click OK to close the Advanced TCP/IP Settings dialog box.

10. Click OK to close the Internet Protocol (TCP/IP) Properties dialog box.

11. Click OK to close the Local Area Connection Properties dialog box.

Exam Essentials

Know NetBIOS name restrictions. Understand the 15-character limit and character restrictions on NetBIOS names. Also be aware of older names with only 14 characters and the underscore for networks that support LAN Manager.

Know each server's Properties dialog box and how to configure each through the four tabs. Understand the functions that you manage through the four tabs: General, Intervals, Database Verification, and Advanced.

Know how to configure the Windows 2000 client to use WINS. Understand the settings in the Advanced TCP/IP dialog box.

Key Terms and Concepts

extinction interval The time period that controls how long a released WINS record remains marked as "released" before it's marked as "extinct."

extinction timeout   The time period that controls how long an extinct record remains in the database before it's removed.

renew interval   The time period that controls how often a WINS client has to renew its registration.

verification interval   The time period that regulates how long a stale record owned by another server can remain in the database before it's verified to determine whether the registration is still valid.

WINS burst handling   The number of simultaneous requests that your WINS server can handle can be configured and is called burst handling.

Sample Questions

1. What WINS database options do you have for the WINS snap-in in the server's Properties box? (Choose all correct answers.)

A. Where you want your WINS directory to be backed up

B. Where you want to store your WINS database

C. Whether you want your WINS database to be backed up during server shutdown for additional fault tolerance

D. Whether you want to verify WINS database consistency every definable period

Answer: A, B, C, D. All of the above and more verification options are available in the Database Verification tab.

2. What is the name of the period for which a released WINS record remains marked as "released" before it's marked as "extinct"?

A. Extinction interval

B. Release interval

C. Time to live

D. Half-life

Answer: A. You may need to know defaults for these time intervals on the exam. The extinction interval's default is four days.

Manage and monitor WINS.

WINS is like the other two naming services, DHCP and DNS, in that the similarity between monitoring/managing them and occasional troubleshooting makes these objectives blur. WINS is fairly trouble-free in most circumstances, though, with the possible exception of an occasional corrupt database. In addition, from time to time you may find registration problems, most of which are easy to isolate and fix.

Critical Information

The WINS snap-in maintains a database of statistical information that you may find useful. This information includes the numbers of successful and failed registrations—itself a good measure for how busy your WINS servers are—as well as more esoteric information, such as the numbers of successful and failed WINS queries.

By default, these statistics are hidden, but you can reveal them by selecting a WINS server in the snap-in and then choosing the Show Server Statistics command (from the Action menu or the context menu). This command displays a floating window that displays the pertinent statistics.

If you want to clear the statistics, perhaps because you've restarted the server or have made some other change and want a clean start, use the Show Server Statistics command, but click Reset instead of OK.

If you want to control how often the statistics are updated, check out the General tab of the server Properties dialog box.

Viewing WINS Records

It's often useful to peek at the WINS records in your database, particularly if you know or suspect that something's wrong with a particular record. For anything but a very small WINS database, however, sifting through the records manually is prohibitively time-consuming. You can search the database in two different ways. In each case, you choose the server of interest, right-click its Active Registrations node, and then choose the appropriate command:

- The Find By Name command allows you to query the database for WINS records that start with or contain a particular string of characters.

- The Find By Owner command allows you search for all the WINS registrations held by a particular owner. This command is the fastest way to see which records any given server owns, and you can use the filtering options in the Find by Owner dialog box to screen out records that don't interest you. The Record Types tab allows you to search or filter records for a particular type of server, such as a domain controller or RAS server.

Compacting the Database

The WINS server periodically goes through its database and cleans it up, deleting records that are no longer needed. This process, called *online compaction*, works well, but it can't reclaim space that's no longer used; it just removes unused records without reclaiming the space that they used to occupy. To really purge your WINS database, you need to compact it while the WINS service is stopped. The jetpack.exe utility allows you to do this. Jetpack takes two parameters: the name of the database file (normally, the name is either dhcp.mdb or wins.mdb) that you want to compact and the name of the temporary file you want it to use. Look at the following example:

```
Jetpack wins.mdb junk.mdb
```

This code compacts the WINS database into a file named junk.mdb; when the compaction succeeds, junk.mdb is renamed wins.mdb, and you can safely restart the WINS service. The following procedure walks you through the necessary steps.

Necessary Procedures

This section describes how to reclaim the space that's no longer used in your WINS database:

Compacting the WINS Database with Jetpack

Follow these steps:

1. Log on to the console of your WINS server.

2. Open the WINS snap-in (Start ➤ Administrative Tools ➤ WINS).

3. Right-click the WINS server that you're on; then choose All Tasks ➤ Stop command.

4. Open a command prompt (Start ➤ Run ➤ cmd.exe).

5. Change to the WINS database directory (by default, winnt\system32\wins).

6. Type **dir *.mdb,** and note the size of the wins.mdb file.

7. Type **jetpack wins.mdb temp.mdb.** Let Jetpack do its thing.

8. Type **dir *.mdb,** and note the size of the wins.mdb file. Did the size change?

9. Switch back to the WINS MMC console, right-click the server, and choose the All Tasks ➤ Start command.

Exam Essentials

Managing and monitoring WINS is a fairly simple affair, but be sure that you are clear on the essential points in this section:

Know that the WINS snap-in has a database of statistical information for your use.   This information includes a record of successful and failed WINS registrations and the numbers of successful and failed WINS queries.

Know two methods of conducting searches in the WINS database.
Understand how to search by name and how to find by owner, as well
as how to filter records for different types of servers.

Know how to reclaim space from your database with the
jetpack.exe **utility.**   Be familiar with compacting the WINS database by using the Jetpack procedure.

Key Terms and Concepts

online compaction   A process in which the WINS server periodically
goes through its database and clean it up, deleting records that are no
longer needed.

Sample Questions

1. Which of the following are common WINS problems?

A. Registration problems

B. NDS integration problems

C. Database corruption problems

D. DHCP coordination problems

Answer: A, C. Even these two maladies occur infrequently.

2. Which two of the following are types of WINS record searches?

A. Find by date

B. Find by owner

C. Find by domain

D. Find by name

Answer: B, D. Know how to use the filters in the Owners tab of
the Find by Owner dialog box and the Record Types tab of the
Find by Owner dialog box.

Chapter

6

Installing, Configuring, Managing, Monitoring, and Troubleshooting IP Routing in a Windows 2000 Network Infrastructure

---

MICROSOFT EXAM OBJECTIVES COVERED IN THIS CHAPTER:

▶ **Install, configure, and troubleshoot IP routing protocols.** *(pages 253 – 287)*

- Update a Windows 2000-based routing table by means of static routes.
- Implement Demand-Dial Routing.

▶ **Manage and monitor IP routing.**
(pages 288 – 298)

- Manage and monitor border routing.
- Manage and monitor internal routing.
- Manage and monitor IP routing protocols.

Network routing used to be like the Internal Revenue Service: poorly understood and greatly feared. Organizations with large networks had people whose job was to stroke the routers and keep them happy and functional. As the use of IP and IPX internetworking has grown, of course, so has the demand for easy-to-install, easy-to-configure routers. Not every small business that wants to connect to the Internet or connect two remote offices can afford a fancy router and a certified professional to administer it.

Microsoft's first attempt to solve this problem was the version of the *Routing and Remote Access Service (RRAS)* included in the Windows NT 4.0 Option Pack, which is the direct ancestor of the RRAS components included in Windows 2000. The Windows 2000 version of RRAS is a fully functional multiprotocol router. It can handle routing IP, IPX, and AppleTalk traffic, and it can be extended by third parties to add network protocols or routing methods.

The idea behind using RRAS for routing is that you can put RRAS on a Windows 2000 machine and use it as a router in addition to whatever else you have it doing. Although RRAS supports routing for IPX and AppleTalk networks, this chapter sticks with IP routing, because that's what Microsoft has as an objective in the exam.

This chapter explores the ubiquitous categories of installing, configuring, and troubleshooting IP routing protocols. Within the initial objective, you also see how to update a Windows 2000-based routing table by means of static routes and how to implement demand-dial routing.

The second chapter objective—managing and monitoring IP routing—includes a discussion of border routing and internal routing, as well as managing and monitoring IP protocols.

Install, configure, and troubleshoot IP routing protocols.

- **Update a Windows 2000-based routing table by means of static routes.**
- **Implement Demand-Dial Routing.**

You need to be comfortable with binary notation and math to understand IP addressing and subnetting, and many texts will go into greater detail than you will find in these notes. This section begins with a review of these details to situate your understanding of the objectives. (For more information on IP addressing and subnetting, see *TCP/IP: 24Seven*, by Gary Govanus (Sybex 1999).

Critical Information

Understanding IP addressing is critical to understanding how IP routing works. An *IP address* is a numeric identifier assigned to each machine on an IP network. The address designates the location of the device to which it is assigned on the network. This type of address is a software address, not a hardware address, which is hard-coded in the machine or network interface card.

Understanding IP Addressing

An IP address is made up of 32 bits of information. These bits are divided into four sections (sometimes called octets or quads) containing one byte (eight bits) each. Three methods are used for specifying an IP address:

- Dotted-decimal, as in 130.57.30.56

- Binary, as in 10000010.00111001.00011110.00111000

- Hexadecimal, as in 82 39 1E 38

All these examples represent the same IP address. For this exam, you need to have a good understanding of IP addressing, along with facility at subnet masking. You can find a good explanation of these skills in the companion, *MCSE: Windows 2000 Network Infrastructure Administration Study Guide* by Paul Robichaux (Sybex 2000).

TIP New to Microsoft, but old to Cisco, is the way that address ranges are written. An address of 131.107.2.0 with a subnet address of 255.255.255.0 is listed as 131.107.2.0/24, because the subnet mask contains 24 ones. An address listed as 141.10.32.0/19 would have a subnet mask of 255.255.224.0, or 19 ones (default subnet mask for a Class B address, plus 3 bits). This format is the new nomenclature used in all Microsoft exams.

Understanding IP Routing

IP routing is simple to understand at the most basic level: Packets have addresses, and the process of routing involves getting a packet from its source address to its destination address. The mechanics of how that happens are a little more complicated, though.

Routing is the process of delivering traffic to the correct destination. We use real-world routing concepts all the time: The U.S. interstate highway system, road-construction detours, and postal letters marked with a forwarding address all use routing in a way that we understand fairly well. Network routing is analogous, but not exactly identical, to these real-world routing systems.

NOTE Although Windows 2000 supports routing IPX, AppleTalk, and IP, only IP routing is discussed in this book. It's the most widely used system and the only one with objectives in the exam.

In very simple networks, no routing is necessary. More complex systems support, and even require, routing. Routing combines the idea that each packet on a network has a source and destination with the idea of associating routes with costs. Paradoxically, it usually is cheaper to fly from New York City to Los Angeles than it is to fly the shorter distance from L.A. to San Francisco. Following this principle, routing systems allow administrators to attach a *metric,* or cost, to each leg of a route. Later in this chapter, you see how routing systems use this metric information to calculate the most efficient route for packets to take.

NOTE   The actual way in which the metric information is used in calculations varies between RIP version 1, RIP version 2, and OSPF. The important point to remember is that all three protocols use metrics to figure out the best route in any situation.

Using Routing in Windows 2000

Windows 2000 includes, and improves on, the routing capabilities included with Windows NT 4.0. Each of the routable protocols that Windows 2000 supports can be routed via the Routing and Remote Access Service (RRAS). In addition, AppleTalk can be routed if you install the Services for Macintosh (SFM) package. Windows NT supported simple IP routing, but it couldn't share routing information with dedicated routers. Because a router needs to know where its "neighbors" are to figure out what the network topology looks like, this omission was critical. Windows 2000 fixes this problem, as well as several other limitations, by including a laundry list of routing features:

- It supports versions 1 and 2 of the Routing Information Protocol (RIP), as well as the Open Shortest Path First (OSPF) protocol. Third-party vendors also sell add-on products that allow RRAS to handle the Border Gateway Protocol (BGP), a complex protocol that is used in large routers that connect directly to the Internet backbone.

- It supports *unicast routing*, in which one machine sends directly to one destination address. It also supports *multicast routing*, in which one machine sends to an entire group within a network.

- It supports *network address translation (NAT),* a service that allows multiple LAN clients to share one public IP address and Internet connection.

- It allows *demand-dial routing*. Demand-dial routes normally bring up only the associated link when outbound traffic is addressed to a network on those routes, although you can configure them to persist. Demand-dialing allows the effective use of impermanent connection methods, such as analog modems and ISDN, to mimic a dedicated Internet connection.

Understanding How Routing Works

This chapter will continue to discuss routing theory and practice, confined to IP routing, even though the same concepts apply to IPX/SPX and AppleTalk routing. The basic idea is that each packet on a network has a source address and a destination address, which means that any device that receives the packet can inspect its headers to determine where the packet came from and where it's going. If such a device also has some information about the network's design and implementation—such as how long it takes packets to travel over a particular link—it can change the routing intelligently to minimize the total cost.

NOTE According to the OSI model, a gateway and a router are two different things functioning at different layers. Microsoft redefines the terms, however, using them interchangeably. You might learn them as synonymous terms for purposes of the exam.

Static Routing

Static routing systems don't make any attempt to discover other routers or systems on their networks. Instead, you tell the routing engine how to get data to other networks; specifically, you tell it what other networks are reachable from your network by specifying their network addresses and subnet masks, along with a metric for that network. This information goes into the system's *routing table*, a big list of routes that are known to other networks. When an outgoing packet arrives at the routing engine, the engine can examine the routing table to select the lowest-cost route to the destination. If no explicit entry for that network appears in the routing table, the packet goes to the default gateway, which then is entrusted with getting the packet where it needs to go.

Static routing is faster and more efficient than dynamic routing. Static routing works well when your network doesn't change much. You can identify the remote networks to which you want to route and add static routes to them to reflect the costs and topology of your network. In Windows 2000, you maintain static routes with the `route` command, which allows you to see the contents of the routing table or modify it by adding static routes to and removing static routes from individual networks.

Dynamic Routing

By contrast with static routing, dynamic routing doesn't depend on your adding fixed, unchangeable routes to remote networks. Instead, a *dynamic routing* engine can discover its surroundings by finding and communicating with other nearby routers in an internetwork.

This process, usually called *router discovery*, enables a new (or rebooted) router to configure itself. The two major dynamic-routing protocols in Windows 2000 are Routing Information Protocol (RIP) and the Open Shortest Path First (OSPF). Both protocols have advantages and disadvantages, but they have some common features and functionality.

Each router (a hardware device, a Windows 2000 machine, or whatever) is connected to at least two separate physical networks. When the router starts, the only information it has is drawn from its internal routing table. Normally, that means the router knows about all the attached networks, as well as whatever static routes have been previously defined. The router then receives configuration information that tells it about the state and topology of the network.

As time goes on, the network's physical topology can change. The process by which this adjustment happens is what makes routing dynamic, and it's also the largest area of difference between the two major dynamic-routing protocols for IP.

THE ROUTING INFORMATION PROTOCOL (RIP)

RIP is like NetBEUI in that it's simple and easy to configure but has performance limitations that restrict its usefulness on medium-size to large networks. RIP routers begin with a basically empty routing table, but they immediately begin sending out announcements that they know will reach the networks to which they're connected. These announcements can be broadcast or multicast. Routers on other networks that hear these announcements can add those routes to their own routing tables. The process works both ways, of course; the hypothetical router hears announcements from other routers and then adds those routes to its list of places it knows how to reach.

In addition to sending and receiving announcements, RIP 2 routers have the capability to receive triggered updates. When you know that your network topology is changing (perhaps because you've added connectivity to another network), you can send out a trigger that contains information about the changes. This trigger forces all the RIP routers you own to assimilate the changes immediately. Triggered updates also are useful because routers that detect a link or router failure can update their routing tables and announce the change, making their neighbors aware of it sooner rather than later.

Microsoft's RIP implementation supports both version 1 and version 2 of RIP. The primary difference between the two versions is the manner in which updates are sent: RIP 1 uses broadcasts every 30 seconds, and RIP 2 uses multicasts only when routes change.

Speaking of changes, you can use the RRAS snap-in to set up two kinds of filters that screen out some types of updates. *Route filters* allow you to choose which networks you want to admit knowing about and which ones you want to accept announcements from. *Peer filters* give you control of which neighboring routers your router listens to.

RIP also incorporates features that attempt to prevent routing loops. A *routing loop* occurs when routes in a set of routers point in a circle. RIP offers several methods for resolving and preventing loops, including the split-horizon and poison-reverse algorithms. Despite the cool names, knowing how these methods work is not important for passing the exam; it's enough to know what they're for and that RIP implements them to protect against routing loops.

THE OPEN SHORTEST PATH FIRST (OSPF) PROTOCOL

RIP is designed for fairly small networks: it can handle only 15 router-to-router hops. If you have a network that spans more than 16 routers at any point, RIP won't be able to cache routes for it; some parts of the network will appear to be (or actually will be) unreachable. The *Open Shortest Path First (OSPF)* protocol is designed for use on large or very large networks. OSPF is much more efficient than RIP, but it also requires more knowledge and experience to set up and administer.

RIP routers continually exchange routing data with one another, a system that allows incorrect route entries to propagate. Instead of doing that, each OSPF router maintains a map (table) of the grouped routers in the internetwork. This map, called a *link state map*, provides a continually updated reference on the state of each internetwork link. Neighboring routers group into an *adjacency* (think neighborhood or group); within an adjacency, routers synchronize any changes to the link state map. When the network topology changes, whichever router notices it first floods the internetwork with change notifications. Each router that receives the notification updates its copy of the link map and then recalculates its internal routing table.

The *SPF* in OSPF refers to the algorithm that OSPF systems use to calculate routes: routes are calculated so that the shortest path, the one with the lowest cost (the lowest cost is considered to be the shortest path, whether it is or not), is used first. SPF-calculated routes are always free of loops, which is another nice advantage over RIP.

Microsoft's OSPF implementation supports (but doesn't require) the use of *route filters*, so any Windows 2000 OSPF router can choose to accept routing information either from other OSPF routers or other types of routers. In addition, a desirable feature not always available in OSPF routers is that you can change any of the OSPF settings and have them take effect immediately without having to stop and restart the router.

Multiprotocol Routing

RRAS provides a multiprotocol router—which is a fancy way of saying that the RRAS routing engine can handle multiple network protocols and multiple routing methods on multiple NICs, all without breaking a sweat. RRAS provides some specific features that are of interest when the conversation turns to network routing. These features include the following:

- It can bring up connections to specific networks when the router receives packets addressed to those networks. This process is called *demand-dial routing*, and it allows you to use on-demand links instead of nailed-up connections. ISDN and PPTP connections can be demand-dialed or you can use demand-dial interfaces to make long-distance connections only when they're needed.

- You can establish *static routes* that specify where packets bound for certain networks should go. The most common use of this feature is to link a remote network with your LAN. The remote network gets one static route that basically says, "Any traffic leaving my subnet should be sent to the router." RRAS handles it from there.

- It provides *dynamic routing*, using versions 1 and 2 of the Routing Information Protocol (RIP) and the Open Shortest Path First (OSPF) protocol. These protocols provide two different ways for your router to share routing information with other routers near it in network space.

- It provides *packet filtering* to screen out undesirable packets in both directions.

UNDERSTANDING INTERNETWORKS

An *internetwork* is just a network of networks. The internetwork is the collection of all these networks, any of which could stand alone. (Don't confuse an internetwork with the Internet; the Internet that we all use is actually just a very large, very complex internetwork.)

As you study the configuration of routing protocols, you'll examine different configuration choices for routers and how these choices affect the overall performance and reliability of the internetwork.

UNDERSTANDING ROUTING TABLES

A *routing table* is a database that stores route information. Think of this table as being a road map for the internetwork. The routing table lists which routes exist between networks, so that the router or host can look up the necessary information when it encounters a packet bound for a foreign network. Each entry in the routing table contains the following four pieces of information:

- The network address of the remote host or network

- The forwarding address to which traffic for the remote network should be sent

- The network interface that should be used to send to the forwarding address

- A cost, or *metric*, that indicates what relative priority should be assigned to this route

The actual format in which these entries are stored isn't important (in fact, it's not visible in RRAS); what's important for you to know is that every routing table entry contains this information.

Routing tables can contain these three kinds of routes:

- *Network routes,* which provide a route to an entire network.

- *Host routes*, which provide a route to a single system. Think of these routes as shortcuts. They provide a slightly more efficient way for a router to "know" how to get traffic to a remote machine, so they're normally used when you want to direct traffic to remote networks through a particular machine.

- *Default route*, which is where packets go when there's no explicit route for them. This route is similar to the default gateway that you're used to configuring for TCP/IP clients. Any time a router encounters a packet bound for some remote network, it first searches the routing table; if it can't find a network or host route, it uses the default route instead. This setup saves you from having to configure a network or host route for every network.

UNDERSTANDING BORDER ROUTING

Border routing is what happens when packets leave your internetwork and go to another one someplace else. In a border-routing network, some routers are responsible for handling packets inside the area; others manage network communication with other areas or groups. These border routers are responsible for storing routes to other borders that they can reach over the backbone. Because this arrangement represents a huge number of potential routes, border routing normally uses dynamic routing protocols such as OSPF and RIP 2 to allow a border router in one adjacent area to discover routes in another.

UNDERSTANDING INTERNAL ROUTING

Internal routing is a generic term that refers to the process of moving packets around on your own internetwork. Internal routers can use static or dynamic routing techniques to build the routing table for their local area.

Router Protocols

Both RIP and OSPF are dynamic router-configuration protocols, but there are some subtle differences between the two.

RIP   A RIP-capable router periodically sends out announcements— "Here are the networks I know how to route to"—while simultaneously receiving announcements from its peers. This exchange of routing information makes each router able to learn what routers exist on the network and which destination networks each of them knows how to reach. Each route has an associated cost; the cost is the *sum* of the costs for each router in the route. RIP attempts to do least-cost routing by searching its routing table to find the lowest-cost route that will reach a particular destination. (If you really want hard-core details on the RIP protocol itself, see RFC 2453, the authoritative source on how RIP works.)

RIP has two operation modes. In *periodic update mode*, a RIP router sends out its list of known routes at periodic intervals (which you define). The router marks any routes that it learns from other routers as RIP routes, which means that these routes remain active only while the router is running. If the router is stopped, the routes vanish. This mode is the default for RIP on LAN interfaces, but it's not suitable for demand-dial connections, because you don't want your router bringing up a connection just to announce its presence.

In *auto-static mode*, the RRAS router broadcasts the contents of its routing table only when a remote router asks for it. Better still, the routes that the RRAS router learns from its RIP neighbors are marked as static routes in the routing table, and they persist until you delete them manually—even if the router is stopped and restarted or if RIP is disabled for that interface. Auto-static mode is the default for demand-dial interfaces. (The opposite of auto-static mode is periodic mode, in which the router sends out updates when it has something to share.)

OSPF   Like RIP, OSPF is designed to allow routers to share routing data dynamically. The actual process by which those routes are discovered and shared is dramatically different, however. OSPF networks are broken into areas; an area is a collection of interconnected networks. Think of an area as being a subsection of an internetwork. Areas are interconnected by backbones. Each OSPF router keeps a link-state database only for the areas to which it's connected. Special OSPF routers called *area border routers* interlink areas.

Installing RRAS

Now that you've reviewed the basics of IP routing, you're ready to look at the main exam objectives. The RRAS components are installed on computers running Windows 2000 Server and Advanced Server, whether or not you choose to activate them. Before your server can route IP packets, you have to activate and configure RRAS. This process normally is handled through the RRAS Server Setup wizard. The "Necessary Procedures" section later in this chapter leads you through the process of installing the Routing and Remote Access Service. The two other members of the objective triumvirate are configuring and troubleshooting.

Configuring IP Routing

When the summary page of the RRAS setup wizard appears, it reminds you to do either two or three of the following things:

- Add demand-dial interfaces if you want to support demand dialing.

- Give each routable interface a network address for each protocol it carries. If you're using TCP/IP and IPX on a computer with three NICs, for example, each NIC that participates in routing needs to have distinct TCP/IP and IPX addresses.

- Install and configure the routing protocols (such as OSPF or RIP for IP, in this case) on the interfaces that should support them.

These three steps form the core of what you must do to make your RRAS server into an IP router. You begin by examining how RRAS treats interfaces.

Setting IP Routing Properties

The IP Routing node in the RRAS console has several subnodes, including the General node. When you select the General node and choose the Properties command, you see settings that apply to all installed IP routing protocols on the server. These settings aren't earth-shattering in and of themselves, but they give you some additional control of how routing works.

THE GENERAL TAB

First up is the General tab, which probably should be called the Logging tab, because that's all it contains. You use four radio buttons to control what information the IP routing components of RRAS log. These buttons are:

- Log Errors Only, which instructs the server to log IP routing-related errors and nothing else. This option gives you adequate indication of problems *after* they happen, but it doesn't point out potential problems noted by warning messages.

- Log Errors and Warnings (the default), which instructs RRAS to log error and warning messages to the event log without adding informational messages. If you get into the habit of reviewing your event logs carefully, these warning messages may give you welcome fore-warning of incipient problems.

- Log the Maximum Amount of Information, which causes the IP routing stack to log messages about almost everything it does. This option gives you a great deal of useful fodder when you're trouble-shooting, but it can flood your logs with minutiae if you're not careful; don't turn it on unless you're trying to isolate and fix a problem.

- Disable Event Logging, which turns off all IP routing event log-ging. Don't choose this option without a good reason, because it will keep you from being able to review the service's logs in case of a problem.

THE PREFERENCE LEVELS TAB

The Preference Levels tab gives you a way to tweak the router's behavior by telling it what class of routes to prefer. In the discussion of routing earlier in this chapter, you read that the router selects routes based on cost metric information. That's true, but another fac-tor comes into play: the preference level of the routing source. The default configuration for RRAS causes it to prefer local and static routes to dynamically discovered routes. You can change the router's class preference by selecting the class that you want to tweak and then clicking the Move Up and Move Down buttons.

NOTE   The Multicast Scopes tab is for setting and managing multicast scopes.

Using the *route print* Command

The route add command is used to add a new static route from the command line. The route print command, however, can show you all or part of the routing table from the command line. Just typing **route print** in a command window gives you a dump of the entire routing table. (Adding a wildcard IP address, as in **route print 206.151.***, displays only routes that match 206.151.)

Troubleshooting

A comprehensive overview of IP-routing troubleshooting could easily fill a book this length—or two. Microsoft's online help system is fairly good at suggesting probable causes and solutions for most routing problems, and you have to know only the most blatant problems (and their solutions) for the exam. To wit, when you suspect that your RRAS server isn't routing traffic properly, begin by verifying the following:

- The RRAS service is running and configured to act as an IP router.

- The router's TCP/IP configuration is correct (including a static IP address).

- You have IP routing protocols attached to each interface where you need them.

Next, you need to verify the following routing-specific settings and behaviors:

- If you're using OSPF, make sure that the Enable OSPF on This Interface check box is turned on in the interface's OSPF Properties dialog box.

- Make sure that your router is receiving routes from its peers by opening the routing table and looking at the Protocol column. Entries marked as OSPF or RIP tell you that at least some peers are getting routing information through. If you don't see any RIP or OSPF routes, that's a bad sign.

- You need to have a static default route enabled if you want your router to forward routes that it doesn't understand to a specific connection. To do so, add a new static route with a destination of 0.0.0.0, a net mask of 0.0.0.0, and either a demand-dial or LAN interface as appropriate for your network setup. You can send any IP address that is not within your internetwork to the Internet, for example.

Updating with Static Routes

When you use static routes, there's some good news and some bad news. The good news is that they're simple to manage and configure, because they don't participate in any kind of automatic discovery process. Static routes are conceptually simple; they combine a destination network address with a subnet mask to provide a list of potential destinations. The destination addresses are reached through a particular interface on your router, and they're sent to a specified gateway. Finally, a metric is associated with the static route.

You create new static routes in two ways: by using the route add command from the command line or by right-clicking the Static Routes node in the RRAS console and then choosing the New Static Route command.

Using *route add*

The route add command allows you to add new static routes; you can specify whether these routes remain in the routing table after the system reboots. Routes that stick around in this manner are called *persistent routes*. The command itself is simple:

```
route add destination mask netMask gateWay metric
interface
```

You specify the destination, net mask, gateway, metric, and interface name in the command line. All these parameters are required, and route add does some basic sanity checking to make sure that the net mask and destination match and that you haven't left out anything. One speed bump: you have to specify the interface as a number, not as a name. Luckily, the route print command lists its interfaces and the associated numbers.

Using RRAS

When you create a new static route by using the RRAS console, all you have to do is choose the New Static Route command; you see the Static Route dialog box. You have to provide the same parameters as with the route add command—the interface that you want to use to connect, the destination and network mask, the gateway for the outbound packets, and a metric. If you're creating a route that's not bound to a LAN interface, you can check the Use This Route to Initiate Demand-Dial Connections check box to specify that the route should bring up a new demand-dial connection on the specified interface.

Creating and Managing Interfaces

The Routing Interfaces node in the RRAS snap-in shows a summary of the routable interfaces available on your machine for *all* protocols. It lists all the LAN and demand-dial interfaces, plus two special interfaces maintained by RRAS: Loopback and Internal. Each of the interfaces displayed has a type, a status (either enabled or disabled), and a connection status associated with it.

You can right-click each of the interfaces to get a context menu that contains some useful commands, including Disable, Enable, and the ever-popular Unreachability Reason (which tells you why an interface is marked as "unreachable").

Managing LAN Interfaces

Each LAN interface has properties of its own. These interfaces, which appear when you select the General node below the IP Routing node in RRAS, correspond to the LAN interfaces you defined in RRAS. These interfaces allow you to set general properties for the interface; when you add specific routing protocols to the interface, you can configure those protocols individually. To see the properties for an interface, just select the General node in the console, select the interface of interest in the right pane, and choose the Action ➤ Properties command.

The General Tab

The General tab allows you to set some useful parameters for the entire interface, including whether this interface will send out router discovery advertisements so that other routers on your network can find it.

The controls in the General tab are:

- The Enable IP Router Manager check box, which controls whether this interface allows IP routing. When this check box is checked, the administrative status of this interface appears as "up," indicating that it's available for routing traffic. When the check box is unchecked, the interface is marked as "down," and it won't route any packets; neither will other routers be able to communicate with it.

- The Enable Router Discovery Advertisements check box, which controls whether this router broadcasts *router discovery messages*. These messages allow clients to find a nearby router without any manual configuration on your part. When this check box is enabled, the controls below it become active, so you can set the following options:

  - How long advertisements are valid, as in the Advertisement Lifetime (Minutes) field. Clients ignore any advertisement that they receive after its lifetime expires.

  - What preference level is assigned to the use of this particular router. Clients use routers with higher preferences first; if multiple routers have equal preference levels, the client can randomly select one.

  - The minimum and maximum time intervals for sending advertisements. RRAS sends out advertisements at a randomly chosen interval that falls between the minimum and maximum; under the default settings, RRAS sends an advertisement every seven to 10 minutes.

- The Input Filters and Output Filters buttons, which allow you to selectively accept or reject packets in the specified interface. You can accept all packets that don't trigger a filter or accept only those packets that match filter criteria. Each type of filter can use the source or destination IP address and net mask as filter criteria.

- The Enable Fragmentation Checking check box, which tells your router to reject any fragmented IP packets instead of accepting them for processing. Because flooding a router with fragmented IP packets is a popular denial-of-service attack, you may want to check this check box.

The Configuration Tab

The Configuration tab may seem to be out of place in the Interface Properties dialog box, because it essentially duplicates what you see when you edit the properties of a LAN interface from the Network and Dial-Up Connections folder. You use this tab to set the IP address, subnet mask, and default gateway for an interface if you want it to use a different set of parameters from the ones defined for the interface. The Advanced button allows you to specify multiple IP addresses and default gateways, just as the TCP/IP Properties dialog box does.

NOTE The Interface Properties dialog box has two other tabs, but they're related to multicasting, which is beyond the scope of this exam.

Implementing Demand-Dial Routing

When you install RRAS, it automatically creates an interface for each LAN connection it can find. You're on your own, however, if you want to create new demand-dial interfaces. Fortunately, you can create these interfaces easily with the Demand Dial Interface wizard, which you activate with the New Demand-Dial Interface command (available when you right-click the Routing Interfaces node in the RRAS console).

Naming the Interface

The first step in the wizard is the Interface Name page, where you specify the name you want the new interface to have. This is the name you'll see in the RRAS console, so you should choose some name that identifies the source and destination of the connection. This naming is particularly useful when you want to use one RRAS console somewhere in a network to manage many RRAS servers; having an easy way to see which link you're working with can be very valuable.

Choosing a Connection Type

Demand-dial interfaces can use a physical device (such as a modem or an ISDN adapter) or a virtual private networking (VPN) connection. You can have a demand-dial connection that opens a VPN tunnel to a remote network when it sees traffic destined for that network. Depending on which option you choose here, the remaining wizard pages will differ.

Connecting with a Physical Device

Assuming that you choose to use a physical device as the basis for your network, the next step in the wizard prompts you to choose a device (such as a modem or ISDN terminal adapter) to use for this demand-dial interface. If the device that you want to use doesn't already exist, you need to add it; for that reason, you're probably best off adding and configuring modems and so on before setting up RRAS.

Connecting Via a VPN

If you specify that you want to use a VPN connection, the next step is to specify what type of VPN connection to use. You do so through the VPN Type page, which offers the following three choices:

- The Automatic radio button, which tells RRAS to figure out the connection type when negotiating with the remote server. This option is the most flexible choice, so it's selected by default.

- The Point-to-Point Tunneling Protocol (PPTP) radio button, which tells RRAS that this connection will always use PPTP.

- The Layer 2 Tunneling Protocol (L2TP) radio button, which indicates that you want this connection to always use L2TP.

The next step is the same for both VPN and physical connections, even though the wizard pages are labeled differently. For VPNs, you see a page titled Network Address; for ordinary dial-up connections, the page is labeled Phone Number. In either case, you should enter the phone number or IP address (whichever is appropriate) of the remote router.

Setting Routing and Security Options

The next step for both types of router connection is the Protocols and Security page, which contains several configuration check boxes:

- The Route IP Packets on This Interface and Route IPX Packets on This Interface check boxes control whether this interface will handle the specified packet types. By default, IP routing is enabled, but IPX routing isn't.

- If you want to add a user account so that a remote router (running RRAS or not) can dial in, check the Add a User Account So a Remote Router Can Dial In check box. When this check box is active, you also can choose to require the remote router to authenticate itself (using the same credentials) when you call it—just check the Authenticate Remote Router When Dialing Out check box.

- Some routers can handle PAP, CHAP, or MS-CHAP authentication, but others can handle only PAP. If your remote partner falls into the latter group, make sure that Send a Plain-Text Password If That Is the Only Way to Connect check box is checked.

- If the system that your RRAS server is calling isn't running RRAS, it may expect you to interact with it manually, perhaps through a terminal window. This is the purpose of the last check box, Use Scripting to Complete the Connection with the Remote Server. Check this check box, and you get a terminal window after the modem connects so that you can provide whatever commands or authenticators you need.

Setting Dial-In Credentials

If you choose to allow remote routers to dial in to the RRAS machine you're setting up, you have to create a user account with appropriate permissions. The Demand Dial Interface wizard handles the account-creation process for you, assuming that you fill out the Dial-In Credentials page. Microsoft recommends that you pick a username that makes evident which routers use the link. You can use the International Civil Aviation Organization (ICAO) airport identifiers, city names, or whatever else you like, so long as you can figure out what is what and where.

Setting Dial-Out Credentials

If you want your router to initiate calls to another router, you need to tell your local RRAS installation what credentials to use when it makes an outgoing call. Unlike the Dial-In Credentials page, RRAS makes no attempt to do anything with the credentials you provide in this page. (Actually, it checks the two password fields to make sure that you typed the same password in each one, but that's it.) The credentials you provide here must match the credentials that the remote router expects to see; otherwise, your router won't be able to authenticate itself to the remote end.

Creating and Removing RIP and OSPF Interfaces

After you create the physical interfaces (using either demand-dial or LAN interfaces), the next thing you have to do is create an interface for the routing protocol you want to use. You do so by right-clicking either the RIP or OSPF node in the RRAS console and then choosing the New Interface command. That command displays the New Interface dialog box, which simply lists all the physical interfaces that are available for the selected protocol. If you have two NICs in a computer and have already bound RIP to both of them, you can add OSPF to either or both, but when you try to add another RIP interface, you get an error message.

When you select the interface that you want to use, and if RRAS can create the interface, it adds the interface to the appropriate item in the console and opens the corresponding Properties dialog box.

You can remove a RIP or OSPF interface by selecting it in the appropriate folder and then pressing the Delete key, by choosing the Action ➤ Delete command, or by choosing the Delete command from the context menu.

Setting RIP Interface Properties

RIP interfaces have their own properties, all of which are specific to the RIP protocol. You adjust these settings by selecting the RIP interface and choosing the familiar Properties command from the context or Action menu.

THE GENERAL TAB

The General tab of the RIP Interface Properties dialog box allows you to control the router's operational mode, which protocols it uses to send and accept packets, and a couple of other useful things.

Here's what you can do with the General tab:

- The Operation Mode pull-down menu controls the router's mode. By default, demand-dial interfaces are set to auto-static update mode, whereas LAN interfaces are set to use periodic update mode.

- The Outgoing Packet Protocol pull-down menu controls what kind of RIP packets this router sends out. If your network has all RIP version 2 routers, choose RIP Version 2 Multicast to make RRAS send out efficient RIP multicasts. If you have version 1 routers or a mix of version 1 and version 2, there are options for those routers, too. The fourth choice, Silent RIP, is useful when you want your RRAS router to listen to other routers' routes but not advertise any of its own. Typically, you use Silent RIP when you're using RRAS to connect a small network (such as a branch office) that doesn't have any other routers to a larger network.

- Use the Incoming Packet Protocol pull-down menu to specify what kinds of RIP packets this interface accepts. You can choose to accept only RIP version 1 packets, only RIP version 2 packets, both version 1 and version 2 packets, or none. The default setting accepts both version 1 and version 2 packets.

- The Added Cost to Routes field allows you to control how much this router will increase the route cost. Normally, it's best to leave this option set to 1, because setting it too high may increase the interface's cost so much that no one will use it (unless, of course, that's what you want to happen).

- The Tag for Announced Routes field gives you a way to supply a tag included in all RIP packets sent by this router. RRAS doesn't use RIP tags, but other routers can use them.

- The Activate Authentication check box and Password field give you an identification tool to use with your routers. If you turn on authentication, all incoming and outgoing RIP packets must contain the specified password. Therefore, all this router's neighbors need to use the same password. The password is transmitted as clear text, so this option doesn't provide any security.

THE SECURITY TAB

The Security tab helps you regulate which routes your RIP interface accepts from and broadcasts to its peers. There are good reasons to be careful about which routes you accept into your routing table; a malicious attacker can simply flood your router with bogus routes and watch as your routers send traffic off on a wild goose chase. Likewise, you may not want to advertise every route in your routing table, particularly if the same routers handle both Internet and intranet traffic. You can use the controls in this tab to discard routes that fall within a particular range of addresses, or you can accept only those routes that fall within a particular range.

The default setting accepts all routes, but you can change the security setup by using these controls:

- The Action pull-down menu allows you to specify whether you want to impose settings on incoming routes that your router hears from its peers or on outgoing routes that it announces. Depending on which of these options you choose, the labels of the three radio buttons below the pull-down menu change.

- The From and To fields; the Add, Edit, and Remove buttons; and the address range list are all used to specify which set of addresses you want to use with the restriction radio buttons.

- The restriction radio buttons in the center of the dialog box control the actions applied to incoming or outgoing routes:

  - The default setting, Announce All Routes (outgoing) or Process All Routes (incoming) does just that. All routes are accepted or announced, no matter the source.

  - Choosing Announce All Routes in the Ranges Listed (outgoing) or Accept All Routes in the Range Listed (incoming) causes RRAS to ignore any routes that fall outside the specified ranges. You normally use this option when you want to limit the range of routes over which your router can exchange traffic.

- The Do Not Announce All Routes in the Range Listed (outgoing) and Ignore All Routes in the Ranges Listed (incoming) settings tells RRAS to ignore any routes that fall within the specified ranges. This option is useful for filtering out routes that you don't want to make available or those that you don't want to use to reach remote systems.

THE NEIGHBORS TAB

The Neighbors tab gives you a finer degree of control of how this particular interface interacts with its peer RIP routers. By specifying a list of trusted neighbor routers (an OSPF concept that Microsoft mixed into its RIP implementation), you can choose to use neighboring routers' routes in addition to, or instead of, broadcast and multicast RIP announcements.

You see the following radio buttons in the Neighbors tab:

- Use Broadcast or Multicast Only, which tells RRAS to ignore any RIP neighbors. This option is the default setting. When this option is enabled, any router that can successfully broadcast or multicast routes to you can load its routes into your routing table.

- Use Neighbors in Addition to Broadcast or Multicast, which tells RRAS to accept routes from RIP peers as well as from the neighbors you specified.

- Use Neighbors Instead of Broadcast or Multicast, which indicates that you don't trust RIP announcements that your router picks up from the Internet; instead, you're telling RRAS to trust only those neighbors that are defined in the neighbor list.

Speaking of the neighbor list, you manage the list of trusted neighbor routers by using the IP address field; the Add, Edit, and Remove buttons; and the list itself. These controls are enabled when you specify that you want to use neighbor-supplied routing information; when the controls are activated, you can add router IP addresses to the neighbor list.

THE ADVANCED TAB

The Advanced tab contains 12 controls that govern some fairly esoteric RIP behavior. But you need to know what these controls do and how they work for the exam, so read on.

The first three controls are active only when you turn on periodic update mode in the General tab. These controls are:

- The Periodic Announcement Interval (Seconds) field, which controls the interval at which periodic router announcements are made.

- The Time Before Routes Expire (Seconds) field, which controls how long the route stays in the routing table before it's considered to be expired. The arrival of a new RIP announcement for the route resets the timer; it is marked as invalid only if it reaches the expiration timer without being renewed through a new announcement.

- The Time Before Route Is Removed (Seconds) field, which controls the interval between the time when a route expires and the time when it's removed.

The next group of check boxes control update processing and loop detection:

- The Enable Split-Horizon Processing check box turns on split-horizon processing, in which a route learned by a RIP router on a network is not rebroadcast to that network. Split-horizon processing helps prevent routing loops, so it's enabled by default.

- The Enable Poison-Reverse Processing check box (which is active only when the Enable Split-Horizon Processing check box is checked) modifies the way that split-horizon processing works. When poison reverse is turned on, routes learned from a network are rebroadcast to the network with a metric of 16, a special value that tells other routers that the route is unreachable. This option also prevents routing loops while keeping the routing tables up to date.

- The Enable Triggered Updates check box indicates whether you want routing-table changes to be sent out immediately when they're noticed (the default). Triggered updates help keep the routing table up to date with minimum latency.

- The Send Clean-Up Updates When Stopping check box controls whether RRAS sends out announcements that mark the routes it was handling as unavailable. This option lets RIP peers know immediately that the routes it was servicing are no longer usable.

The last set of controls govern what happens with host and default routes:

- By default, RRAS ignores any host routes it sees in RIP announcements. Check the Process Host Routes in Received Announcements check box if you want RRAS to honor those routes instead of ignoring them.

- The Include Host Routes in Sent Announcements check box directs RRAS to send host route information as part of its RIP announcements; normally, it doesn't.

- The Process Default Routes in Received Announcements and Include Default Routes in Sent Announcements check boxes have the same function as their host-route counterparts.

- The Disable Subnet Summarization check box is active only if you have RIP version 2 specified as the outbound packet type for the router. When subnet summarization is turned off, RIP won't advertise subnets to routers that are on other subnets.

Necessary Procedures

You need to practice the following procedures to install RRAS, to add and remove static routes and to create a demand-dial interface:

Installing an RRAS Remote-Access Server

Follow these steps to install an RRAS remote-access server:

1. Open the RRAS MMC console (Start ➢ Programs ➢ Administrative Tools ➢ Routing and Remote Access).

2. In the left pane of the MMC, select the server that you want to configure. Right-click the server; then choose the Configure and

Enable Routing and Remote Access command. The RRAS setup wizard appears. Click the Next button.

3. In the Common Configurations page of the wizard, make sure that the Network Router radio button is selected; then click the Next button. The Remote Client Protocols page appears, listing the protocols that currently are installed on your RRAS server.

4. If this list contains all the protocols you want to route, leave the Yes, All of the Required Protocols Are on the List button selected. If you need to add or remove protocols, click the No, I Need to Add Protocols button. Click the Next button. If you specified that you need to tweak the protocol list, the wizard stops at this point. Otherwise, the Demand-Dial Connections page appears.

5. The Demand-Dial Connections page is there only to ask whether you want to use demand-dialed connections; you still have to set up the connections (either manually or by using the Demand-Dial wizard) after you complete the RRAS Setup wizard. If you choose to use demand-dial connections, the wizard automatically sets up your RRAS installation so that it can take incoming demand-dial calls as well. In that case, congratulations—you've just built a remote-access server.

6. If you chose *not* to use demand-dial connections, click the Next button; you see the wizard summary page. The remaining steps apply only if you indicate that you want to use demand-dial interfaces.

7. If you chose to use demand-dial connections, the next page you see is the IP Address Assignment page, which controls how RRAS assigns IP addresses to incoming demand-dial calls. If you want to use DHCP (either a DHCP server on your network or the built-in address allocator), leave the Automatically radio button selected. If you want to choose an address range, select the From a Specified Range of Addresses button. Then click the Next button.

8. If you chose to pass out IP addresses manually, the next page that appears is the Address Range Assignment page. You use this page to specify which IP address ranges you want to hand out to incoming calls (whether demand-dial or from remote-access users). Use

the New, Edit, and Delete buttons to specify the address ranges you want to use.

Adding and Removing Static Routes

Follow these steps to add and then remove a static route (you remove it only to make sure that it doesn't interfere with any other machines on your network):

1. Open the RRAS MMC console (Start ➤ Programs ➤ Administrative Tools ➤ Routing and Remote Access).

2. In the left pane of the MMC, select the server that you want to configure. Expand it until you see the Static Routes node below IP Routing.

3. Right-click the Static Routes node; then choose the New Static Route command. The Static Route dialog box appears.

4. Choose the interface you want to use from the Interface pull-down menu. You can use the internal interface or any other interface you've already defined.

5. Enter the destination address and a subnet mask.

6. For the gateway address, enter the IP address of your RRAS server.

7. Click the OK button. The RRAS console reappears.

8. Right-click the Static Routes item; then choose the Show IP Routing Table command. The IP Routing Table window appears. Verify that your new static route is present in the table.

9. Select the Static Routes item. Notice that the right pane of the MMC changes to list all static routes that you've defined. Compare the list with the contents of the IP Routing Table window.

10. Right-click the static route that you added; then choose the Delete command to remove it.

Creating a Demand-Dial Interface

In this exercise, you create a simple demand-dial interface. This exercise requires you to have the phone number, username, and password for the remote end (your ISP or whomever you're calling).

1. Open the RRAS MMC console, select the server on which you want to create the interface, and select its Routing Interfaces node.

2. Right-click the Routing Interfaces node; then choose the New Demand Dial Interface command. This command starts the Demand Dial Interface wizard. Click the Next button in the first wizard page (and after each of the subsequent steps).

3. In the Interface Name page, specify a name for the interface.

4. In the Connection Type page, select the Connect Using a Modem, ISDN Adapter, or Other Physical Device radio button.

5. In the Protocols and Security page, make sure that the Route IP Packets on This Interface check box is the only one checked.

6. In the Dial Out Credentials page, fill in the username, domain (if any), and password needed to connect to the remote network.

7. When the wizard summary page appears, click the Finish button to create the interface.

Exam Essentials

Know IP addressing.   Understand the three IP address formats: hexadecimal, binary, and dotted-decimal. Be clear about the hierarchical nature of IP addresses and how the network and node information is contained in the different address classes.

Know how to calculate the subnet addresses for the different classes of IP addresses.   Understand information hiding and how to figure subnet masks for each class. This procedure is described in *MCSE: Windows 2000 Network Infrastructure Administration Study Guide* by Paul Robichaux (Sybex 2000).

Know that Windows 2000 supports routing IPX and AppleTalk, as well as the IP routing that you have studied for these objectives. Understand that the same basic procedures you learn with IP will work on these other protocols, with minor differences in configuration details.

Know how routing protocols use the metric or cost to choose the best routes. Understand the different parameters that go into choosing metrics for different routes.

Know the difference between static and dynamic routing. Be familiar with the various configurable parameters that enable dynamic and static routing, as well as the protocols you would use for each.

Know the requirements and steps involved in demand-dial routing. Understand that you can control costs such as metered ISDNs and long-distance connection time with demand-dial connections.

Know that RRAS supports packet filtering to screen out undesirable packets in both directions. Understand the two principal packet-filtering methods.

Know what a routing table contains and the different types of routes that are possible. Understand network, host, and default routes.

Know how to install and configure RRAS. Understand how to set the properties that affect all IP routing protocols on the server.

Know the principal steps in basic IP routing troubleshooting. Understand at least the basics in this large field.

Know how the Static Routes node in the RRAS console and the *route add* and *route print* commands help you update a Windows 2000-based routing table by means of static routes. Understand that static routes that remain after booting are called persistent routes.

Know how to manage routing interfaces by configuring the RRAS console node. Understand that these interfaces, which appear when you select the General node below the IP Routing node in RRAS, correspond to the LAN interfaces you defined in RRAS.

Know how to implement demand-dial routing. Understand that you can create these demand-dial interfaces, which are necessary for routing, easily with the Demand Dial Interface wizard. You activate this wizard by choosing the New Demand-Dial Interface command.

Key Terms and Concepts

adjacency   A neighborhood of adjacent routers that synchronizes any changes to the link-state map.

area   A contiguous group of network resources that contains one or more physical subnets.

area border router   A special *OSPF* router that connects adjacent *areas.*

area router   An OSPF router that is restricted to routing traffic between machines inside a single area.

auto-static update mode   An *RIP* update mode in which the RIP router broadcasts the contents of its *routing table* only when a peer router asks for it. (See also *periodic update mode.*)

backbone   A connecting trunk allowing all areas to connect to any other area; this task can be accomplished with tunnels. A *tunnel* is a private virtual circuit between a client and a server that uses the Internet as a transportation medium.

Border Gateway Protocol (BGP)   A complex protocol that is used in large routers that connect directly to the Internet backbone.

border routing   A process of passing packets from one *internetwork* to another.

default response rule   An IP filtering rule that governs what the IP filtering stack does when no more-explicit filter rule applies.

default route   The route that packets take when no explicit route exists. If a router encounters a packet bound for some remote network whose route cannot be resolved in the routing table, it takes the default route.

default subnet mask   A way of saying that networks don't have a subnet address. Not all networks need to have subnets and, therefore, don't need to use subnet masks. In this event, they are said to have a *default subnet mask*.

demand-dial interface   A network interface that routes packets over a connection that's established only when there is traffic to pass over it. The *interface* is the functionally connecting place and method. These interfaces are usually built with dial-up connections.

demand-dial routing   Routing accomplished by the use of an impermanent connection, such as an analog modem or ISDN, to imitate a dedicated Internet connection.

dynamic routing   Routing that can discover its surroundings by finding and communicating with other nearby routers.

hierarchical address   An addressing scheme in which different fields address different information, accommodating growth and leading to hierarchical routing, which makes internetworking much more efficient.

host route   A route provided to a single system; normally used when you want to direct traffic to remote networks through a particular machine.

inbound port mapping   A mapping that controls where requests from outside your network should be routed.

information hiding   The use of subnetting that hides one network and various routes from an internetwork.

internal routing   The process of moving packets around on your own internetwork.

internetwork   A network made up of multiple network segments that are connected by some device, such as a router. Each network segment is assigned a network address. Network-layer protocols build routing tables that are used to route packets through the network in the most efficient manner.

IP address   A four-byte number that uniquely identifies a computer on an IP *internetwork*. InterNIC assigns the first bytes of Internet IP addresses and administers them in hierarchies. Huge organizations such as the government and top-level ISPs have Class A addresses, large organizations and most ISPs have Class B addresses, and small companies have Class C addresses. In a Class A address, InterNIC assigns the first byte, and the owning organization assigns the remaining three bytes. In a Class B address, InterNIC or the higher-level ISP assigns the first two bytes, and the organization assigns the remaining two bytes. In a Class C address, InterNIC or the higher-level ISP assigns the first three bytes, and the organization assigns the remaining byte. Organizations not attached to the Internet are free to assign IP addresses as they please.

metric   The cost information used to calculate the most efficient route for packets to take.

multicast routing   A process in which one machine sends to an entire network or group within a network.

multiprotocol routing   Routing that allows a Windows 2000 computer to accept packets from other computers on its local network, sort out the correct destinations, and route the packets accordingly.

node address   A place descriptor for every network node that must have a unique IP address or subnet address.

Open Shortest Path First (OSPF)   A protocol designed for use in large or very large networks; it's more efficient but harder to set up and administer. The routes are calculated so that the shortest path (the one with the lowest cost) is used first.

packet filtering   A method of *eliminating* packets. You can use the RRAS snap-in to set up two kinds of filters—*route filters* and *peer filters*—that screen out some types of updates.

peer filters   Packet filters that give you control of which neighboring routers your routers listen to.

periodic update mode   An *RIP* update mode in which *routing table* updates are sent automatically to all other RIP routers in the *internetwork*. (See also *auto-static update mode*.)

route filters   Packet filters that allow you to choose which networks you want to admit knowing and which ones you want to accept announcements from.

routing loop   A circuitous path or routing loop occurs when routes in a set of routers point in a circle, trapping packets in an endless circle.

router   A network-layer device that moves packets between networks. Routers provide *internetwork* connectivity.

Routing and Remote Access Service (RRAS)   A Windows 2000 component that provides multiprotocol routing and dial-up access.

Routing Information Protocol (RIP)   An IP routing protocol that allows routers to exchange information about the presence and capabilities of other routers on the network. (See also *OSPF.*)

routing table   A table of information maintained by an IP router. Each entry in the table contains a destination network ID, gateway address, and *metric*.

static route   A specification of where packets bound for certain networks should go.

static routing   A fixed route that doesn't make any attempt to discover other routers or systems on the networks.

subnet addressing   An extension of the IP addressing scheme that allows a site to use a single IP network address for multiple physical networks. Outside the site using subnet addressing, routing continues as normal by dividing the destination address into a network portion and local portion. Routers and hosts inside a site using subnet addressing interpret the local portion of the address by dividing it into a physical-network portion and a host portion.

subnet mask   A number mathematically applied to *IP addresses* to determine which IP addresses are part of the same subnetwork as the computer applying the subnet mask.

unicast routing   A system in which one machine sends directly to one destination address.

Sample Questions

1. Wiley is setting up a RRAS router at a remote site so that it can connect back to the corporate LAN. He needs which of the following interfaces?

   A. A demand-dial interface for connecting the remote and LAN routers

   B. RIP or OSPF for routing discovery

   C. A and B

   D. None of the above

   Answer: A. RIP and OSPF are optional; you can use static routes on a remote dial-up router to avoid fooling with dynamic routing protocols.

2. Julia set up a new RRAS router that seems to be functioning properly, but it isn't routing traffic. She's already verified that RRAS is running and properly configured. Which of the following are possible causes of the problem? (Choose all that apply.)

   A. No routes are being learned from peer routers.

   B. The router is not being authenticated.

   C. No RIP neighbors are defined.

   D. No static default route exists.

   Answer: A, D. RIP neighbors are optional. If no routes are arriving, or if there's no static default route, the router may not be able to route traffic.

Manage and monitor IP routing.

- **Manage and monitor border routing.**
- **Manage and monitor internal routing.**
- **Manage and monitor IP routing protocols.**

The second IP routing exam objective deals with the familiar secondary categories of managing and monitoring IP routing. In addition, you learn about managing and monitoring border routing, as well as internal routing. Managing and monitoring the protocols makes up the final subobjective for this section.

Much of the explanatory text and some of the previous procedures could be used to manage the IP routing on your network. Additional information and procedures are covered in the following sections.

Critical Information

Managing IP routing is fairly simple: if you understand how the options described earlier in this chapter work, you know about 75 percent of what you need to know to keep IP routing working smoothly. All the remaining skills you need center on monitoring your routers to make sure that traffic is flowing smoothly and troubleshooting the occasional problem.

Monitoring IP Routing Status

Several status displays are built into the RRAS console. Knowing that these displays exist and what they display makes it much easier to see all the health and status data that RRAS maintains. Each command shows something different.

General ➤ Show TCP/IP Information   As you would expect, this command shows a broad general selection of IP routing data, including the number of routes in the route table, the number of IP and UDP datagrams received and forwarded, and the number of connection attempts. You can use the Select Columns command (right-click the TCP/IP Information window) to customize what you see in this view.

Static Routes ➤ Show IP Routing Table   This command shows the entire contents of the routing table, including the destination, net mask, and gateway for each route. This version of the routing table doesn't show where the route came from (whether it was learned by RIP or OSPF).

RIP ➤ Show Neighbors   This command shows you which RIP neighbors exist. For each router, you can see how many bad packets and bad routes that neighbor has tried to foist off on your router.

OSPF ➤ Show Areas   This command shows a list of all the defined areas. (Keep in mind that there is only one defined area per interface.) For each area, you can see whether that area is up or not, as well as the number of shortest-path computations performed on the link.

OSPF ➤ Show Link-State Database   This command presents a view of the entire contents of the link-state database, which is far outside the scope of this book. If you want to know more about the format of the link-state database and what its fields mean, see *CCNP: Advanced Cisco Router Configuration Study Guide* by Todd Lammle, Kevin Hales, and Donald Porter (Sybex 1999).

OSPF ➤ Show Neighbors   This command shows everything RRAS knows about the OSPF neighbors of this router, including the type of neighbor (point-to-point, broadcast, or NBMA), the neighbor's state, and its router ID.

OSPF ➤ Show Virtual Interfaces   This command shows a list of virtual interfaces for this OSPF router. Unless you have a fairly complicated OSPF network, this list is likely to be blank.

Setting OSPF Interface Properties

OSPF has its own set of properties that you can set on OSPF-enabled interfaces. These properties are both simpler and more complex than RIP; there aren't as many of them, because OSPF is largely self-tuning, but the properties that you *can* set tend to be somewhat more obscure.

The General Tab

The General tab of the OSPF Properties dialog box controls, among other things, whether OSPF is enabled on a particular interface address.

Here's what you can do with the controls in the General tab:

- The Enable OSPF for This Address check box, combined with the address pull-down menu, specifies whether OSPF is active on the *selected* address. Because a single interface can have multiple IP addresses, you use this check box and pull-down menu to specify which IP addresses are OSPF-capable. The settings you make in the OSPF Properties dialog box apply to the IP address you select here.

- The Area ID pull-down menu allows you to select the OSPF area of which this interface is part. There's a simple rule: one IP address can be in one area. If you have multiple IP addresses defined, however, each address can be in a separate area.

- The Router Priority field controls the priority of this interface relative to other OSPF routers in the same area. OSPF supports the concept of a designated router in an area; that router serves as the default router for the area it's in. The router with the highest priority becomes the designated router unless there is an existing designated router when this router is installed.

- The Cost field controls the metric attached to this router's routes in the link-state database.

- The Password field works just as it does for RIP; all routers within an area can share a common plain-text password for identification. This feature does nothing for access control (especially because the default password is the easy-to-guess 12345678).

The Network Type controls influence how this router interacts with its peers, but to understand what these controls do, you have to know some more buzzwords. A *broadcast router* is one that can talk to any number of other routers—such as a typical LAN router, which can see any number of other routers on the LAN. A *point-to-point router* is one that has only one peer. A typical DSL installation, for example, has one router on your end and one on the ISP end; that's a point-to-point configuration. The third option, *non-broadcast multiple access (NBMA)*, is a little harder to define. An NBMA router allows a single router to talk to multiple peers without using a broadcast, as in an ATM or X.25 network. You use these radio buttons to specify the kind of network in which your router is participating. If you set the router to NBMA mode, you can use the NBMA Neighbors tab to specify the routers to which your NBMA router should talk.

The NBMA Neighbors Tab

If you think back to the description of RIP neighbors, you learned that Microsoft recycled an OSPF concept for use in RIP. The NBMA Neighbors tab, then, should look like the RIP Neighbors tab; as it happens, the two are very similar. The pull-down menu at the top of the tab allows you to choose the IP address whose neighbors you're configuring. After you choose an IP address, you can use the remaining controls in the tab to specify the IP addresses and priorities of the NBMA neighbors to which you want this router interface to talk.

The Advanced Tab

The Advanced tab contains several parameters that didn't fit anywhere else in the OSPF configuration user interface. The first thing you'll probably notice is that you can specify which IP address you're configuring. Past that point, you need to use the six fields that give you access to some inner OSPF workings.

The six fields of the Advanced tab include the following:

- Transit Delay (Seconds), which specifies how long you think it will take a link-state update to propagate outward from this router. The OSPF engine uses this value to decide how stale route information is when it arrives.

- Retransmit Interval (Seconds), which is for your best estimate of the round-trip delay required for two routers to communicate. If it takes longer than this interval for a packet to arrive, it is retransmitted.

- Hello Interval (Seconds), which controls how often OSPF routers send out "Here I am" packets to discover other routers. This value must be the same for all routers in the same network; lowering the interval speeds the discovery of topology changes at the expense of generating more OSPF traffic.

- Dead Interval (Seconds), which controls the interval after which a router is marked as "dead" by its peers. Microsoft recommends using an integral multiple of the hello interval for the dead interval. If your hello interval is set to the default 10 seconds, for example, the default dead interval of 40 seconds works well.

- Poll Interval (Seconds), which controls how long an NBMA router waits before attempting to contact an apparently dead router to see whether it's really dead. This interval should be set to at least twice the dead interval.

- Maximum Transmission Unit (MTU) Size (Bytes), which regulates how big an OSPF IP packet can be. Your best bet is to leave this value alone.

Managing Routing Protocols

Routing protocols typically don't take a great deal of management; after you install RIP or OSPF, the protocol engine takes care of exchanging routes with remote routers. Unlike what you may be accustomed to with dedicated routers, using a router OS such as Cisco's IOS, there's no way to directly edit the contents of the routing table generated by dynamic routing protocols. As a result, your management of these protocols is essentially limited to installing them, configuring them to meet your needs, and monitoring them as they run.

Installing RIP and OSPF

You add routing protocols from the General subnode below the IP Routing node in RRAS. This procedure is quite different from the way you manage network protocols in Windows NT, but it makes sense; there's no reason to install RIP or OSPF unless you're using RRAS, so it's logical that you would install it from there. An exercise in the "Necessary Procedures" section later in this chapter explains how to install the RIP and OSPF protocols.

Setting RIP Properties

The RIP protocol is essentially self-tuning. After you configure an RRAS router to use the RIP protocol, it quietly goes off, looks for peer routers, and exchanges routing information without much effort on your part. You can change a small group of settings through the RIP Properties dialog box (which you open by selecting the RIP node below IP Routing in the RRAS console and then choosing the Action ➤ Properties command).

THE GENERAL TAB

The General tab has the same logging controls as the General tab of the IP Routing Properties dialog box, but it has an additional control that you can use. The Maximum Delay (Seconds) control governs how long the router waits to send an update notification to its peers.

THE SECURITY TAB

The Security tab allows you to control what router announcements your router accepts. By default, the RRAS RIP implementation happily ingests routes supplied by any other router; you can restrict this behavior by supplying either a list of routers to trust or a list of routers whose routes you want to reject.

Setting OSPF Properties

You can set some OSPF-specific properties by selecting the OSPF node below the IP Routing item in the RRAS console and then opening the OSPF Properties dialog box.

NOTE   If the descriptions in this section seem to be brief, it's because you need to know what these settings do, not necessarily how the guts of these protocols work, to pass the exam.

THE GENERAL TAB

The General tab of the OSPF Properties dialog box contains the logging controls that you've already seen twice, plus two controls that you'll probably have occasion to use. These controls are the following.

- The Router Identification field, which allows you to enter an IP address that your router uses to identify itself. Although it's not a good idea to assign a bogus IP address as your router's identifier, you may want to choose the public IP address even for internal interfaces.

- The Enable Autonomous System Boundary Router check box, which controls whether your OSPF router advertises routes that it finds from other sources (including its static routes and routes it learns via RIP) to the outside world. The External Routing tab won't be enabled unless you check this box; check it only if you want this particular RRAS router to try to exchange OSPF routing information with its peers.

THE AREAS TAB

The Areas tab lists the OSPF areas that your router knows about. You can add, edit, or remove areas by clicking the corresponding buttons below the list box.

THE VIRTUAL INTERFACES TAB

Recall that OSPF conceptually divides networks into areas, some of which are part of the backbone and some of which aren't. Because a nonbackbone router isn't connected to the backbone, there has to be some other way to allow backbone and nonbackbone routers to share routing information. There is a way: the virtual link. A *virtual link* connects a backbone-area border router and a non–backbone-area border router. When the link is created, the two routers can share routing information just as though they were connected to the same physical network. You use the Virtual Interfaces tab to create and edit these virtual links.

THE EXTERNAL ROUTING TAB

OSPF isn't the only potential source of routing information; your router can acquire routes from several other sources. You may not want all those routes to be accepted and used, though. When you use OSPF, you can control which additional routing sources the OSPF components use by checking the appropriate check boxes in the External Routing tab. The two radio buttons at the top of the tab— Accept Routes From All Route Sources Except Those Selected and

Ignore Routes From All Route Sources Except Those Selected—allow you to control the meaning of the check boxes in the Route Sources list. By default, OSPF will accept all routes from all sources. To turn off individual route sources (static routes, for example), check the appropriate box. If you want to reject all route sources *except* for a particular group, select the Ignore Routes radio button and then check the route sources that you *do* want to use.

NOTE   The External Routing tab is active only if you check the Enable Autonomous System Boundary Router check box in the General tab.

The Route Filters button allows you to ignore or accept individual routes. This option is a handy way to screen out particular routes without disallowing entire classes of route-source information.

Necessary Procedures

You need to practice the following two procedures for monitoring route status and installing the RIP and OSPF protocols.

Monitoring Routing Status

To monitor routing status, follow these steps:

1. Open the RRAS MMC console (Start ➤ Programs ➤ Administrative Tools ➤ Routing and Remote Access).

2. In the left pane of the MMC, select the server whose status you want to monitor. Expand it until you see the IP Routing node.

3. Select the Routing Interfaces node. Notice that the right pane of the MMC now lists all known interfaces, along with their status and connection state.

4. Select the General node below IP Routing. Notice that the right pane of the MMC updates to show the IP routing interfaces, their IP addresses, their administrative and operational states, and whether IP filtering is enabled.

5. Right-click the General node; then choose the Show TCP/IP Information command. Check the number of IP routes displayed.

6. Right-click the Static Routes node; then choose the Show IP Routing Table command. Notice that the number of routes listed corresponds to the route count in the TCP/IP Information window and that some of the routes listed are generated automatically.

Installing the RIP and OSPF Protocols

Follow these steps to install the RIP and OSPF protocols:

1. Open the RRAS MMC console (Start ➤ Programs ➤ Administrative Tools ➤ Routing and Remote Access).

2. In the left pane of the MMC, select the server that you want to configure. Expand it until you see the General node below IP Routing.

3. Right-click the General node; then choose the New Routing Protocol command. The New Routing Protocol dialog box appears.

4. Select the routing protocol that you want to install; then click the OK button. The RRAS console refreshes its display, revealing a new node, labeled with the chosen protocol, below the IP Routing node.

5. Right-click the General node; then choose the New Routing Protocol command.

6. When the New Routing Protocol dialog box appears, select the next protocol; then click the OK button.

Exam Essentials

Know the different routing protocols supported in Windows 2000 and how to manage and monitor them. Understand the minutiae involved in installing and implementing RIP, RIP2, and OSPF.

Know the distinctions and parameters involved in border routing and internal routing. Be familiar with the different settings and protocols you use with each type of routing.

**Know that the Network Type controls influence how routers inter-
acts with their peers.**   A *broadcast router* is one that can talk to any
number of other routers. A *point-to-point router* is one that has only
one peer. A *non-broadcast multiple access (NBMA)* router allows a
single router to talk to multiple peers without using a broadcast.

Know the status controls that are built into the RRAS console.
Understanding what these controls display makes it much easier to
see all the health and status data that RRAS maintains.

**Know the parameters in the OSPF configuration user interface
Advanced tab.**   Be familiar with the delay, packet size, and interval
parameters you can set in this tab.

Key Terms and Concepts

broadcast router   A router that sends out broadcasts.

dead interval   A field that controls the interval after which a router
is marked as "dead" by its peers. Microsoft recommends using an
integral multiple of the hello interval for the dead interval.

hello interval   A field that controls how often OSPF routers send out
"Here I am" packets to discover other routers. This value must be the
same for all routers on the same network; lowering the interval speeds
the discovery of topology changes at the expense of generating more
OSPF traffic.

NBMA router   A single router that can talk to multiple peers without using a broadcast, as in an ATM or X.25 network.

non-broadcast multiple access (NBMA)   A single router that can
talk to multiple peers without using a broadcast.

point-to-point router   A router that has only one peer.

poll interval   A field that controls how long an NBMA router waits
before attempting to contact an apparently dead router to see
whether it's really dead. This interval should be set to at least twice
the dead interval.

retransmit interval   A period of your best estimate of the round-trip delay required for two routers to communicate. If it takes longer than this interval for a packet to arrive, the packet is retransmitted.

transit delay   A field that specifies how long you think it will take a link-state update to propagate outward from this router. The OSPF engine uses this value to decide how stale route information is when it arrives.

virtual link   A link that connects a backbone-area border router and a non–backbone-area border router.

Sample Questions

1. Which of the following statements is true of a border router?

   A. It acts as a gateway between routing areas.

   B. It routes traffic in the internal routes of an area.

   C. It cannot be used to interface with RRAS.

   D. All of the above.

   Answer: A. Border routers connect adjacent routing areas; they don't route anything inside an area.

2. Which of the following statements are true of the RIP and OSPF protocols? (Choose all that apply.)

   A. They can coexist on a single RRAS server.

   B. They can coexist on a single RRAS server, provided that it has at least two NICs.

   C. They can share routing data in the same routing table.

   D. They can be used to interoperate with non–Windows 2000 routers.

   Answer: A, C, D. RIP and OSPF can happily coexist on a single machine with one NIC and one routing table and they can exchange data with any standards-compliant RIP or OSPF router.

Chapter

7

Installing, Configuring, and Troubleshooting Network Address Translation (NAT) in a Windows 2000 Network Infrastructure

MICROSOFT EXAM OBJECTIVES COVERED IN THIS CHAPTER:

▶ **Install Internet Connection Sharing.** *(pages 300 – 310)*

▶ **Install NAT.** *(pages 310 – 317)*

▶ **Configure NAT properties.** *(pages 317 – 321)*

▶ **Configure NAT interfaces.** *(pages 321 – 327)*

U ntil recently, Microsoft didn't offer a way for several people to share a single connection to the Internet. Linux and Mac OS users have been able to do this for a while, and several third parties have shipped products such as WinGate. As part of Windows 98 Second Edition, Microsoft included a feature called *Internet Connection Sharing*, or *ICS*. The idea behind ICS is simple: If you have more than one computer and the computers are networked together, one computer can act as a gateway to the Internet. This concept is simple, but some behind-the-scenes magic has to happen to implement it.

ICS actually implements a service called *network address translation (NAT)*. In this chapter, you get a deeper understanding of why NAT is the workhorse behind ICS and how it works, in both ICS and as NAT in the full-blown version. You also gain an understanding of how to install, configure, and manage both NAT and ICS in Windows 2000. You learn to install ICS and NAT and to configure both the NAT properties and interfaces, all for separate exam objectives.

Install Internet Connection Sharing.

B ecause every IP packet contains address information, you probably can guess how NAT got its name: It's a service that translates between your own network's addresses and addresses that are usable on the Internet. With either ICS or NAT, your entire network uses a single IP address on the Internet. All outgoing traffic passes through the NAT machine on its way out. All inbound traffic is likewise addressed to the NAT machine, which is responsible for passing it back to the proper computer on your local network.

Critical Information

The job of a NAT server seems to be simple enough at first glance: allow a group of computers to masquerade behind a single IP address. In fact, NAT is sometimes called "IP masquerading" in the Unix world. Some subtleties, however, make it more complex than a first glance indicates. You can start exploring the process by looking at a simple representation of a network using NAT to connect to the Internet. In this network are six workstations and a NAT server, each with addresses in the 10.10.1.x range. Notice that the only machine connected to the Internet is the NAT server and that it actually has a second IP address assigned—both small but very important details, as you'll see soon.

NOTE   In the rest of this chapter, *NAT* refers to the protocol used both by the ICS and NAT services in Windows 2000, but those components are called by their correct names.

Understanding Private Addressing

In the early days of the Internet, it must have seemed that the IP addressing scheme would provide a large-enough address space for the foreseeable future. It's fairly clear that the designers of IP addressing never expected the explosive growth of the Internet. Each device directly connected to the Internet normally needs its own address, and addresses have become scarce. As a workaround, the Internet Network Information Center (InterNIC), in conjunction with the Internet Assigned Numbers Authority (IANA), designated some address ranges as *private addresses*.

These addresses cannot receive traffic from or send traffic to the Internet. In every other respect, though, they're ordinary IP addresses. The idea behind private addresses is that you can use them to configure a network that's not connected to the Internet. That idea seems to be a useful one until you want to hook your network up to the Internet. That's where NAT comes in: it translates between public and private addresses.

RFC 1597 (titled Address Allocation for Private Internets) designates the three private address ranges:

- 10.0.0.0 with a subnet mask of 255.0.0.0
- 172.16.0.0 with a subnet mask of 255.240.0.0
- 192.168.0.0 with a subnet mask of 255.255.0.0

You can use any of these address spaces with impunity, because no router is allowed to route Internet traffic to or from those addresses. The NAT server uses a public IP address to communicate with the Internet and a private IP address for the local network.

Using NAT Editors

The approach NAT uses works fine for data when the IP address information is all in the packet headers, but it falls down for protocols that embed addressing information in the packet payload. File Transfer Protocol (FTP), for example, embeds IP address data in the payload, as do NetBIOS over TCP/IP and Point-to-Point Tunneling Protocol. The approved solution is for the NAT machine to inspect the packet payloads and change any addressing data that it finds. But this solution works only with certain data types; a special component called a *NAT editor* is responsible for changing data in the protocols that it supports. Windows 2000 includes NAT editors for FTP, PPTP, NBT, and Internet Control Message Protocol (ICMP). It also includes a similar capability called *NAT proxying* for videoconferencing (the H.323 protocol) and the Windows Remote Procedure Call (RPC) interprocess communications tool.

Understanding Differences

Up to this point, this chapter has treated ICS and NAT as though they are identical, because they're extremely similar: They both implement NAT, but with differing levels of bells and whistles. Microsoft expects you to know the differences, including the following:

- **What they run on.** ICS is available on Professional, Server, and Advanced Server, whereas NAT requires Windows 2000 Server or Advanced Server.

- **How you configure them.** Checking one check box in the Sharing tab of a network adapter configures ICS. NAT requires you to use the Routing and Remote Access snap-in, and with NAT, many more configuration options are available.

- **How many public IP addresses they can use.** With ICS, you expose a single public IP address. NAT can expose several public IP addresses, which is useful if you want to tie specific public IP addresses to individual machines on your LAN.

- **How many networks they can link.** ICS links one LAN to one public IP address, but NAT can link many LANs (provided that each LAN has their own interfaces) to many public IP addresses.

Installing Internet Connection Sharing

ICS is simple to install and use, provided that you make the right decisions during installation. It's easy to configure, too. ICS's ease of use and management comes at the expense of some functionality, though.

Unlike almost every other service described in this book, ICS isn't installed via the Windows Components wizard. To install it, all you do is check one check box in a Properties dialog tab. Thereafter, the installation process is invisible, save for the changes ICS makes in your existing TCP/IP configuration.

ICS is intended for connecting small-office/home-office (SOHO) networks to the Internet. In particular, it's designed for small networks that don't already have a full network infrastructure and that have a single connection to the Internet. Because ICS installs its own DHCP server and because it requires you to use the 192.168.* address block, it's not suitable for networks that already have their own DHCP server, that use static IP addresses, or that run DNS servers or Windows 2000 domain controllers.

To install ICS, you must have administrative privileges on the target machine.

Understanding the ICS Install

Now that you understand how the underlying protocol works, you may be curious to see what happens on a machine when you install Internet Connection Sharing. ICS is a NAT implementation, but it leaves out some of the powerful features included in the full-blown NAT version.

Suppose that you have a Windows 2000 Professional machine connected to your cable modem via an Ethernet NIC. You decide to install ICS so that you can add network connections for two other machines in your house, so you buy the necessary supplies and hardware to construct a LAN for your house. As part of the process, you add a second NIC to your Windows 2000 machine so that it can run ICS. Although this isn't strictly required, ICS *does* require you to have two independent network interfaces. One interface can be a modem or a NIC; the other must be a NIC.

When you install ICS, you attach it to one of the adapters—the one that's connected to the Internet. When you do so, a few things change in your machine and adapter configurations:

- The *other* adapter (the one connected to your LAN) gets a new IP address of 192.168.0.1 and a subnet mask of 255.255.255.0.

- The Internet Connection Sharing service is started and set to run automatically at boot time.

- The DHCP address allocator service is enabled. The allocator gives out IP addresses in the range 192.168.0.1 to 192.168.0.254, using the standard 255.255.255.0 subnet mask. Think of this service as though it's a baby DHCP server, because there's no way to configure any of the options that you studied in the objectives in Chapter 2.

- If you're using a dial-up connection on the Internet-connected adapter, automatic dialing is enabled.

These changes don't do anything special to the clients on your network; you must configure each of them manually to use DHCP so that they can get the necessary settings from the *DHCP allocator*. ICS also doesn't make any changes in the adapter connected to the Internet.

Installing ICS

Installing ICS is easy; it's literally a one-check-box operation. When you open the Network and Dial-Up Connections window, you see one icon for each adapter (real or dial-up) that you have installed. Find the adapter that you normally use to connect to the Internet and right-click it; then choose the Properties command from the context menu. When the Properties dialog box opens, click the Sharing tab.

To enable ICS, just click the check box labeled Enable Internet Connection Sharing for This Connection. If you want Internet traffic from other computers on your LAN to bring up the connection automatically (as you normally will), make sure that the Enable On-Demand Dialing check box is checked, too. That's all you have to do to set up a basic ICS configuration, apart from configuring each client to use DHCP.

WARNING   Installing ICS interrupts any TCP/IP connection you have set up, so don't do it in the middle of any operations you don't want interrupted.

Configuring ICS Options

After you enable ICS, you'll have access to the Settings button at the bottom of the Sharing tab. This button allows you to configure two separate, but related, groups of settings that have to do with what entries are preloaded into the NAT table on your ICS computer. These settings include the following:

- The Applications tab controls *outbound port mapping*. Changing the settings in this tab allows you to add entries to the NAT table so that computers on your network can make connections to remote services on the Internet.

- The Services tab controls *inbound port mappings*. By adjusting the settings in this tab, you can control where requests from outside your network should be routed.

The Applications Tab

The Applications tab allows you to create predefined routings for Internet services that you want your users to be able to access. You may want to allow users on your network to access streaming audio and video sent from servers using Apple's QuickTime, for example. QuickTime implements the Internet-standard Real Time Streaming Protocol (RTSP, defined in RFC 2326), but you have to make some adjustments to your NAT server to allow RTSP traffic to come inside. RTSP uses TCP port 554 and UDP ports 6970 through 6999. To make this work, click the Add button in the Applications tab, which then displays the Internet Connection Sharing Application dialog box.

Fill out the dialog box as follows:

- Use the Name of Application field to specify some meaningful name that you'll recognize later.

- Use the Remote Server Port Number field (and the TCP and UDP radio buttons) to specify the port number and type that your machines will use when making connections to the outside world.

- Use the Incoming Response Ports fields to specify which TCP and UDP ports outside servers will use when sending data back to a client on your network.

The Services Tab

The Services tab allows outside computers to access some of the services on your network. Suppose that you've set up a small home office, and you're using ICS to connect to the Internet. By making the appropriate entries in the NAT table, you can redirect incoming Web requests to one machine, incoming mail to another, and incoming FTP requests to a third. You can't edit the NAT table by hand, but you can achieve the same effect with this tab.

Microsoft helpfully added the six most common services: FTP for file transfer; Telnet for remote administration; IMAP3, IMAP4, and POP3 for remote mail access; and SMTP for sending and receiving mail. Because all these services use well-known port numbers, you must first check the check boxes next to the services you want to enable. That act in and of itself probably won't be sufficient, however, because checking the boxes doesn't specify which computer on your LAN should get the traffic. To do that, you need to click the Edit button. By specifying the local DNS name or its IP address in the dialog box that appears, you instruct the NAT software to route incoming packets for that port to the server you specify.

You also can add new services. Suppose that you're using Exchange 5.5 as a Network News Transfer Protocol (NNTP) server, and you want outside hosts to be able to reach it. NNTP uses TCP port 119, so you'd click the Add button and fill out the resulting dialog box.

Necessary Procedures

In the preceding sections, you saw that ICS is simple to install. Make sure that you understand the steps in the following procedure.

Installing Internet Connection Sharing

Follow these steps to install ICS on Windows 2000 Professional, Server, or Advanced Server:

1. Open the Network and Dial-Up Connections window (Start ➤ Settings ➤ Network and Dial-Up Connections).

2. Right-click the icon for the adapter that's connected to the Internet (bearing in mind that you can share a dial-up or VPN connection, too); then choose the Properties command. The adapter's Properties dialog box appears.

3. Click the Sharing tab. If you don't see the tab, you're probably trying to share an unsharable connection, such as the Local Area Connection, or because you're not logged on as an administrator.

4. In the Sharing tab, make sure that the Enable Internet Connection Sharing for This Connection check box is checked. If you want demand dialing turned on, make sure that the Enable On-Demand Dialing check box is checked as well.

5. Click the OK button.

Exam Essentials

Know the functionality of both ICS and NAT. Understand that NAT is the underlying protocol working in both, but ICS works on Windows 2000 Professional, while NAT as a service does not; both services work on 2000 Server and Advanced Server.

Know about private addresses and their ranges. Understand the ranges and subnet masks used with private addresses and how NAT translates and fronts for them.

Know the functioning of NAT Editors and their responsibility to change data in the protocols that they support. Understand that different software addressing makes a NAT editor necessary if the associated packets are going to find their destinations.

Know the IP addresses and minimal IP assignments that come from the DHCP address-allocator service. Understand why this service must remain an internal service on a private network.

Know the process for installing ICS and the options you can configure in the Applications and Options tabs. Be familiar with how to configure these ICS options.

Key Terms and Concepts

address pool   The range of IP addresses that the DHCP server can actually assign.

addressing component   A portion of the *Internet Connection Sharing* or *Network Address Translation* services that assigns IP addresses to clients; takes the place of a DHCP server.

DHCP allocator   A service that gives out IP addresses in the range 192.168.0.1 to 192.168.0.254, using the standard 255.255.255.0 subnet mask. There's no way to configure any regular DHCP options.

inbound port mapping   An addressing component that controls the ports to which requests from outside your network should be routed.

Internet Connection Sharing (ICS)   A Windows 2000 feature that allows a small network to be connected to the Internet through a single connection. The computer that dials into the Internet provides network address translation, addressing, and name resolution services for all the computers on the network. Through Internet connection sharing, the other computers on the network can access Internet resources and use Internet applications, such as Internet Explorer and Outlook Express.

NAT Editor   A component responsible for changing data in the protocols that it supports.

NAT interface   A network interface that supports Network Address Translation services for LAN clients.

NAT proxying   A NAT editing function for videoconferencing (the H.323 protocol) and the Windows Remote Procedure Call (RPC) interprocess communications tool.

Network Address Translation (NAT)   A service that allows multiple LAN clients to share a single public IP address and Internet connection by translating and modifying packets to reflect the correct addressing information.

outbound port mapping   An addressing component that controls the ports to which requests from inside your network should be routed.

private addresses   Addresses that cannot receive traffic from, or send traffic to, the Internet. In every other respect, though, they're ordinary IP addresses. The idea behind private addresses is that you can use them to configure a network that's not connected to the Internet. If you want to connect these machines to the Internet, you can use NAT to translate between public and private addresses.

Sample Questions

1. A private address is one that _____.

A. Is not broadcast to the Internet

B. Does not use the 192.192.* address space

C. Cannot be used to exchange data with Internet addresses

D. Is reserved for use by Internet Service Providers

Answer: C. Internet hosts aren't allowed to send or receive traffic to addresses that fall in the private range.

2. Which of the following are differences between Internet Connection Sharing and NAT? (Choose two.)

A. ICS runs only on Windows 2000 Professional.

B. ICS can share only a single public IP address.

C. NAT has more-flexible configuration options.

D. NAT requires a DSL or cable-modem connection.

Answer: B, C. ICS runs on all Windows 2000 family members, but NAT is available only on Windows 2000 Server and Advanced Server. ICS shares only one public IP address; NAT has many more configuration settings that you can change. ICS and NAT both work on dial-up modems, DSL, cable modems, and any other device that you can use to connect to the Internet.

Install NAT.

It's fair to describe ICS as "NAT Lite," because it offers many of the same features in a pretty, not-so-filling package. Earlier in this chapter, you saw that the primary differences between the ICS and NAT implementations in Windows 2000 are related to scale and scope. The good news is that the actual configuration isn't much more difficult; there's just more of it.

Critical Information

"Installing" NAT is a bit of a misnomer, because NAT is actually treated as another routing protocol that you install under the aegis of the Routing and Remote Access Service (RRAS). In that light, when you install NAT, what you're really doing is activating some components that provide services within the RRAS framework. You must install and run RRAS before you install NAT, of course.

Knowing NAT Components

Microsoft's documentation discusses three separate, but related, components that contribute to the NAT implementation. It's important to understand these components so that you'll understand the buzzwords used in their docs and on the exams. These components include the following:

Translation   The translation component handles the NAT functions themselves, including maintaining the NAT table for inbound and outbound connections.

Addressing   This component is what Microsoft calls the "DHCP address allocator" in its ICS documentation. Like the DHCP allocator, the *addressing component* is just a stripped-down DHCP server that assigns an IP address, a subnet mask, a default gateway, and the IP address of a DNS server.

Name Resolution   When you install and configure NAT, it begins to act as a DNS server for the other machines on the local network. That service is provided by the *name resolution component*. When a client resolver makes a DNS query, it goes to the name-resolution component on the NAT server, which forwards it to the DNS server defined on the Internet-connected adapter and returns the reply. Think of this component as being a proxy for DNS.

Just because you install these components doesn't mean you'll have to use them all, of course. You always need the translation component, because it actually implements the NAT functionality. If you're running a DHCP server *or* the DHCP relay agent on your private LAN, you can't use the NAT addressing component concurrently. Likewise, if you're running an internal DNS server, you cannot use the name-resolution component.

Here's what those options *really* mean:

- The Use the Selected Internet Connection radio button and the corresponding list of adapters that Windows 2000 thinks are connected to the Internet allow you to choose an adapter to share. Choosing this radio button and then selecting an adapter is roughly equivalent to picking an adapter in the Network and Dial-Up Connections folder, opening its Properties dialog box, and clicking the ICS check box in its Sharing tab. Notice that the button displays dial-up connections even though the dialog box says "adapter." Therefore, this button is the one to use if you want to press an existing VPN or dial-up connection into service.

- The Create a New Demand-Dial Internet Connection button tells the wizard that you want to create a new demand-dial connection to use as your Internet pipeline. When you choose this option, it triggers the Demand Dial Interface wizard, which you met in Chapter 6. When you complete the wizard, it automatically adds a NAT interface for the new demand-dial connection.

Installing NAT When RRAS Is Already Running

If you've already configured RRAS to handle IP or IPX routing, you'll probably want to know how to configure NAT without deactivating RRAS (which wipes out its configuration information) and reactivating it to start the wizard. The steps are described in the "Necessary Procedures" section. Be aware that this procedure covers only the installation—not the process of adding a NAT interface and configuring it.

Necessary Procedures

You can now practice installing and activating NAT with the following necessary procedures.

Installing NAT on a Running RRAS Server

Follow these steps to install NAT on a previously installed RRAS server:

1. Open the Routing and Remote Access snap-in (Start ≻ Programs ≻ Administrative Tools ≻Routing and Remote Access).

2. Locate the server on which you want to enable NAT. If its icon has a little red down arrow, right-click it, choose the Enable and Configure Routing and Remote Access Service command, and then proceed with the RRAS wizard as described in the preceding section.

3. Expand the server's configuration until you see the General node (*serverName* ≻ IP Routing ≻ General).

4. Right-click the General node; then choose the New Routing Protocol command. The New Routing Protocol dialog box appears.

5. Select Network Address Translation in the list of routing protocols; then click the OK button. The IP Routing node now has a child node named Network Address Translation.

Understanding the Overall NAT Process

ICS hides many of the necessary gory details from you, but Microsoft assumes that if you're tough enough to run NAT, you can take a little extra time to do some of the things that ICS does for you. Most of these steps are familiar to you from the material in Chapter 6, but some of it is specific to NAT configuration. Here's what you need to do:

1. Install RRAS and enable it. If you use the RRAS wizard, this step is your last one. The wizard takes care of the other steps for you. If not (if you're installing NAT on an existing RRAS box, for example), read on.

2. If you're not using a permanent connection (that is, not something that's always up, such as a dedicated analog line, ISDN line, DSL, or cable-modem connection), you need to configure your dial-up connection to reach your ISP by following these steps.

A. Create a demand-dial interface to reach your ISP by using the Demand Dial wizard.

B. Use RRAS to make the dial-up port routable, as you did in Chapter 6.

3. Configure the local network adapter properly. Give it an appropriate private IP address and network mask, and make sure that no default gateway is specified.

4. Add a static IP route on the adapter that's connected to the Internet. The destination address must be 0.0.0.0, and the subnet mask also should be 0.0.0.0. This step forces RRAS to send all traffic across that interface, which is what you want for Internet connectivity.

5. Add NAT as a routing protocol inside RRAS.

6. Add two NAT interfaces: one for your Internet adapter and one for the local network adapter.

7. If you want to use the addressing or name-resolution components, you have to configure them.

Activating NAT and RRAS

RRAS is installed by default with Windows 2000 Server and Advanced Server, but it's not activated. Therefore, if you haven't already turned it on according to the directions in Chapter 6, you need to do so. There are two ways to set up NAT: use the Routing and Remote Access Service wizard to lead you through the process, or start a bare-bones RRAS server and add NAT manually.

In either case, here's what you need to do:

1. Open the Routing and Remote Access Service snap-in (Start ≻ Programs ≻ Administrative Tools ≻ Routing and Remote Access).

2. When the RRAS snap-in opens, navigate to the server you want to manage. If you see a little red spot on the computer icon, RRAS is inactive on that machine.

3. Right-click the inactive machine; then choose the Configure and Enable Routing and Remote Access command. This command starts the Routing and Remote Access Service wizard, about which you learned in Chapter 6.

4. Dismiss the first page of the wizard by clicking the Next button.

5. In the Common Configurations page of the wizard, you see radio buttons that allow you to specify the role you want this server to play. If you want to configure the server manually later, choose the Manually Configured Server radio button. If you want the wizard to lead you through the process, make sure that the Internet Connection Server radio button is selected; then click Next.

6. When you complete the preceding five steps, the next question is simple. The Internet Connection Server Setup page asks you to specify whether you want to set up ICS or NAT. If you select the ICS radio button, a snippy little dialog box tells you to set it up by using the Network and Dial-Up Connections folder. To set up NAT properly, then, make sure that the Set Up a Router With the Network Address Translation (NAT) Routing Protocol radio button is selected. Then click the Next button.

7. The next step of the wizard requires you to pick the connection that you want to share. You can specify how you want the connection to be made. Your two choices are to use an existing Internet connection or to create a new demand-dial connection.

Exam Essentials

Know how to perform a NAT installation.   Understand the necessity of having RRAS up and running before the NAT implementation.

Know the three NAT components and the distinctions on a network that will determine their use.   Understand the translation component, the addressing component, and the name-resolution component. Be clear that the latter two act analogously to DHCP and DNS and would not be needed if you already had those services on your network.

Key Terms and Concepts

addressing component   The component that is just a stripped-down DHCP server and assigns an IP address, a subnet mask, a default gateway, and the IP address of a DNS server.

name-resolution component   The component that acts as a DNS server for other machines on the local network; it works as a proxy for DNS.

translation component   The component that handles the NAT functions themselves, including maintaining the NAT table for inbound and outbound connections.

Sample Questions

1. You have just attached your server to a dedicated connection between a satellite and your company's home office. The dedicated connection is providing you three addresses. All clients must have direct access to a DOS-based database to enter and retrieve information. What is the best way to attach your 18 clients to the database?

A. ICS

B. Proxy DNS

C. Proxy server

D. NAT

Answer: D. Because transparent access to a database is required, the best solution is NAT. ICS would change port addresses, which would be unacceptable in a database access. A proxy server normally is used for caching and single-address access and is incompatible with non–ODBC-compliant databases.

2. You control whether the NAT addressing component is enabled by using the _____.

   A. General tab of the NAT Interface Properties dialog box

   B. Translation tab of the NAT Properties dialog box

   C. Address Assignment tab of the NAT Properties dialog box

   D. Name Resolution tab of the NAT Properties dialog box

   Answer: C. You control NAT addressing per server, not per interface, so you have to use the Address Assignment tab of the NAT Properties dialog box.

Configure NAT properties.

Some properties pertain to all NAT interfaces and connections on your RRAS NAT server. You modify these settings through the NAT Properties dialog box, which you display by right-clicking the Network Address Translation node in the RRAS console and then choosing the Properties command.

Critical Information

The Properties dialog box has four tabs: the General tab, the Translation tab, the Address Assignment tab, and the Name Resolution tab.

The General Tab

The General tab is fairly uninteresting; it simply allows you to change the amount of event-logging information that the NAT software writes to the system event log. The default setting is to log errors only, but you can choose any of three other levels: no logging, logging only of errors and warnings, and logging of everything. More-detailed log information is useful when you're trying to troubleshoot a problem, but it can bulk up your event log quickly, so don't turn up logging unless you're trying to find and fix a problem. Turning this feature off completely also may be a problem.

The Translation Tab

The Translation tab is more interesting. It allows you to set scavenging times for port mappings, and it gives you access to an application-mapping dialog box. The controls in the Translation tab do the following:

- The Remove TCP Mapping After and Remove UDP Mapping After fields allow you to control how long entries remain in the NAT table after their last use. The default behavior is to keep TCP mappings for 24 hours and UDP mappings for one minute.

- The Applications button allows you to open the Applications dialog box so that you can add, remove, or edit application mappings. Any mappings you create with ICS are preserved for NAT and vice versa. This setting helps smooth the way if you start with ICS and later migrate to a more sophisticated NAT implementation.

The Address Assignment Tab

The Address Assignment tab controls whether the NAT addressing component is used. Recall that the NAT addressing component is just a baby DHCP server; you don't need to use it if you already have a DHCP server on your private network, but you can use it if you want to streamline the number and kinds of services you have installed.

The controls in this dialog box are simple. The Automatically Assign IP Addresses By Using DHCP check box controls whether the addressing component is active. If it is, the IP Address and Mask fields control the address range that's handed out. You have no way to change the default gateway address (it's always the private IP address of the NAT machine), default DNS server, or any of the other DHCP options.

You can, however, exclude IP addresses that you don't want to be assigned by the allocator. To do so, click the Exclude button in the Address Assignment tab; this button displays the Exclude Reserved Addresses dialog box. In this dialog box, you see a list of any reserved

IP addresses. You can modify the list contents with the ever-present Add, Edit, and Remove buttons. Doing this is functionally equivalent to creating an exclusion range in the DHCP snap-in when you're using the "real" DHCP server.

NOTE To allow inbound connections from the Internet, you need to exclude the IP address of the target machine in the Exclude Reserved Addresses dialog box and then assign that IP address statically to the target. After you've done so, you'll be able to configure a special port pointing to the target.

The Name Resolution Tab

You can choose to use the NAT name-resolution component, or not, via the Name Resolution tab. When you turn on the component, its address is passed out by the addressing component, and client computers send all their DNS queries to the NAT computer that acts as a DNS proxy. You still can configure each individual client with the IP address of an external DNS server, but then you may not be able to resolve the names of hosts on your private LAN.

The Name Resolution tab has two check boxes that control how resolution works. The first, Clients Using Domain Name System (DNS), normally is checked—a good thing, because it controls whether the name-resolution component is active. The second check box, Connect to the Public Network When a Name Needs to Be Resolved, specifies whether you want the Internet connection to be brought up just for DNS queries. The Demand-Dial Interface pull-down menu allows you to choose which demand-dial interface (if any) you want to be brought up when a DNS query requires bringing the link up.

Necessary Procedures

Be sure to not confuse these property configurations with the interface configuration. Following is the procedure for configuring NAT properties.

Configuring NAT Properties

In this exercise, you set the logging level for the NAT components to a more reasonable value. You also turn on client name resolution. To configure NAT properties on a server, follow these steps:

1. Open the Routing and Remote Access snap-in (Start ➤ Programs ➤ Administrative Tools ➤Routing and Remote Access).

2. Expand the RRAS tree until you see the Network Address Translation node (RRAS ➤ *serverName* ➤ IP Routing ➤ Network Address Translation).

3. Right-click Network Address Translation; then choose the Properties command.

4. In the General tab, change the logging setting by selecting the Log Errors And Warnings radio button.

5. Switch to the Name Resolution tab; then check the Clients Using Domain Name System (DNS) check box.

6. Click the OK button.

Exam Essentials

Know that there is a benefit for small users to use ICS and then move to NAT.   Understand that the settings in these users' NAT tables will migrate.

Know that if you choose to implement NAT with the "real" DNS server, it may not be able to resolve the names of hosts on your private LAN.

Know that the NAT properties that you can configure involve tabs for the three primary NAT components you learned for the preceding objective and logging.   Understand that you must decide whether to use the NAT components or the "real" DHCP and DNS.

Key Terms and Concepts

This objective doesn't have any new terminology or concepts, but you do learn the practical steps necessary to configure these properties.

Sample Questions

1. True or false: There is no positive reason to start with a small ICS deployment before moving to a full-blown NAT deployment.

Answer: False. For one thing, you can use ICS on Professional and not have the necessity of Server or Advanced Server, but in addition to that, you can develop your NAT table with ICS and still use it with NAT at a later date.

2. The NAT logging default is to record:

A. All warnings and activities

B. Log errors only

C. Log turned off

D. Log all DNS queries

Answer: B. This default is probably a good one, because it is too late to turn on after the errors occur.

Configure NAT interfaces.

You know from your exploration of RRAS in Chapter 6 that you have to add an interface in RRAS before it can do anything with packets bound to or from that interface. NAT is no different; before you can use NAT on your local network, you must add a *NAT interface* by using the RRAS interface. The actual process of adding a new NAT interface is fairly simple, provided that you know which adapter to put the interface on.

Critical Information

Just as you do with ICS, you have to distinguish between adapters that are connected to your local network and those that are connected (or that can connect) to the Internet. NAT links these two interfaces, so you actually need to create both of them. ICS is smart enough to create both interfaces automatically, but RRAS requires you to do it yourself. There's a simple rule to follow:

- Create an interface for your local network adapter first, specifying it as such.

- Create the Internet adapter interface second. If you're using a dial-up connection, you also need to add some routing information.

Removing NAT Interfaces

You can remove any NAT interface easily—just select it and then choose the Action ➤ Delete command (or the corresponding command in the context menu). RRAS asks you to confirm that you want to remove the interface. If you remove an interface that has active connections, they'll be closed immediately, so don't do this if you (or your network users) are in the middle of something that you don't want to be interrupted.

Setting NAT Interface Properties

Each NAT interface has its own set of properties. Unsurprisingly, you can edit these properties by right-clicking an interface and then choosing the Properties command from the context menu. This process works just like it does for the interface types you saw in Chapter 6.

The General Tab

The General tab allows you to designate what kind of NAT interface this is. Normally, you need to add a pair of NAT interfaces: one for the adapter that's connected to the Internet and the other for your local adapter. As a result, you have reason to use the radio buttons in the General tab. These buttons include the following:

- Private Interface Connected to Private Network, which you use to specify that this interface is bound to the adapter on your local network.

- Public Interface Connected to the Internet, which specifies that this adapter is connected to the Internet. That means (duh!) that you use it only on the adapter that you use to connect to the Internet, whatever type of adapter it is.

- Translate TCP/UDP Headers, which controls whether the built-in NAT editors do their thing on IP address data in the packet headers. If you turn this option off, other clients on your local network won't be able to exchange data with Internet hosts. This option should always be turned on for a public interface.

The Address Pool Tab

You may remember from an earlier discussion in this chapter that the number of supported IP addresses is one of the differences between NAT and ICS. The Address Pool tab is where you inform NAT which IP addresses it should expect traffic to come from. You can assign *address-pool* information as a range or as a collection of individual addresses. No matter how deep the pool is, you manage it from this tab by using the list of addresses (or ranges) and the Add, Edit, Remove, and Reservations buttons.

When you add a new range of addresses, you specify the start address, the subnet mask, and the end address. If you're using a single address, just specify it alone. RRAS tries to be helpful and calculate the correct ending address based on the start address and subnet mask that you specify. When you edit a range, you can tweak any of these settings; removing a range from the address pool removes it from the public IP address set that can be used to reach machines on your internal LAN.

WARNING   Removing an address from the address pool *does not* prevent outside hosts from reaching your NAT server; it just prevents the NAT server from routing packets any further on your LAN.

The Reservations button allows you to reserve individual IP addresses from the public range and add static mappings in the NAT table that point to particular hosts inside your network. This process adds a degree of efficiency to the NAT process. The only tricky part of adding a reservation is getting the matching addresses into the Add Reservation dialog box. You need to specify a single public IP address that maps to a single private IP address. If you want incoming traffic to reach through the NAT box and to the target machine, you also must check the Allow Incoming Sessions to This Address check box.

The Special Ports Tab

You can edit the NAT table in a second way: you can specify the ports to which inbound traffic should be mapped. This procedure allows you to take traffic coming to any port on any of your public IP addresses and direct it to a specified port on any machine in your private network. You could channel any incoming Web requests to a single machine, for example, by mapping port 80 on the public interface to port 80 on your internal Web server. You could do the same with SMTP or any other TCP or UDP protocol. All this flexibility is yours for the asking, thanks to the Special Ports tab. In the example shown in the figure, the Secure Sockets Layer (SSL) port is mapped to 192.168.0.240, so that any SSL connection attempt from the outside world is channeled automatically to a single machine on the private network. The *Special Ports tab* lists the *port mappings* you have in effect; you can add, edit, and remove these mappings by using the buttons at the bottom of the tab.

When you add or edit a special port, you use the Edit Special Port dialog box. You use the controls in this dialog box to set up the special port mapping that you want to take effect. These controls include the following:

- The Public Address group allows you to specify what public address can receive traffic for this specific port. The On This Interface radio button (the default choice) accepts traffic on the specified port for all public IP addresses in the address pool. If you instead select the On This Address Pool Entry radio button, the public IP address that you provide is the only one for which this port mapping will be active.

- Use the Incoming Port field to specify the port number that the outside world will be using.

- Use the Private Address field to specify the private address to which incoming traffic on the magic port will go.

- Use the Outgoing Port field to specify the port that will be used for outbound traffic generated by hosts on your local network.

Necessary Procedures

This is a simple objective with a single necessary procedure. Learn how to add and configure public NAT interfaces by practicing this procedure.

Adding and Configuring Public NAT Interface

Follow these steps to add and configure a public NAT interface:

1. Open the Routing and Remote Access snap-in (Start ➤ Programs ➤ Administrative Tools ➤Routing and Remote Access).

2. Expand the RRAS tree until you see the Network Address Translation node (RRAS ➤ *serverName* ➤ IP Routing ➤ Network Address Translation).

3. Right-click Network Address Translation; then choose the New Interface command. The New Interface for Network Address Translation dialog box appears.

4. Select the adapter that you want to use; then click OK. The NAT Properties dialog box appears.

5. Select Public Interface Connected to the Internet; then click the OK button.

6. (Optional) If you want to specify an address pool for NAT clients, switch to the Address Pool tab and click the Add button. In the Add Address Pool dialog box, specify the starting address and subnet mask to be used for the pool; then click the OK button.

7. (Optional) If you want to create port-mapping entries (as described later in the chapter), switch to the Special Ports tab and use the Add button to create them.

Exam Essentials

Know that NAT allows multiple addresses to be connected to the Internet and that you configure these addresses by right-clicking an interface and choosing the Address tab. Understand that RRAS tries to be helpful and calculate the correct end address based on the start address and subnet mask that you specify.

Know that the Special Ports tab allows you to take traffic coming to any port on any of your public IP addresses and direct it to a specified port on any machine in your private network. Understand that this process can result in some very handy situations for your network users, based on what they need to access from Internet packets.

Key Terms and Concepts

NAT interface A network interface that supports Network Address Translation services for LAN clients.

Sample Questions

1. The Translate TCP/UDP Headers radio button controls whether the built-in NAT editors do their thing on IP address data in the packet headers. You would turn this option off if:

   A. You want multiple Internet connections.

   B. You need to disconnect to troubleshoot an addressing problem.

   C. You want to configure the addresses in the headers manually.

   D. You want to configure FTP at a specific port.

Answer: B. If you turn this option off, other clients in your local network won't be able to exchange data with Internet hosts. This option should always be turned on for a public interface.

2. To allow inbound data to reach a particular target machine, you must do which of the following?

   A. Make the target machine a NAT server.

   B. Create a special port.

   C. Disable the addressing component.

   D. Add a static route to the target machine.

   Answer: B. A special port ties a source port to the private address of one of the machines on your network.

Chapter

8

Installing, Configuring, Managing, Monitoring, and Troubleshooting Certificate Services in a Windows 2000 Network Infrastructure

---

MICROSOFT EXAM OBJECTIVES COVERED IN THIS CHAPTER:

▶ **Install and configure Certificate Authority (CA).** *(pages 331 – 359)*

▶ **Issue and revoke certificates.** *(pages 360 – 379)*

▶ **Remove the Encrypting File System (EFS) recovery keys.** *(pages 379 – 381)*

Some security services require a way to authenticate users or protect data in transit. To name just one example, secure e-commerce depends on having some way to obscure credit-card numbers and expiration dates in transit, so that they can't be easily stolen. IPSec connections, for example, can be set to require that each end of the connection authenticate itself; the Secure Sockets Layer, used to protect and secure Web traffic, is another example. Authentication and confidentiality can be implemented in several ways, ranging from simple password exchanges to elaborate hardware-assisted security systems. One way is to use *digital certificates*, which can provide both authentication and confidentiality. In fact, certificates are used throughout Windows 2000: IPSec, Kerberos authentication, Internet Information Server, and the Encrypting File System (EFS) all use them.

A *certificate authority*, or CA, is a service that allows you to issue new certificates, revoke or cancel old ones, and monitor and control which certificates are doing what. Microsoft's CA implementation, Microsoft Certificate Server (MCS), began life as part of IIS. The Windows 2000 version is a fully functional CA that you can use to issue certificates inside or outside your organization.

This chapter explores the basic terms and concepts that underlie MCS and the certificate-services exam objectives. It explains why encryption is important, how it's used to meet everyday business needs, and what MCS is and what it does.

In preparing for the first objective, you learn to install MCS and the accompanying Certificates and Certificate Authority snap-ins (wizards make these installation procedures easy). You then learn the specifics of configuring MCS to issue certificates, and you read a discussion of how you request, revoke, and manage certificates from the Certificates snap-in. Finally, you learn to remove the Encrypting File System (EFS) recovery keys, which is the final exam objective in this chapter.

Install and configure Certificate Authority (CA).

Knowing how to configure MCS depends on your understanding of what it does and how it works. If this were a security book, it would go into pages and pages and pages of detail on the cryptographic algorithms and nitpicky details of MCS. But because this is an *Exam Notes* book, designed to prepare you for the Windows 2000 Network Infrastructure exam, it focuses on the essentials of the plumbing that underlies MCS and how it interacts with other parts of the system.

Critical Information

When most people hear the words "encryption" or "cryptography," they immediately think of secret-key cryptography. In a secret-key system, two people who want to communicate use a single shared key that must be kept secret. The same key is used to encrypt and decrypt data, so if a user loses the secret key or if it's stolen, the data that it encrypts becomes vulnerable. Secret-key systems tend to be fast and flexible, but their dependence on a single key makes them better suited for applications in which you can change the key frequently, such as IPSec. In addition, secret-key systems can be used only for encryption, not authentication.

Instead of the single secret key used in a secret-key system, public-key systems use *two* keys, combined into a single keypair:

- A *public key*, which is designed to be spread around freely

- A *private key* (also called a *secret key*), which must be held only by its owner and should never be publicly disclosed

These keys complement each other. If you encrypt something with your public key, it can be decrypted only with the corresponding private key (which only you hold), and vice versa. The security of these keys depends on the mathematical relationship between the public and private keys. You can't derive one from the other, so passing out the public key doesn't introduce any risk of compromising the private key.

What You Can Do with a Public Key

Two fundamental operations are associated with public key cryptography: *encryption and signing*.

- *Encryption* hides data so that only the intended party can read it.

- *Signing* uses encryption to prove the origin and authenticity of some piece of data.

- In combination, signatures and encryption can be used to provide three features that customers demand, particularly for business-to-business e-commerce. These features include the following:

Privacy   Properly encrypted data can't be read by anyone except the intended recipients. Because public keys can be posted freely, complete strangers can communicate privately just by retrieving one another's public keys and using them to exchange encrypted messages.

Authentication   Transactions and communications involve two parties. Much of the time, it's desirable for one end or the other (or maybe both) to verify the other's identity. Secure Web sites, for example, allow users to verify that the server's identity is as claimed. One way to implement authentication uses public keys: the client can encrypt a challenge message by using the server's public key and then send it to the server. If the server can decrypt and answer the message correctly, it demonstrates that the server has the proper private key, thus proving its identity.

Authentication also allows you to verify that a piece of data wasn't tampered with after it was sent. This kind of authentication usually is implemented as a digital signature, using the public-key signing operations mentioned earlier in this chapter. Suppose that you want to digitally sign e-mail messages that you send out announcing new revisions of your book. To do so, you use software built into your Eudora e-mail client that does the following:

A. It examines the message content you provide and passes it through a special type of algorithm called a hash algorithm. *Hash algorithms* generate a unique "fingerprint" (or hash) for any block of data. It's practically impossible to produce two different messages that have an identical hash.

B. It encrypts the message and the fingerprint by using your private key.

Anyone who wants to verify that the message is from you can perform the same steps in reverse. First, your software decrypts the message by using your public key; then it computes a hash for the message. If the new hash and the decrypted version match, the recipient has proof that (a) you sent the message and (b) the message hasn't been modified.

Nonrepudiation   Nonrepudiation is one aspect of "conventional" business that e-commerce users often overlook. If someone signs a paper contract and give you a copy, it's fairly hard for that person to later say, "Hey, I didn't sign that." Digital signatures can provide the same legal binding for electronic transmissions, and they're being used for that purpose increasingly often.

What About Certificates?

Think of a digital certificate as being a carrying case for a public key. A certificate contains the public key and a set of attributes, such as the key holder's name and e-mail address. These attributes specify something about the holder: her identity, what she's allowed to do with the certificate, and so on. The attributes and the public key are bound together, because the certificate is digitally signed by the entity that issued it. Anyone who wants to verify the certificate's contents can verify the issuer's signature.

Certificates are one part of what security experts call a *public-key infrastructure (PKI)*, which sounds more complicated than it actually is. The PKI has to be able to do the following three things.

- **Manage keys.** A PKI makes it easy to issue new keys, review or revoke existing keys, and manage the trust level attached to keys from different issuers.

- **Publish keys.** A PKI offers a way for clients to find and fetch public keys and information about whether a specific key is valid. Without the ability to retrieve keys and know that they are valid, your users can't use of public-key services.

- **Use keys.** A PKI provides an easy way for users to use keys—not just by moving keys around where they're needed, but also by providing easy-to-use applications that perform public-key cryptographic operations for securing e-mail, network traffic, and other types of communication.

What's in a PKI?

The plumbing infrastructure in your house or apartment has a large number of components: sinks, toilets, supply pipes, municipal pumping stations, and so on. Likewise, a PKI has several components that you can mix and match to achieve the desired results. Microsoft's Windows 2000 PKI implementation offers the following functions:

- **Certificate authorities,** which issue certificates, revoke certificates that they've issued, and publish certificates for their clients. Big CAs such as Thawte and Verisign may perform this service for millions of users; with MCS, you can set up your own CA for each department or workgroup in your organization if you want to. Each CA is responsible for choosing what attributes it will include in a certificate and what mechanism it will use to verify those attributes before issuing the certificate. CAs also build and maintain lists of revoked certificates (known as *certificate revocation lists*, or *CRLs*).

- **Certificate publishers,** which make certificates and CRLs publicly available, inside or outside an organization.

- **Management tools,** which allow you, as administrator, to keep track of which certificates were issued, when a given certificate expires, and so on. The Certificate Services snap-in allows you to do these things, and more, for MCS.

- **PKI-savvy applications,** which allow you and your users to do useful things with certificates, such as encrypt e-mail or network connections. The best-known examples of PKI-savvy applications are Web browsers (such as Internet Explorer and Netscape Navigator) and e-mail applications (such as Outlook and Outlook Express). Windows 2000 includes the *Encrypting File System (EFS)*, a PKI-aware file system that can encrypt and decrypt files for you automatically.

Why EFS Is Your Friend

EFS is a little-talked-about Windows 2000 feature that's actually very cool. It encrypts files and folders transparently to you and your applications, so that when you're logged in, everything in an EFS-encrypted folder looks like a normal document. To everyone else, of course, it's unreadable gibberish. (Windows 2000 produces an "Access Denied" message when you try to open someone else's EFS files.)

EFS files are always encrypted on disk, because EFS actually is a filesystem driver that sits between the standard disk drivers and the applications.

EFS supports recovery, so that you always have a way to recover access to files that have been encrypted. It provides this support by encrypting the key used to protect the file twice: once for the owner and once for the Administrator account (or whoever else has recovery authority). By default, administrators can act as recovery agents, but you can customize recovery access as much as you want, up to and including removing it.

These components work together to provide a full set of PKI services.

Certificate Hierarchies

How can you determine whether a certificate is valid? The answer lies in the concept of a *certificate hierarchy*. In a hierarchy, each certificate authority signs the certificates that it issues, using its own private key. Each CA has its own certificate, which contains the CA's public key. This CA certificate is itself signed by a higher-level CA. You can stack up any number of CAs in a hierarchy, with each CA certifying the authenticity of the certificates it has issued. Eventually, though, there must be a top-level CA, called a *root certificate authority*. Because there's nobody above the root CA in the hierarchy, there's nobody to vouch for its certificate. Instead, the root CA signs its own certificate, asserting that it is the root.

The root CA is the CA at the top of the hierarchy; CAs lower in the hierarchy are called intermediate or subordinate CAs.

Enterprise and Stand-alone CAs

Until now, you've been reading about only one type of CA. But MCS supports two different *types* of CAs, and each type can operate in one of several different *roles*.

Which type of CA you install determines whom you can issue certificates to and what the certificates can be used for, so it's important to understand the distinctions between them. The only real configuration difference between the two is which set of policies are enforced, but the operational differences are important.

THE ENTERPRISE CA

The *enterprise* CA acts as part of the PKI for an enterprise. It issues and revokes certificates for end users *and* intermediate CAs according to the policy and security settings that you apply to the CA. As you'd expect of something labeled "enterprise," enterprise CAs require Active Directory access, though they don't necessarily have to be installed on an AD domain controller.

MCS machines acting as enterprise CAs have five special attributes:

- All users and computers in their domains always trust them.

- Certificates issued by an enterprise CA can be used to log on to Windows 2000 domains if you're using *smartcards* (those little credit-card-like things that actually pack an embedded microprocessor and cryptographic software).

- Enterprise CAs publish certificates and CRL information to Active Directory, from which any client in the enterprise can get them.

- Enterprise CAs use certificate *types* and *templates* to construct the content of newly issued certificates.

- Enterprise CAs always either reject or approve a certificate request; they never mark a request as pending and save it for human inspection. The CA makes this decision based on the security permissions in the security template and on permissions and group memberships in Active Directory.

THE STAND-ALONE CA

Stand-alone CAs don't require Active Directory access, because they're designed to do nothing but issue certificates for external use. In other words, a stand-alone CA is made to issue certificates to people who aren't part of your organization, such as Internet users or business partners.

Stand-alone CAs are similar to enterprise CAs in most respects, with a few differences:

- Stand-alone CAs automatically mark incoming certificate requests as "pending," because the CA doesn't have access to Active Directory information to verify them.

- Certificates issued by a stand-alone CA can't be used for smartcard logons (though you may store them on a smartcard).

- Certificates and CRLs generated by the stand-alone CA aren't published anywhere; you must distribute them manually.

NOTE   You *can* install a stand-alone CA on a server that participates in an Active Directory organization. If you do, the CA will be able to publish certificate information if its server is a member of the Certificate Publishers group.

Some Windows 2000-Specific Terms to Know

Besides knowing the general terms used to talk about PKI components and their capabilities, you have to know some specific terms that Microsoft uses in its products and on its exams. Most, but not all, of these terms are the same as those used by other PKI vendors.

Cryptographic Service Providers

Microsoft ships a set of cryptographic libraries with every copy of Windows NT, Windows 95/98, and Windows 2000. These libraries implement basic, low-level crypto operations, including both *secret-* and *public-key encryption*. They expose a set of application programming interfaces that Microsoft calls the CryptoAPI. Applications, and the operating systems themselves make CryptoAPI calls when they need some cryptographic work done. The libraries themselves are known as *cryptographic service providers,* or *CSPs*.

Policy and Exit Modules

MCS supports using predefined sets of instructions that tell the CA what to do with incoming requests and how to proceed when a request is approved. The rules that govern how the CA handles an incoming request are built into policy modules, and rules that specify where and how a newly issued certificate is published are built into exit modules.

A *policy module* is a set of instructions that tells the CA what to do with incoming certificate requests. Microsoft's standard policy module does these three things:

- It processes each incoming request or marks it as pending, depending on whether you're operating an enterprise or a stand-alone CA.

- It adds an attribute to the certificate that specifies where the issuing CA's certificate can be obtained. This attribute allows clients that want to verify the new certificate to get the issuer's certificate at the same time.

- It adds an attribute that specifies where the issuing CA's CRLs are available to clients.

An *exit module* allows the CA to do something with a certificate after it's been issued. Microsoft's standard exit module, for example, can publish new certificates to Active Directory, store them in a shared folder, or e-mail them back to the requestor. It also publishes CRLs for the issuing CA, if you enable that feature.

Certificate Trust Lists

The *Certificate Trust List*, or *CTL*, is a way for PKI administrators to decide whom they trust. When you put a CA certificate on the CTL for your domain, you're explicitly telling your users' PKI clients that it's OK to trust certificates issued by that CA. The CTL actually lives in Active Directory, and as an administrator, you can control who may (and may not) make changes in the CTL for a site, domain, or organizational unit.

Certificate Attributes

Each certificate contains some combination of attributes. The X.509 standard defines which attributes are mandatory and which are optional. (The standard calls optional attributes *extensions*, and so does Microsoft.) MCS follows the standard closely; any certificate that it generates is guaranteed to contain all the mandatory attributes. MCS uses nine significant attributes. The certificate template, used when the certificate was generated, determines the exact combination and contents of these attributes in a certificate.

How to Install MS Certificate Server

The actual process of installing and configuring MCS is fairly straightforward. Some planning is necessary, however, to avoid making the wrong configuration choices at installation; MCS doesn't allow you to change some of its settings after it's installed.

Four Questions to Answer

Before you install a CA anywhere on your network, you must know the answer to four questions that the setup program will ask as part of the setup process:

- What type of CA are you installing: enterprise or stand-alone? You can't install an enterprise CA unless you've already set up and tested Active Directory.

- What role do you want the CA to play? At one point in the installation process, you choose between stand-alone and enterprise CAs; after that point, the installation options diverge.

- Do you want to use any CSPs other than the default Microsoft modules? If you install the optional (and North America-only) High Encryption Pack for Windows 2000, you can take advantage of CSPs that are cryptographically stronger than the ones included with Windows 2000.

- Do you want to allow end users to request certificates by using the Web interface included with MCS? This interface makes it easier for users to get certificates, which may or may not be what you choose.

How to Manage the Certificate Server

After you've installed the Certificate Server and the CA snap-in, you're ready to configure and manage your CA. When you open the CA snap-in in the MMC, you see that it contains several items. The snap-in interface looks very much like every other MMC snap-in. In the left half of the console window, you see one node for each CA running on the server you're managing.

If you expand any of those CA nodes, you see the following five folders below it:

- Revoked Certificates, which holds all certificates that have been revoked by this CA. Once revoked, a certificate can't be unrevoked; it stays on the CRL forever.

- Issued Certificates, which lists the certificates that this CA has issued since its installation. Double-clicking a certificate shows its properties; right-clicking a certificate allows you to revoke it.

- Pending Requests, which lists the requests that are queued on the CA, waiting for you to approve or disapprove them. Enterprise CAs never have any items in this list, but stand-alone CAs may display zero or more requests at any given time.

- Failed Requests, which lists all the requests that failed *or* were rejected, including the CN, e-mail address, and submission date of the failed request.

- Policy Settings, which shows the certificate templates that are available for use on this server. You can change the set of available templates by right-clicking the Policy Settings folder and then choosing the New ➤ Certificate to Issue or Delete command. Double-clicking a template shows you the certificate purposes available with that certificate, but you have no way to change the template directly.

Each folder expands into a list, and you can customize the list's columns and fields via the commands in the View submenu of the context menu. To do so, right-click the folder; then choose the Choose Columns and Customize commands until you have the list configured the way you want it. You also can define filters by choosing the View ➤ Filter command.

Controlling the CA Service

Because MCS is just another Windows 2000 service, you can configure it to start when you want. The installer automatically configures the service to start when the system starts; for extra security, you can set it to start manually so that it can issue certificates only when you want.

As with every other Windows 2000 service, you can use the Services item in the Computer Management snap-in to start and stop the services, set recovery options for it when it stops, and change the account used to run it. You also can perform most of these functions, plus some other useful ones, directly from the Certification Authority snap-in. When you right-click a CA, you gain access to several commands that simplify your day-to-day management tasks. The following sections describe the primary commands that appear in the All Tasks submenu of the context menu that you get when you right-click the CA.

RETARGET CERTIFICATION AUTHORITY

The first command appears when you right-click the Certification Authority node, not an individual CA. The Retarget Certification Authority command allows you point the snap-in to a different CA. You may remember that during installation, you have to specify which CA you want to manage; this command is how you change it. When you use this command, you'll be able to browse the network and change to any CA to which you have management rights.

START SERVICE AND STOP SERVICE

In addition to starting and stopping the CA from the Services item in Computer Management or from the command line, you can choose the Start Service and Stop Service commands from the context menu. These operations take effect immediately; you don't get a chance to change your mind or confirm your command.

BACKUP CA AND RESTORE CA

Doing a solid backup of the CA's data is a two-step process, and it involves two separate tools. Although this process seems to be more complicated than necessary, doing good backups is critical; if you lose the CA's certificates, you won't be able to issue, renew, or revoke certificates for that CA's domain. Backing up data is pointless, of course, unless you have the ability to restore it when you need it.

Backing Up the CA   The two-step process of backing up the CA is conceptually simple. First, you use the Certification Authority Backup wizard to make a usable copy of the CA's data. Because the CA keeps its files open when it's running, you can't just copy the files unless you stop the service, but the wizard can copy the needed data while the service is running. To begin this first step, right-click the CA; then choose the Backup CA command. After an introductory wizard page, you see the Items to Back Up page. Use this page to specify what you want to back up.

The following settings specify what should be backed up:

- The Private Key And CA Certificate setting specifies that you want to back up the CA's private key and the associated certificate. If you choose this option, the wizard asks you for a password, which it uses to encrypt the private key and certificate data and then store it in a PKCS#12 file.

- The Configuration Information check box specifies that you want the CA's settings to be backed up, too. Servers that are part of Active Directory store their information in AD, so this check box is disabled. If you're using a stand-alone CA and want its configuration to be saved, be sure to check this check box.

- The CA keeps log files that record certificate issuance and revocation; it also keeps a queue of pending requests. If you want this information backed up, check the Issued Certificate Log and Pending Certificate Request Queue check box.

- If you choose to back up the log and queue files, you can further specify whether you want to back up the entire set of files at each backup (the default) or only those items that have changed since the previous backup (by checking the Perform Incremental Backup check box).

- The Back Up to This Location field (and the associated Browse button) allows you to specify where you want the backed-up data to go. You must specify an empty directory; in that location, the wizard puts a file named <caName>.p12 (containing the private key and certificate) and a directory named DataBase (which contains the actual logs, queues, and CA database). You can't store multiple backups in the same directory without overwriting them.

After you've chosen the appropriate settings, click the Next button. If you chose to back up the private key material, you'll be prompted to enter a password to secure the data on disk. When you've done that (if necessary), you see a summary wizard page; clicking its Finish button actually performs the backup.

When you've used the CA Backup wizard to make a backup of your CA data, the second step is to use Windows 2000 Backup to back up your CA data to disk, tape, CD-R, or whatever you use for backup. Don't skip this step—all that the CA Backup wizard does is make a clean copy of the CA's data on your local machine, where it's no more protected than the original data was.

Restoring the CA   A *restore* reverses the backup process, returning the target machine to its original backed-up state. Thus, restoring CA data is the reverse process of the backup process: First, you restore your backed-up CA data from its storage media, using Windows 2000 Backup or whatever; then you open the Certification Authority Restore wizard by choosing the Restore CA command. The wizard allows you to restore whatever you've backed up, in any combination you choose.

You can restore just the queue; the queue and the logs; or the queue, the logs, and the key material.

There are some differences in the actual process, though. First, the CA service has to be stopped for you to use the Restore wizard; the wizard offers to do this for you. The meat of the wizard is the Items to Restore page. Using the check boxes on this page, you specify what you want to restore. You also must use the Restore from This Location controls to tell the wizard where to find the specific backup from which you want to restore.

Renewing the CA Certificate

Like real-world credentials, certificates eventually expire. When you control the CA, you get to control the expiration interval for certificates that it issues, which can be handy. CA certificates aren't exempt from this process, so it's likely that you'll need to renew your CA certificates periodically. For subordinate CAs, renewal is accomplished by requesting a new certificate from the issuing CA, but root CAs get to renew their own certificates. This task can be accomplished in two ways:

- The CA can bind its existing keys to a new certificate. This option is the most common, because it allows you to keep reusing the existing keys for signature verification and signing.

- The CA can generate a new key pair and use it to create a new certificate. This option is useful when you want or need to generate a new key. In essence, this process is equivalent to creating a new CA, because it creates a new key and certificate.

To begin the renewal process, just right-click the CA whose certificate you want to use and then choose the Renew CA Certificate command. You are reminded that the CA must be stopped to renew the certificate; then you see a dialog box. You use this dialog box to specify whether you want to create a new key pair for the new certificate; you can't change the CSP or key length, though.

How to Install and Configure CAs

CAs have several configurable properties that control how they behave. Most of these settings have reasonable default values, but you may need to change them at times. All the CA's properties, including its policy and exit module settings, are available through the Properties dialog box that appears when you select a CA and choose the Properties command (from the Action menu or the context menu).

Setting General Properties

The first thing you see in the CA Properties dialog box is the General tab. Most of the information is strictly for reference; although the tab shows you the name and description of the CA, along with the CSP and hash algorithm in use, you can't change those settings. You can view the CA certificate's details by clicking the View Certificate button.

Setting Policy Module Properties

The Policy Module tab definitely is more interesting than the General tab, if only because it has controls you can adjust. This tab shows you which policy module is active, and it allows you to configure the current module or change to another one. The selected policy module almost always is the Enterprise And Stand-Alone Policy module that Microsoft supplies with Windows 2000. If you use a third-party product or wrote your own; click the Select button to pick a new policy module from the list of those registered with the system.

The Configure button allows you to set options for whichever policy module you have installed. When you click it, you get a Configuration dialog box with the following two tabs:

- Default Action, which has two radio buttons that give you control of how incoming requests are processed. The Always Issue the Certificate option (the only choice for enterprise CAs) tells the CA to process the request immediately. The Set the Certificate Request Status to Pending option tells the CA to mark the request as pending for stand alones and to stuff it in a queue until you approve or reject it.

- X.509 Extensions, which allows you to tailor two lists of locations: one for where CRLs are published (known as *CRL Distribution Points*, or *CDPs*) and one that specifies where users can get the CA's certificate (known as *Authority Information Access Points*, or *AIAs*). The lists of CDPs and AIAs are encoded as part of the CA certificate, so any client can look at the certificate and figure out which CDPs and AIAs exist for it to use. By default, MCS uses HTTP and LDAP, CDPs and AIAs, but there also are file-system-based URLs. You can click the Add AIA and the Add CDP buttons to specify additional CDPs or AIAs. You can specify literally any URL, but it doesn't make sense to specify a URL unless you plan to actually serve CRLs or CA certificates from it.

WARNING   If you change any of the X.509 extension values by using this tab, you'll have to stop and restart the CA before the changes take effect. This requirement holds for most changes in the CA.

Setting Exit Module Properties

The Exit Module tab is very similar to the Policy Module tab; it shows you which exit modules you've currently configured to work with your CA. A CA can use only one policy module at a time, but it can use several exit modules, which are executed in a series. You could use the Microsoft policy module to publish newly issued certificates to Active Directory and the file system, for example, and then use your own module to publish certificates on a Web page or in an Exchange public folder.

When you click the Configure button, you see a Properties dialog box with two check boxes that give you control of where certificates are published. (Your available options depend on whether your CA computer is part of an Active Directory domain.) These check boxes are:

- Allow Certificates to Be Published in the Active Directory, which is marked by default on servers that participate in an AD domain. To allow the exit module to load certificates into AD when it's present, check this check box.

- Allow Certificates to Be Published to the File System, which allows you to specify that you want new certificates stored in the shared folder you specified when you installed the CA.

Viewing Storage Properties

The Storage tab shows the paths where the CA is keeping its configuration and certificate database files. You can't change these values after the CA is installed, but it might be useful to have a way to double-check the file locations in case you need them, and this tab is the quickest way to do so. You can change one setting in this tab, however. If your CA is a stand-alone CA running on a computer with Active Directory access, checking the Active Directory check box moves the CA's configuration information into the directory.

Setting Security Properties

Like practically everything else in Windows 2000, MCS servers can be assigned their own set of permissions that control who can see and change the information the CA owns. *MCSE: Windows 2000 Network Infrastructure Administration Study Guide* by Paul Robichaux (Sybex 2000) shows the 12 permission settings that you can apply to the CA; each permission allows someone who holds it to do something specific with the CA. Right out of the box, the following four groups have permissions to use the CA:

- Administrators, which has the Manage, Enroll, and Read Configuration rights. Even though Manage enables the other permissions, you can turn it off if you want to allow administrators to enroll users without giving them permission to manage the CA itself.

- Authenticated Users, which has Enroll and Read Configuration permission.

- Domain Admins and Enterprise Admins, which have Manage, Enroll, and Read Configuration permissions.

Configuring Certificate Templates

Part of configuring the CA is telling it which certificate templates can be used and who can use them. When someone requests a certificate from your CA (as described in "Requesting New Certificates" later in this chapter), he can request that the CA use any of the templates you've made available, and the issued certificate are filled out according to the rules in the template. By adding and removing templates, and by setting permissions on the templates that are installed, you get control of what people can do.

Necessary Procedures

You install the Certificate Server by using the Windows Components wizard; because it's just an ordinary system service, the system doesn't do anything out of the ordinary when you install it. When you run the wizard, you can install the CA service itself, the Web enrollment component, or both.

Installing Microsoft Certificate Server (MCS)

Follow these steps to install MCS:

1. Choose Start ➤ Settings ➤ Control Panel ➤ Add/Remove Programs; then click the Add/Remove Windows Components button.

2. Select Certificate Services from the component list. When the warning dialog box appears, click OK. The CA Type Selection dialog box appears.

3. If your server is part of an Active Directory domain, click the Enterprise Root CA button; if it's not, choose the Stand-Alone Root CA button. Click the Next button when you're done.

4. Fill in the fields in the CA Identifying Information page. Make sure to specify a unique name for the CA. Click the Next button when you're done. The Data Storage Location page appears.

5. Write down the database paths for future reference; then click the Next button.

6. Complete the installation by clicking the Finish button.

Installing the CA

When you're ready to install the CA on a computer (after answering the questions listed earlier in the section, of course), here's what to do:

1. Open the Windows Components wizard by opening the Add/ Remove Programs control panel (Start ➤ Settings ➤ Control Panel ➤ Add/Remove Programs) and clicking the Add/Remove Windows

Components icon. The wizard opens, displaying all the components it knows how to install or remove.

2. Select Certificate Services in the component list. You see a warning dialog box, which tells you that you can't change the name of the computer, or move it into or out of an AD domain, after installing the CA. If you want the machine on which you're installing the CA to function as an enterprise CA, make sure that you promote it to a domain controller before continuing the installation.

3. Click the Details button, and uncheck the check boxes for any components that you don't want to install. If you want to install only the Web enrollment components on a network kiosk, for example, uncheck the CA options. Click OK when you're done; then click the Next button to move on to the next wizard step. The CA Type Selection dialog box appears.

4. Here's where your premeditated decision about what type and role you want this CA to fulfill comes in handy. Notice the Advanced Options check box; you'll need to check it if you want to change the CSPs that this CA can use, reuse an existing key pair, or change the default hash algorithm. Click Next after you've filled out the page.

5. If you checked the Advanced Options check box, you see the Public and Private Key Pair Selection page. Apart from allowing you to select the key pair you want to use, this dialog box allows you to choose the CSP, hash algorithm, and key length you want to use with its controls. By default, the Microsoft Base Cryptographic Provider is the standard CSP, though you may have others available, depending on what hardware and software you have installed on your server.

The fields in this dialog box do the following:

- The Cryptographic Service Providers list shows all the CSPs on your machine. Choose the one that you want this CA to use. Be forewarned that if you choose a CSP that doesn't support the RSA algorithm suite (such as the Microsoft Base DSS CSP), your CA may not interoperate properly with CAs from other vendors.

- The Hash Algorithms list allows you to choose the hash algorithm you want to use for computing digital signatures. Don't use MD4. If you can avoid it, don't use MD5, either. Both algorithms have known weaknesses. Instead, accept the default setting of SHA-1.

- The Key Length pull-down menu allows you to select a key length if you're generating a key pair. You can accept the default value of 1,024 bits, or you can go all the way up to 4,096 bits if you need to, provided that your CSP supports longer keys.

- The Use Existing Keys check box allows you to reuse an existing key pair for the CA's key, as long as it was generated with algorithms compatible with your selected CSP. As you choose different CSPs, this check box and the contents of the list below it change to reflect the keys you could use.

- The Import button allows you to import certificates from a PFX/PKCS#12 file, and the View Certificate... button shows you the properties for the selected certificate.

- The Use the Associated Certificate check box allows you to use an existing certificate if the key pair you've selected has one associated with it *and* if it's compatible with your chosen CSP.

When you've set the options that you want to use, click the Next button.

6. The CA Identifying Information page allows you to specify the information needed to uniquely identify this CA. You must specify a unique name for the CA itself, as well as an e-mail address where requests for the CA's services should go. You also should specify names for the organization that owns the CA and the organizational unit it's in; if you want, you could specify information about its physical location, too. The Valid For controls at the bottom of the dialog box allow you to set the validity interval for your CA's certificate. Click the Next button after you've filled in enough information to identify your CA.

WARNING You *cannot* change any of this identifying information after the CA is installed, because it's all encoded in the CA's certificate. Make sure that the information you enter is correct.

NOTE If you choose an organization name that includes special characters (&, *, [,], and so on), the CA has to encode them with Unicode, because the X.509 standard for PKI certificates requires it. This setup may make some older (or broken) applications unable to verify your CA certificate, so Setup warns you and gives you a chance to change the CA name before proceeding.

7. The CA stores its certificates in a database file, and you get to choose where that database lives on disk. Notice that this database contains the CA's certificates, not the certificates that it issues—those are published in Active Directory or wherever else you specify. The Data Storage Location page allows you to choose where on your server these database files reside. The Store Configuration Information in a Shared Folder check box allows you to force the CA to use a shared folder for storing the certificates it emits. This option is handy if you're not using Active Directory or if you have clients that expect to get certificates only from a file on disk somewhere.

The Preserve Existing Certificate Database check box allows you to reinstall the CA on top of an existing installation. If you have a machine that you want to convert from stand-alone to enterprise mode, for example, or if you need to reinstall to change the CA's name or Active Directory membership, checking this check box tells Setup not to erase the old certificates.

WARNING Make sure that whatever location you specify is on an NTFS disk volume and that it gets backed up regularly. If you lose a CA's certificates, you'll have to reissue all the certificates ever issued by that CA.

8. When you're happy with the settings in all the preceding pages, click the Next button. If you're currently using the Internet Information Service (IIS) WWW service, Setup stops it for you so it can finish the installation.

9. When the setup is complete, restart your machine. From then on, the CA service starts automatically whenever the server does.

Installing Certificates and Certificate Authority Snap-Ins

Managing Microsoft Certificate Server involves using two different, but related, Microsoft Management Console (MMC) snap-ins: one for managing certificates and one for managing the CA itself. The process for installing the two snap-ins is identical, and you usually can keep them together in a single console file so that you can quickly manage all certificate-related functionality on a machine at the same time. Here's what to do:

1. Open MMC, either with an existing console file or a new one.

2. Choose the Console ➤ Add/Remove Snap-In command to open the Add/Remove Snap-in dialog box.

3. Click the Add button. The Add Stand-Alone Snap-In dialog box appears.

4. Choose the Certification Authority item in the Available Stand-Alone Snap-Ins list; then click the Add button. The Certification Authority dialog box appears.

5. By default, this snap-in is used to manage the local computer. If you want to retarget the snap-in so that it manages some other computer, choose the Another Computer radio button to specify the

computer that you want to manage. The Allow the Selected Computer to Be Changed When Launching from the Command Line check box enables you to change the snap-in's target at any time.

6. Click the Finish button. You return to the Add Stand-Alone Snap-In dialog box from step 3. This time, choose the Certificates snap-in instead of Certification Authority; then click the Add button. The Certificates Snap-In dialog box appears.

7. Specify which set of certificates the snap-in will be used to manage. By default, the My User Account radio button is selected, but you also can manage computer and service account certificates—just not with the same snap-in. Choose the certificate type that you want to manage; then click the Finish button.

TIP To manage all three certificate types from a single MMC, just add three instances of the Certificates snap-in.

Configuring Microsoft Certificate Server (MCS)

Follow these steps to configure MCS:

1. Open the Certification Authority snap-in from an MMC console session.

2. Right-click the CA that you want to manage; then choose the Properties command from the context menu. The Properties dialog box appears.

3. Click the Exit Module tab; then click the Configure button.

4. Make sure that both the Allow Certificates to Be Published in the Active Directory check box and the Allow Certificates to Be Published to the File System check box are checked; then click the OK button.

5. Click the OK button in the Exit Module tab to close the Properties dialog box.

Configuring the Template Permissions

You set permissions on the CA itself by using the CA Properties dialog box, but to set permissions on the certificate templates, you have to leave the familiar environment of the Certification Authority snap-in. The Active Directory Sites and Services snap-in is where you actually adjust permissions for enterprisewide services, including the use of certificate templates and other PKI components.

To set permissions, follow these steps:

1. Open the Active Directory Sites and Services snap-in.

2. Right-click the Sites node; then choose the View ➢ Show Services Node command.

3. Expand the Services node until you see the Certificate Templates node; then expand it, too. This action fills the right half of the MMC window with a list of installed templates.

4. Right-click the template whose permissions you want to set; then choose the Properties command. When the Properties dialog box appears, switch to the Security tab.

5. Adjust the permissions to suit your needs. To keep users from using the template to request new certificates, make sure that you deny the appropriate groups the Enroll permission.

Enabling Automatic Enrollment

Users aren't the only ones who have certificates; Windows 2000 computers have them, too. Normally, you have to issue certificates for new computers manually as they join your AD domain, but this process is a pain. Instead, you can use automatic enrollment to have the CA generate a new certificate automatically for each computer that joins the domain. To do so, you have to adjust a setting in the Group Policy Object (GPO) for your domain. To adjust this setting, follow these steps:

1. Open the Group Policy snap-in, and use it to select the GPO for which you want to turn on automatic enrollment.

2. Open the GPO's Computer Configuration node; then open the Windows Settings, Security Settings, and Public Key Policies nodes below it. This action exposes four subfolders below the Public Key Policies node.

3. Right-click the Automatic Certificate Request Settings folder below the Public Key Policies node; then choose the New ➤ Automatic Certificate Request command. This command starts the Automatic Certificate Request wizard.

4. Click Next to get past the wizard's introductory page. When the second page appears, it lists all the types of certificates that can be issued to computers automatically. Normally, you use the basic Computer type, but separate types exist for domain controllers and devices that participate in IPSec. Select the template type that you want to use; then click the Next button.

5. Page three of the wizard lists all the CAs available in the AD domain. Choose the one that you want to issue certificates for newly added computers; then click the Next button. The summary page of the wizard appears.

6. Review your choices; then click the Finish button to create the request. The new request appears in the Automatic Certificate Request Settings folder; you can edit or remove it later by selecting it and choosing commands from the Action menu.

Exam Essentials

Know the general principles behind secret- and public-key cryptography.   Understand public and private keys and the fundamental operations of encryption and signing. Be clear about how these operations create a system providing privacy, authentication and non-repudiation.

Know the roles played by digital certificates within Public Key Infrastructure.   Understand the PKI functions of key management, publishing, and use.

Know Microsoft's Windows 2000 PKI components. Understand that Windows 2000 includes certificate authorities, certificate publishing, PKI management tools, and PKI-savvy applications. Be familiar as well with the Encrypting File System (EFS) as a PKI-aware file system that can encrypt and decrypt files automatically and transparently.

Know the functioning of intermediate and subordinate certificate authority within a certificate hierarchy. Understand that the ultimate top-level CA is called a *root certification authority*.

Know the two types of CA supported by Windows 2000. Understand the enterprise and stand-alone CAs and their various functionalities.

Know that Cryptographic Service Providers (CSPs) are sets of libraries that ship with many Microsoft operating systems. Understand that these libraries include application programming interfaces known as *CryptoAPIs*.

Know that MS uses predefined sets of instructions known as policy and exit modules that direct CA functioning. Understand the certificate manipulations that are possible with these policy sets.

Know about Certificate Revocation Lists (CRLs), Certificate Trust Lists (CTLs), and their use. Understand that the CTL actually lives in Active Directory and therefore can be accessed and protected under that aegis.

Know the X.509 mandatory and optional certificate attributes. Be clear about the certificate template's role in configuring these attributes.

Know that Windows 2000 includes 22 certificate templates. Understand what these templates are; and be familiar with who they are for and what they do.

Know the four CA roles and when and where to implement them. Understand the different functions of enterprise and stand-alone CAs and the differences between root and subordinate roles.

Know how recovery keys can protect you against data loss. Understand the distinction between key recovery and key escrow and the fact that Microsoft doesn't support key escrow.

Know how to install MS Certificate Server and the four questions that the setup process asks you.   Understand the issues and the answers to these four questions.

Know how to back up and restore the CA.   Understand how to use the Certification Authority Restore wizard.

Know how to set policy-module properties.   Understand the Default Action tab and the X.509 Extensions tab of the CA's Properties dialog box.

Understand CDPs and AIAs as publishing and distribution locations.   Understand that the X.509 Tab of the Properties Module dialog box of the CA allows you to click the Add AIA and Add CDP buttons to specify additional CDPs or AIAs.

Know the other CA properties that you can configure.   Be familiar with the exit-module properties, the storage properties, and the security properties.

Key Terms and Concepts

authority information access point (AIA)   A list of locations where users can get the CA's certificate and authentication information.

certificate authority (CA)   A server that controls the issuance and use of digital certificates for users and computers in some group.

certificate hierarchy   A "stack" of CAs. Each CA has a parent in the hierarchy that has issued the child its CA certificate. Eventually, this hierarchy works up to a root CA, which has no parent.

certificate revocation list (CRL)   A list of certificates that have been revoked for some reason, such as expiration. Each CA builds and maintains its own CRL.

certificate trust list (CTL)   A certificate list that allows PKI administrators to tell PKI clients to trust certificates issued by a particular set of CAs. The CTL information is stored in Active Directory.

certificates   The codes exchanged to allow for encrypted information interchange. Each party has its own certificate identifying (uniquely) the party sending or receiving information.

CRL distribution point (CDP)   A location that you can configure to find certificate revocation lists (CRLs) in the Policy Modules Tab property box in the X.509 Extensions tab. This allows you to advertise locations where CRLs are published.

Data Encryption Standard (DES)   A frequently used algorithm developed by the U.S. National Bureau of Standards for encrypting and encoding data.

exit module   A module that contains the rules that specify where and how a newly issued certificate is published.

policy module   The module that contains information about how the CA handles an incoming request.

private key   A key that must be held only by its owner and should never be publicly disclosed; also called a *secret key*.

public-key encryption   An encryption technique that uses private-public key pairs. Each actor has a public and a *private key*. Public keys are shared between the two parties and are used to sign and encrypt data. This encrypted data can be decrypted only with a private key.

Public Key Infrastructure (PKI)   A service that provides a fundamental set of services that application programmers can use to deliver privacy, authentication, and nonrepudiation in their applications.

recovery agent   A user who has recovery authority. Recovery agents can recover encrypted files when the original key material is unavailable.

recovery key   A key that allows encrypted data to be unencrypted without the original key.

root certificate authority   The top-level CA, which signs its own certificate, asserting that it is root.

root certificate hierarchy   The hierarchy of certificate authorities that starts at the highest level: the root CA. The root CA is the CA at the top of the hierarchy; CAs lower in the hierarchy are variously called intermediate or subordinate CAs.

secret-key encryption   An encryption technique that works with keys that are shared between two parties but are unknown to an external party. The keys are exchanged via a secure channel. See also *public-key encryption.*

signing   One of the two fundamental operations associated with public-key cryptography (the other is *encryption*). Signing proves the origin and authenticity of some piece of data.

Sample Questions

1. Brooke installed a CA on a Windows 2000 member server. She now wants to join an Active Directory domain. What effect will this change have on the CA installation?

   A. It will have no effect.

   B. The CA will need to be removed and reinstalled.

   C. The CA will need to have its certificate rekeyed for Active Directory.

   D. The parent CA will need to be reinstalled.

   Answer: B. You can't rename a computer or join or leave a domain after the CA is installed.

2. Automatic enrollment allows you to do which of the following?

   A. Automatically create certificates for all user accounts in a domain

   B. Automatically issue certificates to users as their accounts are added

   C. Automatically issue machine certificates to computers as they join an Active Directory domain

   D. Automatically issue certificates for any object that doesn't already have one

   Answer: C. Automatic enrollment causes the group policy mechanism to issue certificates to computers as they're added to a domain. There's no corresponding function for users.

Issue and revoke certificates.

This exam objective discusses subjects related to issuing and revoking certificates.

Critical Information

Although the code that runs them is identical, stand-alone and enterprise CAs have a few differences, which you've already read about. To pass the Microsoft exam, you have to understand how these differences are exposed in the CA management tasks. You need to know how to do two primary things, both of which pertain to handling incoming certificate requests.

Issuing Certificates

Enterprise CAs always process incoming requests automatically. By default, though, stand-alone CAs tag inbound requests as pending and dump them in the Pending Requests folder below the CA's node in the Certification Authority snap-in. When queued, the requests sit there until you approve or reject them.

Setting the Default Action for New Requests

If you don't want requests to be marked automatically as pending, you can change the arrival behavior by adjusting the controls in the Default Action tab, which you access by clicking the Configure button in the Policy Module tab of the CA Properties dialog box. When you make this change, newly arrived requests are treated in accordance with your instructions, but you still need to approve or reject any previously queued requests.

Handling Pending Requests

The process of approving or rejecting a pending request couldn't be easier. Navigate to the Pending Requests folder and select it; when you do, all pending requests appear on the right side of the snap-in window. Right-click the request that you want to approve or reject, and you see commands for either action.

Configuring Revocation and Trust

Issuing certificates is necessary if you want to use a PKI, but it's not the only thing you have to do. To get ongoing use and security out of your PKI, you have to decide which certificates and issuers you trust, and you need to be able to revoke certificates when their useful life span is over. You do these things by using two separate mechanisms:

- The *Certificate Trust List (CTL)* for a domain holds the set of root CAs whose certificates you trust. You can designate CTLs for groups, users, or an entire domain. If a CA's certificate isn't on the CTL, its trustworthiness depends on how you've configured your clients (either explicitly or through a GPO) to behave when presented with an untrusted certificate.

- The revocation function adds the targeted certificate to the CA's *certificate revocation list (CRL)*, and a new CRL is published. Clients are required to check the CRL before using a certificate; if the certificate appears on the CRL, clients may not use it. This mechanism is very similar to the authorization mechanism that retail stores use to verify credit cards.

Trusting Other CAs

The Trusted Root Certification Authorities folder below the Public Key Policies node in the Group Policy snap-in contains a list of root CAs that you trust. Notice that this list isn't the same as a CTL; it's just a list of CAs that individual sites, domains, or organizational units may or may not trust. Because the set of trusted CAs for an Active Directory object is defined as part of the GPO for that object, you can designate exactly which Active Directory objects trust which CAs.

When you've added the foreign CA certificate to your local certificate store, you've instructed your clients to trust any certificate issued by that CA as much as they trust certificates issued by their own CA. This capability is useful, because it allows you to trust CAs operated by other organizations without requiring them to have a common root.

You can modify the Trusted Root Certification Authorities list in three ways: add new CA root certificates to it by importing them, remove a certificate from it, and change the purposes for which the foreign CA is trusted. To do all three of these things, display the Public Key Policies node in the Group Policy snap-in. Then do the following:

- To import a new root CA certificate and add it to the trust list, right-click the Trusted Root Certification Authorities folder; then choose the All Tasks ➤ Import command. Tell the Import Certificate wizard how to find the new certificate; it then loads the certificate into the store and adds it to the trust list.

- To remove a certificate from the folder, right-click it; then choose the Delete command. A confirmation dialog box warns you of the consequences of removing the certificate.

- To edit the list of purposes for which a CA's certificates can be used, right-click the CA's entry in the Trusted Root Certification Authority folder, and open its Properties dialog box. By default, all purposes are enabled for newly added certificates, but you can control how these purposes are used by choosing either the Disable All Purposes for This Certificate radio button or the Enable Only the Following Purposes radio button.

This list of trusted root CAs is distributed by the GPO, which means that it is available automatically to all members of the group. Don't confuse this list with the CTL.

Managing the CTL

The Trusted Root Certification Authorities list shows which foreign CAs you trust. The CTL shows that you trust how those CA's certificates will be used. Normally, you use CTLs to designate trust when your enterprise doesn't have its own CAs. If you do have your own CAs, you'd use the Trusted Root Certification Authorities list to establish the trust list.

When you add a foreign CA to your CTL, you're actually generating a new, digitally signed list that is stored in Active Directory and distributed throughout the domain. You manage CTLs with the Enterprise

Trust folder below the Public Key Policies component in the Group Policy snap-in.

You can do two things with CTLs from the Group Policy snap-in: import a CTL from another machine or create a new one. To perform both actions, right-click the Enterprise Trust folder. Then choose All Actions ➢ Import to use the Import Certificate wizard, or use New ➢ Certificate Trust List to create a new CTL.

Managing Revocation

Certificate revocation is not something to be done lightly, because there's no way to unrevoke a certificate; once revoked, a certificate stays revoked forever.

You can revoke any certificate issued by the CA that you're managing; you cannot revoke certificates issued by other CAs, because you don't have the ability to sign a new CRL for them. To revoke one of the certificates that you've issued, open the Issued Certificates folder in the Certification Authority snap-in; then right-click the certificate and choose the All Tasks ➢ Revoke Certificate command. You'll have the opportunity to choose a reason code for the revocation (the default is unspecified, but you can mark a certificate revoked for a specific reason, such as a change of the user's affiliation or cessation of operations). When you click OK, the certificate is revoked *immediately*.

WARNING   Don't revoke a certificate unless you're sure that you don't need it anymore. Your best bet is to first create a new test certificate and then revoke it.

Publishing CRLs

The CRL is just a signed list of certificate serial numbers. When you revoke a certificate, it's immediately added to the CRL, which is then resigned by the CA. The CRL isn't republished at that instant, however; the CA publishes an updated CRL automatically according to its schedule.

When you right-click the Revoked Certificates folder in the Certification Authority snap-in, you can open the folder's Properties dialog box. The only thing in that dialog box is a group of controls labeled Publication. You can use these controls to adjust the publication interval for CRLs to anywhere from 1 hour to 9,999 years (the default is one week). Microsoft helpfully included some code that tells you when the next scheduled update will take place, so you can judge when that's going to happen.

If you need to publish a CRL manually, you can do so by right-clicking the Revoked Certificates item in the CA snap-in and then choosing the All Tasks ➤ Publish command. The snap-in asks you to confirm that you want to overwrite the existing CRL; if you agree, the CA publishes the CRL to the set of CDPs that you've defined.

WARNING   Clients still have to pick up the CRL from the CDPs, and that process can take some time. Be aware that the time elapsed between your finger's leaving the Publish command and the actual arrival of the new CRL on client machines may vary.

Changing CRL Distribution Points

Certificate requests normally include information that tells the CA where to publish (or distribute) the certificate when it's done. Because since CRLs are solely a function of the CA, however, there's no external source for defining CDPs. You define them yourself in the X.509 Extensions tab of the Policy Module Properties dialog box.

Managing Certificates

Apart from the intricacies of managing your CA, you need to be able to manage certificates for your account—including those issued to you. Windows 2000 implements a database of certificates, or a *certificate store*, for each user and computer account. This database contains end-user and CA certificates and CRLs.

The Certificates snap-in allows you to manage the certificate store associated with your account, with a service account, or with a local computer. The snap-in also allows you to import and export certificates, request new certificates, renew existing certificates, and change various certificate properties.

Using the Certificates Snap-In

After you install the Certificates snap-in, following the procedure described earlier in this chapter, you can begin managing certificates in the store you associated with the snap-in when you installed it. The snap-in works the same way no matter whose certificate store you're managing, but you may not have permission to do everything described in this section.

When you open the snap-in, you see several folders, including the following:

- Personal, which contains a subfolder named Certificates, which in turn contains certificates that belong to you (both those issued to you and those you've imported from elsewhere).

- Trusted Root Certification Authorities, which also contains a Certificates subfolder; it lists the roots you trust. Whether you can modify the contents of this list depends on the settings in the GPOs that apply to your account.

- Enterprise Trust, which contains one folder, labeled Certificate Trust List. Your GPO determines its contents, because the folder is loaded with whatever CTLs the GPO administrators have defined for you.

- Intermediate Certification Authorities, which contains separate Certificates and Certificate Revocation List folders. CA certificates and CRLs from CAs other than your own end up here.

By selecting the certificate that you want to work with, you gain access to several interesting commands.

Viewing and Changing Certificate Properties

The most common task you'll perform in the Certificates snap-in probably is viewing, and maybe even changing, properties for a particular certificate. Because the certificate is a big blob of attribute data signed by the CA, you would be right on the mark if you guessed that each certificate has many interesting properties. Viewing those properties and changing what you can change are two separate tasks:

- To see the certificate's properties, including the full path back to the top of the hierarchy and the certificate's attributes, double-click it or choose the Open command from the context menu.

- To change the purposes for which the certificate can be used, choose the Properties command from the Action or context menu.

This split in behavior seems to be a little confusing—after all, it would make more sense to view all the certificate's properties with the Properties command. It makes more sense when you recall that the certificate's attributes are vouched for by the CA, so there's no way for you to change them without invalidating the CA's signature.

THE GENERAL TAB

The General tab of the Certificate Information dialog box summarizes what purposes the certificate can be used for by listing each purpose as a plainly worded bullet point. In addition, the tab shows the name of the holder, the name of the issuer, and the validity period of the certificate.

This page contains a couple of interesting icons, too: At the bottom of the display area, you see a lock-and-key icon, along with a text message, if you have the private key that matches the certificate. The Issuer Statement button at the bottom of the dialog box allows you to view any message encoded in the certificate by the issuer. These statements, often called *certification practices statements (CPSes)*, normally set forth the terms and conditions under which the CA will issue certificates.

THE DETAILS TAB

The Details tab contains the meat of the certificate. Because each certificate attribute is a combination of an attribute name and a value, the centerpiece of this tab is a list of the attribute names and values. You can view the full contents of any field by selecting it.

You can use the Show pull-down menu to control which attributes are displayed. By default, all attributes then are shown, but you can limit the display by asking to see only required extensions, all extensions, or old-style X.509 version 1 attributes.

THE CERTIFICATION PATH TAB

Every certificate is part of some kind of certificate hierarchy, even if it's a self-signed root certificate. It's often useful to view the full hierarchy for a certificate so that you can see its exact provenance. The Certification Path tab shows you the complete ancestry of the selected certificate. The tab does something else, too: it warns you when one, or possibly more, of the ancestors of the current certificate isn't trusted.

When you select a CA that's above you in the hierarchy, the View Certificate button in the dialog box becomes active. Clicking this button displays a separate Certificate Information dialog box for the selected certificate.

Changing Certificate Purposes

If you use the Properties command on a certificate, you see a dialog box. By choosing the appropriate radio button, you can change what specific tasks this certificate can be used for, as follows:

- The Enable All Purposes for This Certificate option is set by default. When this option is enabled, the certificate can be used for any purpose that's allowed by its issuer. That restriction exists because the issuer controls which purpose flags are encoded in the certificate, so an end user cannot use a certificate for any purpose not provided for by the issuer.

- The Disable All Purposes for This Certificate option essentially shuts off the certificate, preventing its use for anything, without revoking or deleting it. This option is a useful way to disable a certificate temporarily.

- The Enable Only the Following Purposes check box, in conjunction with the list box below it, allows you to mix and match only the purposes for which you want the certificate to be used. The note above the list box tells you that the listed purposes will be drawn from the purpose flags encoded in the certificate.

Requesting New Certificates

Requesting a certificate is simple, because you normally request one only for yourself. When you right-click the Personal folder or its Certificates subfolder, the All Tasks submenu has an additional command: Request New Certificate. When you choose that command, you're actually starting the Certificate Request wizard.

What happens next depends on your CA. If the CA is set to process requests automatically, you immediately get either an error dialog box indicating that the request failed for some reason or a dialog box offering to install the certificate in the store for you automatically. If you're using a stand-alone CA that's set to mark requests as pending, you'll have to come back later and check the status of the request.

Using the Web Enrollment Agent

If you chose to install the Web-enrollment component of the CA, your CA also can issue certificates to Web clients via a Web-based interface—assuming, of course, that your clients are all using Internet Explorer for Windows. By default, the CA pages are at `http://ca-name/certsrv/`, in which `ca-name` is the name of the CA in question. When you load that page, you see a Welcome page that gives you three choices:

- The Retrieve the CA Certificate or Certificate Revocation List button takes you to a set of pages from which you can download the current CRL, the CA's certificate, or the CA's entire certification chain.

- The Request a Certificate button leads you through a series of pages very similar to the ones in the snap-in's certificate wizard. One interesting difference is that you can use the Web interface to feed the CA a PKCS#10-format certificate request generated by another application; you also can take a private key that's already on a smartcard and request a certificate by using that key pair.

- The Check on a Pending Certificate button looks up any pending requests and tells you whether they've been approved.

Rekeying an Existing Certificate

If you need to, you can request that your existing certificate be reissued, either with the same key or a new one. You may want to do this if you lose the private key, but not if you suspect that it's been compromised (in which case the right thing to do is revoke the old certificate). If you want to rekey your existing certificate, do so by right-clicking the target certificate and then choosing either the All Tasks ➤ Request Certificate with New Key command or the All Tasks ➤ Request Certificate with Same Key command. Whichever command you pick takes you through the Certificate Request wizard again; the difference is that the wizard remembers that you want to change the key pair bound to the certificate, not issue a new one.

Renewing a Certificate

Just as when you rekey a certificate, you can renew a certificate in two ways: by keeping the existing key pair or by requesting a new one. When you rekey, the certificate attributes stay the same, but the key pair may change. When you renew, some certificate attributes change. Microsoft includes a Certificate Renewal wizard that you access by right-clicking a certificate and then choosing the All Tasks ➤ Renew Certificate with Same Key and All Tasks ➤ Renew Certificate with New Key commands. In either case, the wizard starts by asking you to choose whether you want to use your CA's default settings or buck the trend by setting your own. Although you might think that the dialog box's text about "settings" and "values" applies to the expiration interval, it doesn't—it's really just a pair of radio buttons that act like the Advanced Options check box in the Certificate Request wizard. If you choose the No, I Want to Provide My Own Settings radio button, you get to pick a CSP and a CA, just as you do when Advanced Options is checked.

Importing, Exporting, and Finding Certificates

Your certificates can be added to your store when you request them, but it's frequently desirable to move certificates in and out of your own personal store. Suppose that one of your users needs to exchange encrypted e-mail with a business partner. Neither you nor the business partner wants to cross-certify your CAs, so the easiest way to make the communications happen is to have your user export his certificate and send it to the other party, and vice versa.

Necessary Procedures

You begin by creating a new certificate trust list. You also learn to issue certificates and revoke them. Finally, you practice requesting a certificate and importing and exporting certificates.

Creating a New CTL

To create a new CTL, follow these steps:

1. Choose the New ➤ Certificate Trust List command to start the Certificate Trust List wizard. Click the Next button.

2. If you want to identify this CTL, enter a prefix for it in the provided field.

3. If you want the CTL to be valid for a fixed period, enter its life span in the Valid Duration fields.

4. If you want to restrict the purposes for which the certificate can be used, check the appropriate boxes in the Designate Purposes list. By default, none of these purposes is specified; you must check at least one purpose to create the CTL.

5. Click the Next button. The Certificates in the CTL page appears. The Current CTL Certificates list shows you which certificates are in the CTL. A new CTL is blank until you add some certificates by using the Add from Store and Add from File buttons. Click the Next button when you're done. The Signature Certificate page appears.

6. You use the Signature Certificate page to designate which certificate will sign the CTL. The Select from Store and Select From File buttons allow you to riffle through your certificate stash until you find a certificate that's marked for use in CTL signing (look for the

purpose marked Microsoft Trust List Signing). Click the Next button after you identify the certificate you want to use.

7. In the next page, you can choose to have the CTL marked with a secure time stamp, which guarantees the authenticity and integrity of the date and time recorded in the CTL. You must have access to, and the URL of, a secure time-stamp service.

8. The wizard's final page allows you to enter a friendly name and description for the CTL. These items are displayed in the Group Policy snap-in whenever the CTL itself is shown in a list.

9. As you might expect, when you complete the wizard, you get the usual summary page. Clicking the Finish button creates the CTL and stores it in Active Directory.

Revoking a Certificate

Follow these steps to revoke a certificate:

1. Open the Certificates snap-in from an MMC console session.

2. Open the Issued Certificates folder; then select the certificate you want to revoke.

3. Right-click the certificate; then choose the All Tasks ≻ Revoke Certificate command.

4. Select a reason code for the revocation; then click the OK button.

Requesting a Certificate

Follow these steps to request a new certificate from within the Certificates snap-in:

1. Open the Certificates snap-in from an MMC console session.

2. Right-click the Personal folder; then choose All Tasks ≻ Request New Certificate. The Certificate Request wizard appears.

3. Right-click the CA you want to manage; then choose the Properties command from the context menu. The Properties dialog box appears. Skip its introductory page by clicking the Next button.

The Certificate Template page appears, listing all the available templates that you can access.

4. The content of the templates list depends on what permissions have been set for templates in your domain. Select a template in the list. If you want to specify that the private key for this certificate should be protected, click the Advanced Options check box. Click the Next button when you're done.

5. If you checked Advanced Options in the Certificate Templates page, the next thing you see is the Cryptographic Service Provider page, which lists all the available CSPs. If you want to use a particular CSP to request this certificate, choose it from the list. More likely, you'll want to check the Enable Strong Private Key Protection check box, which forces the OS to alert you any time an application attempts to use your private key. Click Next when you've made the appropriate changes.

6. If you checked Advanced Options, the next page you see allows you to choose the CA and computer to which your request will be sent. You can change these settings, if you want. Click Next when you're done.

7. The Certificate Friendly Name and Description page allows you to supply a friendly, human-readable name and description for the certificate. This data won't be encoded in the certificate, but it will be stored with the certificate so that you can edit it later, if necessary. Enter this information and click Next. The Wizard Summary dialog box appears.

8. Click Finish to send the request to your CA.

Issuing Certificates

Follow these steps to issue a test certificate:

1. Install the CA and Web components, following the directions in the "Necessary Procedures" section for this chapter's first objective.

2. Open a Web browser, and load the CA enrollment page (`http://`*yourServerName*`/certsrv`). If you're using Windows 2000, the browser identifies you to the CA. If not, you have to log on to the domain; the browser prompts you for credentials.

3. When the Microsoft Certificate Services page appears, choose the Request a Certificate radio button; then click the Next button.

4. In the Choose Request Type page, choose the User Certificate Request radio button; then click the Next button. A summary page appears, telling you that the CA has all the information it needs.

5. Click the Submit button to submit your request.

6. If you have automatic certificate approval turned on, you see a page titled Certificate Issued, with a link reading Install This Certificate. Click this link, and your new certificate is downloaded and installed. If your CA requires approval, you have to go back and approve the request manually.

Importing a Certificate

Importing certificates is the best way to move your certificates from some other computer or program into the Windows 2000 PKI. If you have a Verisign certificate that you've been using with Netscape Navigator on your home PC, for example, you can export it and then import it to your laptop so that you can use it with Internet Explorer.

The Certificates snap-in can import certificates in several formats. In general, the hardest part of using the Import Certificate wizard is remembering where on the disk you put the file; the wizard takes care of all the details for you. To start the wizard, right-click a Certificate Storage folder and then choose the All Tasks ➤ Import command from the Context menu. When the wizard starts, follow these steps:

1. Skip the introductory page by clicking its Next button.

2. Provide the full path and filename of the certificate file that you want to import; then click the Next button. You can import certificates in three formats:

   • PKCS#12 (PFX or P12) files, which are used to store certificates with their associated private keys. Outlook, Outlook Express, and Netscape's tools all produce PKCS#12 files when you export a certificate, as do many third-party PKI components.

- PKCS#7 (P7B, P7C, or CRT) files, which are used to store certificates without keys. A PKCS#7 file can contain an entire certificate chain (including CA certificates) or just a certificate; the application that creates the file gets to decide what goes in it. Almost every PKI component that runs on Windows can produce PKCS#7 files.

- Microsoft's own SST format, which is used sparsely.

3. The next wizard page allows you to choose the store in which you want to put the certificate. You have two choices:

- Choose the Automatically Select the Certificate Store Based on the Type of Certificate radio button to let the snap-in determine the proper store for the certificate based on its type, issuer, and owner information. This option probably is the easiest choice for ordinary use, especially because PKCS#12 and PKCS#7 files can contain multiple certificates.

- Choose the Place All Certificates in the Following Store radio button; then click the Browse button to locate the store you want to use. If you're sure where the certificate goes, this option is the better choice. (In fact, the snap-in sets this option as the default choice if you select a certificate folder before you choose the Import command.)

When you've chosen the destination for the certificate, click the Next button. The wizard displays a summary page.

4. Click Finish to import the certificate. A dialog box indicates whether the import attempt succeeded.

Exporting Certificates

You may find it necessary to export a certificate from your store so that you can import it someplace else. In a welcome display of flexibility, the Certificates snap-in can export certificates and private keys in a wide variety of formats. To export a certificate, you right-click it and then choose the All Tasks ➤ Export command to fire up the Export Certificate wizard. After dismissing the obligatory wizard introduction page, follow these steps:

1. If you're exporting a certificate for which you have a corresponding private key, you see a page asking whether you want to export the private key or just the certificate. If you created your certificate with the XXXXXXX check box set, the Yes, Export the Private Key radio button is unavailable, because you can't export protected private keys.

2. Next, the Export File Format page appears so that you can choose the format for the exported certificate. If you're only exporting a certificate, your choices are:

    *   **Plain binary X.509 format** (labeled as DER Encoded Binary X.509 [.CER]). This format is just a bunch of binary data, so it's well suited for copying around on the network, onto removable disks, and so on. Most programs can accept CER files in this format, so this option is a fairly portable choice.

    *   **X.509 format,** encoded via the base-64 encoding system. Base-64 encoding is used for moving binary data around in e-mail messages; in addition, some PKI components expect to see base-64 certificates only.

    *   **PKCS#7 binary format (P7B).** This format is used by most e-mail security tools, and it can contain many certificates in a single file—something that the CER files can't do. The Include All Certificates in the Certification Chain, If Possible check box causes the exporter to include as many of the intermediate and root CA certificates as possible in the output file, which makes it possible to deliver a complete end-to-end certificate chain to someone in a P7B file.

If you're exporting a certificate with a private key, you get only one choice—PKCS#12 format (in the form of a PFX file)—because the PKCS#12 standard defines a secure way to encrypt a private key and store it along with the certificate. When you use PKCS#12 format, you can use three check boxes to control what else goes in the PFX file:

- The Include All Certificates in The Certification Path If Possible option puts as much of the certificate chain as possible in the PFX file.

- The Enable Strong Protection option turns on strong protection for the exported private key. A protected private key can't be exported, and the operating system notifies you whenever an application requests access to the key. This option works only if you have Windows NT 4.0 SP4 or later, or Windows 2000, both with Internet Explorer 5.0 or later.

- The Delete the Private Key If the Export Is Successful option removes the private key from your local store. Use this option when you want to move a key pair someplace else permanently while leaving the certificate in place for future use.

3. If you're exporting a PFX file, you are prompted to enter and confirm a password.

4. Check the confirmation page to double-check what the wizard is about to do.

5. Click the Finish button when you're done. The certificate is exported, and you receive notice of the operation's success or failure.

Exam Essentials

Know how stand-alone and enterprise CAs handle certificate requests.   Understand that you need to decide on pending stand-alone requests or configure them to follow your default instructions.

Know that if a certificate is not in your CTL, its trustability depends on how you've configured your clients to process untrusted certificates.   Understand that a corollary is the CRL, and clients must check to see whether a certificate is not in this list before they accept one.

Know that transitive trust can be configured in the Trusted Root CA folder below the Public Key Policies node in the Group Policies Snap-in. Also understand that you can modify this list in three ways.

Know how CTLs can substitute for CAs in organizations without one. Understand how to import CTLs and create new ones.

Know how to adjust the automated CRL publishing schedule and why you might do so based on your certificate volume. Also understand how to publish a CRL manually.

Know that the certificate store is a certificate database. Understand how to manage the certificate store with the Certificate snap-in.

Know how to change certificate properties with the Certificate snap-in. Understand that you can first view a certificate's properties and then choose the Properties command to change them.

Know that CPSes are statements encoded in certificates by the issuer. Understand that CPSes normally include the terms and conditions under which the certificate was issued.

Know that you can enable/disable or choose a combination of purposes in a certificate that you want to enable/disable. Understand the radio buttons that you use for this purpose when you choose the Properties command.

Know that you can use smartcards or Web-based interfaces for certificate requests. Understand installing the Web-enrollment component of the CA.

Know the steps for, and differences between, rekeying a certificate and renewing one. Understand that you might keep the existing key pairs in either case or request new ones.

Know how to import/export certificates and the circumstances that might predicate such actions. Understand various situations in which it would be necessary to import or export certificates. Microsoft loves to make up scenarios with these types of details in the exam.

Key Terms and Concepts

certificate store   Certificate storage that holds foreign CA certificates, allowing the clients to trust any certificate in the store without requiring a common root.

Certificate Trust List (CTL)   A list for a domain that holds the set of root CAs whose certificates you trust. You can designate CTLs for groups, users, or an entire domain.

Cryptographic Service Provider (CSP)   A provider of cryptographic services.

Sample Questions

1. Kristen has set up a stand-alone subordinate CA for her users. Users started requesting certificates as soon as the CA was activated, but no user has received a certificate. What is the most likely problem?

   A. The CA is misconfigured.

   B. User requests have been going to the wrong CA.

   C. The certificates have been issued and published but not yet returned to the users.

   D. The requests are marked as pending, so they're sitting in a queue for approval.

   Answer: D. Stand-alone CAs can mark requests as pending, in which case the requests are placed in a queue until the administrator approves or rejects them.

2. Aubrey revoked a user's certificate because she left the company. She came back. What's the best way to reintegrate the user into Aubrey's PKI?

   A. Issue her a new certificate

   B. Rekey her old certificate

C. Manually remove her old certificate from the CRL

D. Regenerate a new CRL

Answer: A. When the certificate is revoked, it can't be unrevoked, even by removing its serial number from the CRL. The only way to get the user back into the PKI is to issue her a new certificate.

Remove the Encrypting File System (EFS) recovery keys.

Earlier in the chapter, you learned about key recovery and how EFS uses it to protect you from losing data if someone encrypts data but then isn't around to decrypt it. Given the need to guarantee recovery, you may well wonder why this chapter includes a section on removing EFS recovery keys in this chapter. The answer, of course, is that doing so is an exam objective—but why? Microsoft decided that the best way to restrict access to EFS is to turn it off when no recovery agents are defined.

Critical Information

By default, the administrator is designated as the recovery agent for a computer the first time he or she logs on to that particular machine. You are free to tweak recovery settings by designating additional recovery agents and modifying the applicable GPOs to regulate who can initiate recovery. For the Windows 2000 network infrastructure exam, the important trick to know is that deleting all the EFS recovery keys turns off EFS in that scope. Removing all the EFS recovery keys on a local machine, for example, turns off recovery on that local machine, but it won't affect any recovery policies imposed by higher-level GPOs.

If you want to turn off EFS, simply follow the steps outlined in the following "Necessary Procedures" section.

Necessary Procedures

This section explains what you need to do to remove the EFS recovery keys and turn off EFS.

Removing the EFS Recovery Keys

To remove the EFS recovery keys, follow these steps:

1. Open an MMC window, and add the Group Policy snap-in, if it's not already present. (To disable EFS on the local machine, add a GPO for the local computer; to disable it for a domain or other unit, use the appropriate GPO.)

2. Open the Public Key Policies node (below Computer Configuration ➢ Security Settings in the GPO).

3. Right-click the Encrypted Data Recovery Agents folder; then choose the Delete Policy command.

4. When asked to confirm the command, click the Yes button.

Exam Essentials

Know how to remove the EFS recovery keys. Understand that doing so won't affect recovery policies on higher-level GPOs.

Key Terms and Concepts

Encrypting File System A Windows 2000 feature that has a PKI-aware file system that can encrypt and decrypt files automatically.

Sample Questions

1. Removing all the EFS recovery keys on a local machine does which of the following things?

A. Turns off recovery on that local machine and affects any recovery policies imposed by higher-level GPOs.

B. Turns off recovery on that local machine, but does not affect any recovery policies imposed by higher-level GPOs.

C. Turns on recovery on that local machine and affects any recovery policies imposed by higher-level GPOs.

D. Turns on recovery on that local machine, but does not affect any recovery policies imposed by higher-level GPOs.

Answer: B. Deleting all the EFS recovery keys turns off EFS in that scope but does not affect the policies of higher-level GPOs.

2. To facilitate recovery, EFS must do which of the following?

A. Leave the secret key unprotected

B. Encrypt the secret key to the owner only

C. Encrypt the secret key to both the owner and all recovery agents

D. Encrypt the secret key to the recovery agents only

Answer: C. The secret key unique to each EFS item has to be encrypted to the owner so that he or she can read it. To support recovery, the item also must be encrypted to each recovery agent.

Index

Note to the Reader: Throughout this index **boldfaced** page numbers indicate primary discussions of a topic.

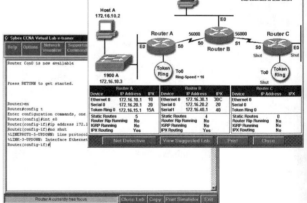

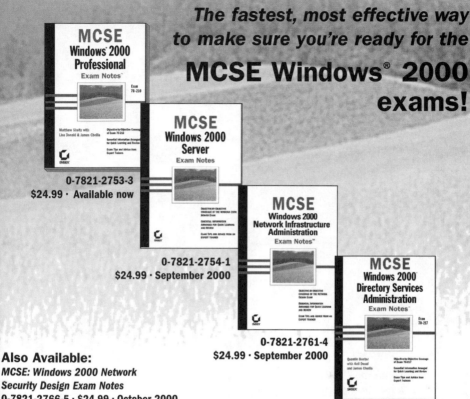

SYBEX BOOKS ON THE WEB

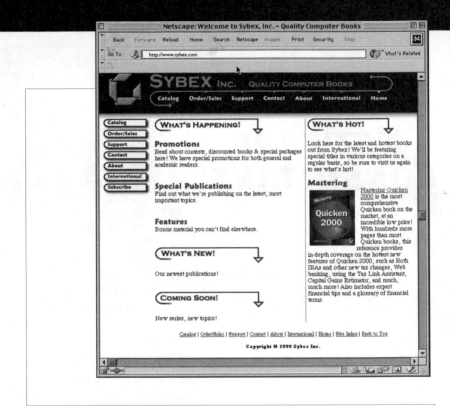

At the dynamic and informative Sybex Web site, you can:

- view our complete online catalog
- preview a book you're interested in
- access special book content
- order books online at special discount prices
- learn about Sybex

www.sybex.com

SYBEX Inc. • 1151 Marina Village Parkway
Alameda, CA 94501 • 510-523-8233